THE UNCANNY X-MEN

THE DARK PHOENIX SAGA

By CHRIS CLAREMONT
JOHN BYRNE
TERRY AUSTIN

Published by MARVEL COMICS, 387 Park
Avenue South, New York, N.Y. 10016.
Copyright © 1984, 1990, 1991. Marvel
Entertainment Group, Inc.
All rights reserved.

Printed in the U.S.A.
ISBN #0-939766-96-5

CONTENTS

THE X-MEN

FIRST OF ALL, let's get one thing straight. I'm not writing this as Stan Lee, Publisher, or Editor-in-Absentia, or even Honorary Living Legend! Nossir! These wondrous words are lovingly being written by an unabashed, unwavering fan of Claremont, Byrne and Austin! Speaking as a typical reader, I just wanna give you my own gut-level feelings about one of the greatest comicbook sagas ever presented—the startling chronicle of Dark Phoenix!

It'll come as no surprise to you to learn that The X-Men is one of Marvel's most popular and best-selling series, and has been so for years. And, if you've been faithfully following the adventures of Professor's Xavier's gregarious little groupies, then you surely know the reason why.

Never in the history of comicdom have there been stories more filled with human interest, believable characterization, and far-out fantasy combined with stark, shattering realism. Never have hard-hitting action-packed adventures been more skillfully intertwined with exciting philosophical concepts and provocative moral issues. And never has any series more accurately symbolized the mighty Marvel credo—"Anything can happen—the more surprising the better—but it must be realistic, it must be dramatic, it must be exciting, and above all, it must be intelligent!"

Sure, any writer can say, "Hey, here's something the fans aren't expecting. Let's do it 'cause it'll be a surprise." But that's the easy way out. One of the reasons the landmark sagas of Claremont, Byrne, et al., are so great is because they don't toss surprises at you for the sake of keeping you off-balance. Every new, daring development in every X-Man thriller is the logical result of what has gone before.

The ultimate fate of Phoenix was one of the most traumatic, unexpected events in the history of illustrated series. Fans throughout the world still debate its many ramifications in heated discussion and arguments. And, if you wanna know the true measure of this series' amazing impact, even in the Bullpen itself the arguments still continue!

Of course, one of the most important qualities that Chris and John have been able to bring to our marvelous mutant magna-series (I can't bear to call such powerful masterworks "mini-series") is the element of flesh-and-blood characterization. If Phoenix didn't seem real, if she wasn't as believable to you as the girl next door, if you didn't feel you knew her, you understood her, you cared for her—then her startling destiny would have meant nothing to you; you'd have shrugged it off and reached for another Twinkie.

(You'll notice, of course, that I refer to Phoenix' fate, or destiny, without telling you what it actually is. There's a reason for that. It just occurred to me that somewhere in the universe there may actually be a culturally-deprived unfortunate who hasn't yet read, or heard about issue #137 of the X-Men. 'Tis for the benefit of that improbable individual that I dare not prematurely reveal the wonderment that yet awaits thee!)

Still, the greatness of the X-Men is exemplified by more than the fate of one of its stars. Have you ever thought of the storylines themselves? I'm constantly amazed by the sheer complexity of the plots, by the way each single element dovetails so perfectly into the whole, by the way we the readers are shown countless seemingly unrelated facts and incidents, and then, as the story progresses, every random thread is cleverly joined together until there are no loose ends. The plotting and conceptualizing are as skillful, as innovatively brilliant as that which you'll find in any award-winning motion picture or best-selling novel. Nuts! Why pussyfoot around? Let's not speak with forked tongue! They're a lot *better* than you'll find in most of today's books or movies!

But let's change the subject before Capricious Claremont and Burgeoning Byrne suspect I'm trying to butter 'em up for a free subscription!

Let's talk about the treats you've got in store for you in the pages that lie ahead. For starters, you'll witness the first time the bedazzling Dazzler has ever guest-starred in the X-Men. And this is no mere token appearance. The gorgeous Dazz is very much a part of the action, the drama, and the cataclysmic chain of events which are destined to shake the superhero world. You'll also see the first appearance of another of Marvel's most unique and empathetic characters, the youthful and extravagantly appealing Kitty Pryde. This is the neophyte Kitty, still discovering her own fantastic powers, still confused and bewildered by the role she seems destined to play in a conflict she cannot fully comprehend. And there's more, much more! You'll see the return of the Beast, the Angel, Lilandra, the gorgeous Majestrix Shi'ar who must battle the man she most loves!

Sheesh! It isn't fair. I could go on yappin' all day, but why merely hint at the brain-blasting thrills in store for you when you can read 'em yourself on the pages that follow? And if it sounds like I'm being noble by cutting this intro short to let you get to the real stuff, forget it! I'm just thinking of me! I'm itchin' to re-read these sagas myself! So let's go, mutie-lover! Wonderment beckons, and the universe entire will be our arena! The best still lies ahead!

Excelsior!

Cyclops. Storm. Banshee. Nightcrawler. Wolverine. Colossus. Children of the atom, students of Charles Xavier, MUTANTS——feared and hated by the world they have sworn to protect. These are the STRANGEST heroes of all!

STAN LEE PRESENTS: THE UNCANNY X-MEN! ™

GOD SPARE THE CHILD...

IT'S ALWAYS HARD TO BID FAREWELL TO THOSE YOU LOVE. FOR THE X-MEN-- GATHERED ON THE RAIN-SLICK LANDING PAD BEHIND MOIRA Mac- TAGGERT'S MUIR ISLAND MUTANT RESEARCH CENTRE -- IT'S HARDER THAN MOST...

...BECAUSE THEY NEVER KNOW IF THIS FAREWELL WILL BE THEIR LAST.

THE "BLACKBIRD'S" FUELED AND CHECKED OUT, SEAN.

I GUESS IT'S TIME WE WERE ON OUR WAY.

AYE. IT'S BEEN GOOD HAVIN' THE LOT O' YE HERE THESE PAST FEW DAYS -- AFTER THAT BATTLE WITH PROTEUS,* WE ALL NEEDED A REST--

-- I'M SORRY TO SEE YE GO, CYCLOPS.

*LAST ISSUE -- ROG.

By CHRIS CLAREMONT and JOHN BYRNE with

| TERRY AUSTIN INKER | TOM ORZECHOWSKI LETTERER | BOB SHAREN COLORIST | ROGER STERN EDITOR | JIM SHOOTER Ed.-IN-CHIEF |

LF608

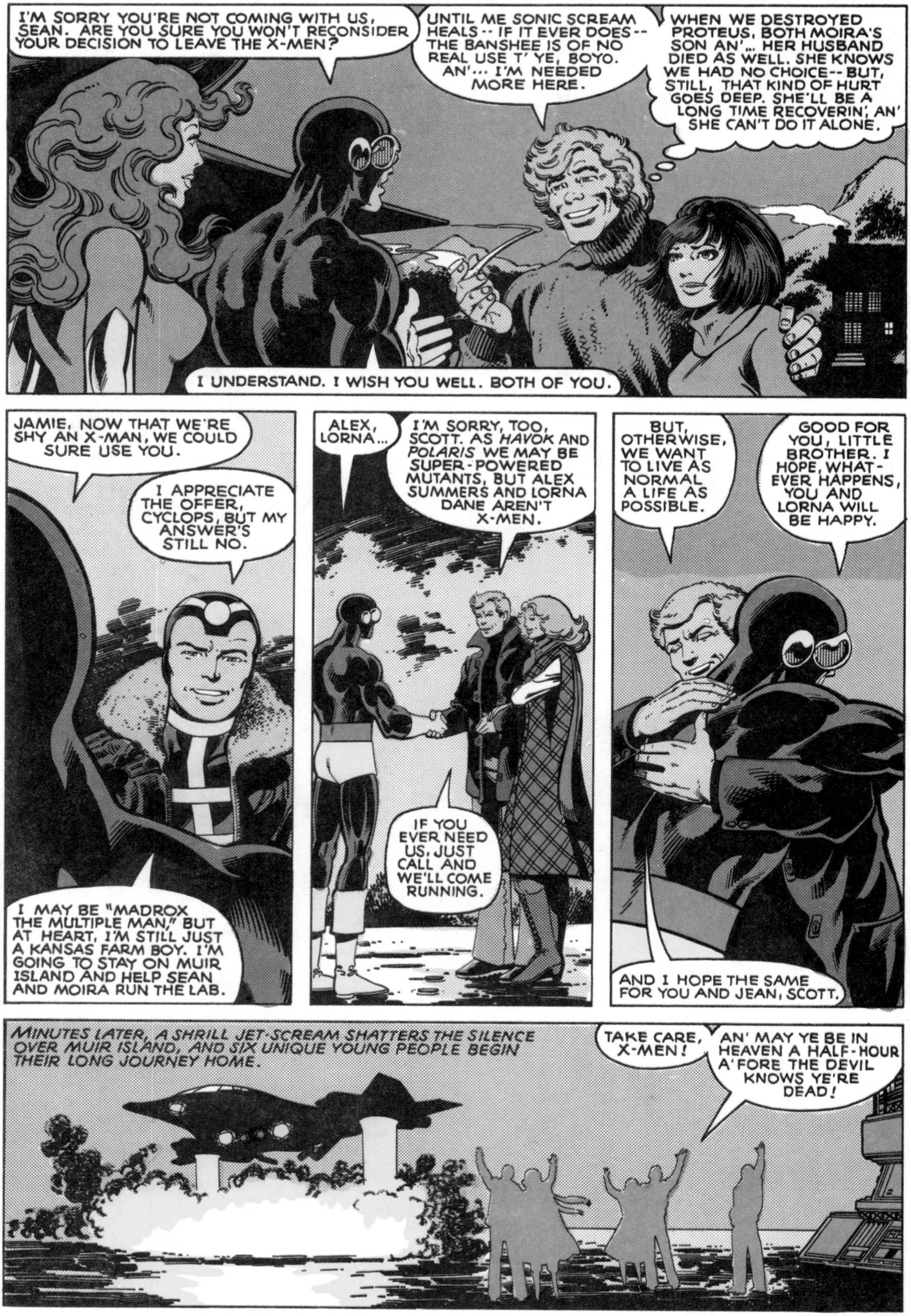
I'M SORRY YOU'RE NOT COMING WITH US, SEAN. ARE YOU SURE YOU WON'T RECONSIDER YOUR DECISION TO LEAVE THE X-MEN?
UNTIL ME SONIC SCREAM HEALS -- IF IT EVER DOES -- THE BANSHEE IS OF NO REAL USE T' YE, BOYO. AN'... I'M NEEDED MORE HERE.
WHEN WE DESTROYED PROTEUS, BOTH MOIRA'S SON AN'... HER HUSBAND DIED AS WELL. SHE KNOWS WE HAD NO CHOICE -- BUT, STILL, THAT KIND OF HURT GOES DEEP. SHE'LL BE A LONG TIME RECOVERIN', AN' SHE CAN'T DO IT ALONE.
I UNDERSTAND. I WISH YOU WELL. BOTH OF YOU.
JAMIE, NOW THAT WE'RE SHY AN X-MAN, WE COULD SURE USE YOU.
I APPRECIATE THE OFFER, CYCLOPS, BUT MY ANSWER'S STILL NO.
I MAY BE "MADROX THE MULTIPLE MAN," BUT AT HEART, I'M STILL JUST A KANSAS FARM BOY. I'M GOING TO STAY ON MUIR ISLAND AND HELP SEAN AND MOIRA RUN THE LAB.
ALEX, LORNA...
I'M SORRY, TOO, SCOTT. AS HAVOK AND POLARIS WE MAY BE SUPER-POWERED MUTANTS, BUT ALEX SUMMERS AND LORNA DANE AREN'T X-MEN.
IF YOU EVER NEED US, JUST CALL AND WE'LL COME RUNNING.
BUT, OTHERWISE, WE WANT TO LIVE AS NORMAL A LIFE AS POSSIBLE.
GOOD FOR YOU, LITTLE BROTHER. I HOPE, WHATEVER HAPPENS, YOU AND LORNA WILL BE HAPPY.
AND I HOPE THE SAME FOR YOU AND JEAN, SCOTT.
MINUTES LATER, A SHRILL JET-SCREAM SHATTERS THE SILENCE OVER MUIR ISLAND, AND SIX UNIQUE YOUNG PEOPLE BEGIN THEIR LONG JOURNEY HOME.
TAKE CARE, X-MEN!
AN' MAY YE BE IN HEAVEN A HALF-HOUR A'FORE THE DEVIL KNOWS YE'RE DEAD!

THEIR NAMES ARE AN UNSUNG ROLL OF HONOR: *NIGHTCRAWLER, CYCLOPS, WOLVERINE, COLOSSUS, STORM, PHOENIX.* IN MANY WAYS, THEY ARE THE BEST HUMANITY HAS TO OFFER. AND, FOR THE MOMENT, ALL IS WELL IN THEIR MADCAP, HELTER-SKELTER WORLD.

NONE ARE AWARE THAT IT IS MERELY THE CALM BEFORE THE HOLOCAUST.

MINE WAS THE HAND THAT SLEW PROTEUS. I KNOW HE WAS EVIL INCARNATE, THAT IT WAS HIS LIFE OR MOIRA'S...

BUT DOES THAT MAKE WHAT I DID... *RIGHT?*

THERE'S NO ANSWER TO PETER RASPUTIN'S ANGUISHED THOUGHTS, ONLY DOUBTS ABOUT HIS LIFE AS THE X-MAN COLOSSUS THAT GNAW INSATIABLY AT HIS HEART AND SOUL...

...AS THE "BLACKBIRD" STREAKS WESTWARD AT FIVE TIMES THE SPEED OF SOUND...

...RAPIDLY OVERTAKING A LARGER, SLOWER CORPORATE JETLINER MARKED WITH THE STYLIZED LOGO OF NEW YORK'S LEGENDARY *HELLFIRE CLUB.*

THE PAINT ON THAT JET'S HULL IS AS BLACK AS THE HEART OF ITS ONLY PASSENGER. FOR THE PAST FEW MONTHS, HE'S GONE BY THE NAME OF JASON WYNGARDE, AND WORN THE FACE OF A GENTLEMAN ROGUE. HE'S ALSO TAKEN GREAT PAINS TO BECOME THE MOST IMPORTANT PERSON IN JEAN GREY'S LIFE.

EACH TIME, IT BECOMES EASIER TO TOUCH JEAN'S MIND -- AS OUR PSYCHIC RAPPORT GROWS EVER CLOSER -- AND WHY NOT?

I'M MERELY GIVING HER A TASTE OF SOME OF HER INNERMOST-- FORBIDDEN --NEEDS AND DESIRES.

WITHIN HER ANGEL'S SOUL -- AS IN ALL OUR SOULS-- LURKS A DEVIL, A *YANG* COUNTERPART TO THE SURFACE *YIN.*

"ALL I'M DOING IS FREEING THAT NEGATIVE PART OF HER *'SELF'* FROM ITS MORAL CAGE."

WYNGARDE SMILES-- CONCENTRATES-- AND, MILES AWAY...

...JEAN GREY'S WORLD SUDDENLY TURNS TOPSY-TURVY.

WHEN AT LAST SHE OPENS HER EYES, THE "BLACKBIRD" AND HER FRIENDS ARE GONE. FOR HER, TIME HAS APPARENTLY SLIPPED BACKWARDS TWO HUNDRED YEARS * AND SHE IS ONCE MORE LADY JEAN GREY, NOW EN ROUTE TO AMERICA WITH THE MAN SHE LOVES AND WILL SOON — MARRY.

OH, NO! DEAR LORD — NO! NOT AGAIN !!

I'M ON A SHIP! EVERYTHING'S CHANGED -- I'VE CHANGED !

* AS IT HAS TWICE BEFORE, IN X-MEN #'s 125 & 126 -- ROG.

HIS NAME IS JASON WYNGARDE. HE'S A KNIGHT OF THE REALM, AND THE MOST MAGNIFICENT MAN SHE HAS EVER KNOWN.

IS ANYTHING AMISS, JEAN? I THOUGHT I HEARD YOU CRY OUT.

I KNOW WE'VE HAD A ROUGH PASSAGE, MY DARLING, BUT WE'LL SOON BE IN NEW YORK.

AND THEN YOU'LL BE MINE. FOREVER!

YES, JASON. OH, YES...

NO! WHAT AM I DOING ?!

THE EMOTIONS HE STIRS WITHIN ME -- SO INTENSE -- MUST BREAK AWAY -- WHILE I CAN !

I ... MY HEAD ACHES SO, JASON. I'LL BE FINE ONCE I'VE HAD A BREATH OF FRESH AIR.

I'LL ACCOMPANY YOU.

NO ! THANK YOU. I ... PREFER TO BE ALONE.

DESPERATELY, HER TELEPATHIC POWERS SCOUR THE SHIP, BUT THEY ONLY CONFIRM WHAT HER SENSES HAVE ALREADY TOLD HER. THIS IS REALITY.

I THOUGHT THESE TIMESLIPS WERE CAUSED BY PROTEUS' REALITY-WARPING POWER.

IT SEEMS I WAS MISTAKEN.

BUT THE ALTERNATIVE IS SO INCREDIBLE -- CAN I ACTUALLY BE PSYCHICALLY SHIFTING IN TIME, RELIVING THE LIFE OF ONE OF MY ANCESTORS ?

I SUPPOSE, FOR THE POWER OF PHOENIX, ANYTHING IS POSSIBLE. THAT SCARES ME.

WHAT REALLY SCARES ME IS THAT THESE TIMESLIPS ARE HAPPENING MORE AND MORE OFTEN. SUPPOSE I'M TRAPPED IN THE PAST? WHAT WILL HAPPEN TO MY BODY IN THE PRESENT?

MILADY...?

THE CAPTAIN! WAIT -- I KNOW THAT VOICE!

"SCOTT!"

I SAW YE COME ON DECK, MA'AM.

IS ANY-THING...

...TROUBLING YOU, JEAN?

SHE'S WHITE AS A SHEET-- ALMOST... TERRIFIED.

I'D LIKE TO HELP.

I DON'T THINK YOU CAN, SCOTT. I DOUBT ANYONE CAN.

AT LEAST LET ME TRY.

I... NEED TO TALK TO YOU. TO EXPLAIN SOME THINGS.

ABOUT YOUR DATING COLLEEN WING? YOU NEEDN'T. I ALREADY KNOW.

I'VE NEVER TAPPED YOUR MIND, SCOTT-- I NEVER WILL-- BUT I COULDN'T HELP PICKING UP STRAY THOUGHTS FROM THE OTHERS.

JEAN, COLLEEN'S A FRIEND-- NO MORE, NO LESS.

I'VE DONE A LOT OF THINKING SINCE YOUR... 'DEATH' IN ANTARCTICA.* I HAVEN'T MUCH LIKED SOME OF THE THINGS I'VE LEARNED ABOUT MYSELF.

*JEAN WAS BELIEVED KILLED IN X-MEN #113--ROG.

ALL MY LIFE, IT SEEMED THAT-- EVERY TIME I TURNED AROUND-- I WAS LOSING PEOPLE I LOVED: MY FOLKS, MY BROTHER ALEX, THE FEW FRIENDS I MADE AT THE ORPHANAGE. EACH TIME, THE LOSS HURT.

LOSING YOU WAS THE LOSS I COULDN'T TAKE.

IF I'D ALLOWED MYSELF TO FEEL ... ANYTHING, THE GRIEF WOULD HAVE BROKEN ME, MAYBE KILLED ME. WHEN I THOUGHT YOU'D DIED... I... IT WAS LIKE MY MIND SHUT PART OF ITSELF OFF.

I FELT... NOTHING.

JEAN, YOU'RE EVERYTHING TO ME-- AS NECESSARY AS THE AIR I BREATHE. I USED TO SAY "I LOVE YOU" WITHOUT TRULY KNOWING WHAT I WAS TALKING ABOUT. I KNOW NOW-- A LITTLE, ANYWAY.

JEAN-- I LOVE YOU.

AND I, YOU, SCOTT. WITH ALL MY HEART.

THEY SPEND THE REST OF THE FLIGHT TOGETHER-- SOMETIMES TOUCHING, SOMETIMES KISSING...

...BUT MOSTLY JUST TALKING WITH AN EASE THEY'D NEVER KNOWN BEFORE, THEIR DIALOGUE CONTINUING EVEN AFTER CYCLOPS TAKES THE "BLACKBIRD'S" CONTROLS TO BEGIN THE DESCENT TO THE X-MEN'S HOME/SCHOOL/HEADQUARTERS.

BECAUSE OF THE TELEPATHIC RAPPORT SHE'S ESTABLISHED BETWEEN THEM, JEAN IS THE FIRST TO REALIZE THAT SOMETHING'S WRONG...

... AS CYCLOPS SUDDENLY SKIDS THE SLEEK AIRCRAFT INTO A SILENT TOUCHDOWN DIRECTLY BEHIND THE MANSION, INSTEAD OF AT THE X-MEN'S HIDDEN LANDING FIELD, OVER A MILE AWAY.

CYKE, WHAT'S UP ?!

INTRUDER ALERT, WOLVERINE! SENSORS HAVE PICKED UP SOMEONE INSIDE THE HOUSE. THE READINGS ARE ALL SCRAMBLED, THOUGH--

-- CAN'T TELL IF IT'S FRIEND OR FOE.

"SO WE'RE GOING TO ASSUME IT'S *TROUBLE!*"

AS THINGS TURN OUT, HOWEVER...

...IT'S QUITE THE OPPOSITE.

PROFESSOR XAVIER-- YOU'RE BACK!

IN THE FLESH, STORM.

GREETINGS, MY X-MEN. IT IS SO VERY GOOD TO SEE YOU AGAIN -- TO KNOW THAT YOU ARE ALL ALIVE AND WELL.

CHARLES XAVIER TRIES TO CONTINUE, BUT WORDS FAIL HIM.

OVER THE YEARS SINCE HE FOUNDED THE X-MEN, HE HAS COME TO REGARD HIS YOUNG MUTANT CHARGES-- BOTH OLD TEAM AND NEW-- MORE LIKE HIS CHILDREN THAN HIS STUDENTS.

LOOKING AT THEM NOW, HE REALIZES JUST HOW GLAD HE IS TO BE HOME, SURROUNDED BY THOSE HE LOVES.

THE DAYS THAT FOLLOW ARE QUIET, LAZY -- PERFECT FOR RELAXATION AND... REFLECTION...

I'M GLAD YOU STAYED UP HERE, JEAN...

PROFESSOR X ASKED ME TO. HE WANTS TO RUN SOME TESTS.

I CAUGHT A STRAY THOUGHT -- I'M THE REASON HE RETURNED TO THE SCHOOL. HE'S WORRIED ABOUT MY ABILITY TO CONTROL PHOENIX'S POWER.

SOMETHING WRONG, JEAN?

HM? NOT SO LONG AS YOU'RE AROUND.

∋Ahem!∈ THAT'S FUNNY -- THE PLACE SEEMS AWFULLY QUIET. PEOPLE SHOULD BE UP AND AROUND BY NOW.

AH-HA! I HEARD SOMETHING BEHIND THIS DOOR.

SCOTT -- WAIT! DON'T YOU REMEMBER?! THAT EXTRA-THICK DOOR LEADS TO--

-- THE DANGER ROOM!

THWAM

WOLVERINE, WHERE ARE YOU GOING?! WOLVERINE!!

EASE UP, MISTER! WHAT'S GOING ON IN THERE?!

I'M NO KID ANYMORE, SUMMERS, AN' I'M NO FLAMIN' AMATEUR -- SO WHERE DOES CHROME-DOME GET OFF TREATIN' ME LIKE ONE?! YOU TELL XAVIER WHAT I TOLD YOU, BUB --

-- WOLVERINE DON'T JUMP THROUGH HOOPS FOR NOBODY!

SOUNDS SERIOUS.

IT IS SERIOUS -- AND I SHOULD HAVE SEEN IT COMING.

I JUST DIDN'T FIGURE THINGS WOULD BLOW UP QUITE SO QUICKLY.

PROFESSOR, CAN I TALK TO YOU? IT'S IMPORTANT.

IN A MOMENT, SCOTT. NIGHT-CRAWLER, NOW WE WILL TEST YOUR AGILITY AND "WALL-CRAWLING" ABILITIES -- STORM, YOUR AIRBORNE MANEUVER-ABILITY -- AND COLOSSUS, YOUR STRENGTH.

SCOTT, NOTIFY WOLVERINE THAT HIS CHILDISH OUTBURST WILL COST HIM TEN DEMERITS.

TEN-- OR TEN THOUSAND, PROFESSOR-- I DOUBT THEY'LL MEAN ANYTHING TO HIM. WOLVERINE'S A GROWN MAN, WITH YEARS OF EXPERIENCE AND TRAINING IN THE USE OF HIS POWERS. THE SAME IS TRUE FOR STORM, MYSELF, AND JEAN.

THE ORIGINAL X-MEN WERE TEEN-AGERS-- WITH NO IDEA HOW TO COPE WITH THEIR MUTANT ABILITIES. WE'RE NOT TEEN-AGERS-- OR BEGINNERS. YOU CAN'T TREAT US LIKE WE ARE.

I TRIED IT THAT WAY. I FAILED.

I AM NOT YOU.

NO, SIR-- BUT YOU ALSO HAVEN'T HAD MUCH CONTACT WITH THE NEW X-MEN SINCE YOU FORMED THE TEAM. I'VE LIVED WITH THEM, WORKED WITH THEM, FOUGHT WITH THEM.

FIRST AND FOREMOST-- WE'RE INDIVIDUALS.

WE CAN'T MESH INTO THE SAME KIND OF TEAM AS THE ORIGINAL X-MEN, BECAUSE WE'RE NOT THE SAME KIND OF PEOPLE.

FORGIVE MY BLUNT- NESS, SCOTT, BUT TO ME THAT BETOKENS A FAILURE OF LEADERSHIP ON YOUR PART. THIS... ANARCHY IS A RESULT OF YOUR FAILURE TO TEACH THESE MUTANTS HOW TO **BE** A TEAM.

PROFESSOR... WE **ARE** A TEAM!

QUIET! YOU'RE CORRECT, I HAVE BEEN REMISS IN MY DUTIES. I HAVE NOT TAUGHT THE NEW X-MEN-- IN PART BECAUSE I TRUSTED YOU TO TAKE THAT RESPONSIBILITY. THAT LAPSE WILL BE SPEEDILY RECTIFIED.

HOW DO I REACH HIM? I KNOW I'M RIGHT, BUT...

RRREEEEE

WE'LL CONTINUE THIS DISCUSSION LATER, SCOTT.

CEREBRO'S CONTACT ALARM! MY SCANNING DEVICE HAS DISCOVERED A NEW MUTANT!

Hmmm-- SCANNER INDICATES TWO MUTANTS, BOTH MANIFESTING ABILITIES UNKNOWN TO CEREBRO'S MEMORY BANKS--

--AND BOTH POTENTIALLY QUITE POWERFUL!

THIS IS CRAZY! TO HIM, I'M STILL THE UNTRIED KID WHO'S ALLOWED ONLY SO MUCH RESPONSIBILITY WITH THE X-MEN AND NO MORE!

ONE IN CHICAGO, ONE IN NEW YORK CITY. THAT MEANS-- IF WE'RE TO CONTACT THEM AS QUICKLY AND EFFICIENTLY AS POSSIBLE -- WE'LL HAVE TO SPLIT THE TEAM.

YOU AND JEAN TAKE THE NEW YORK CONTACT, SCOTT.

I'LL TAKE COLOSSUS, STORM AND WOLVERINE OUT WITH ME TO CHICAGO. I WANT TO SEE HOW THEY OPERATE IN THE FIELD.

MOST IMPRESSIVE, GENTLEMEN.

POOR XAVIER. IF ONLY HE KNEW...

... THAT THE HELLFIRE CLUB HAS A TAP ON HIS PRECIOUS CEREBRO, AND THAT EVERY SCRAP OF DATA IN ITS MEMORY BANKS IS OURS FOR THE ASKING. YOUR MAN, *WARHAWK*, DID HIS BUGGING WORK WELL. *

WHAT'S YOUR NEXT MOVE, SHAW?

WE'LL CONTACT THOSE MUTANTS, JUST AS XAVIER PLANS TO -- ONLY THE HELLFIRE CLUB WILL GET THERE FIRST. AND RECRUIT THEM -- BY HOOK OR BY CROOK.

*FOR THOSE OF YOU WHO WONDERED *WHO* SICCED WARHAWK ON OUR MERRY MUTANTS BACK IN X-MEN #110, AND *WHY*-- WELL, NOW YOU KNOW -- ROG.

AND IF, ALONG THE WAY, WE MANAGE TO ACQUIRE -- OR ELIMINATE--SOME OF THE X-MEN, SO MUCH THE BETTER.

SHAW, YOU MAY BE CHAIRMAN OF THE HELLFIRE CLUB -- AND ONE OF THE MOST POWERFUL INDUSTRIALISTS IN AMERICA--

-- BUT IF YOU THINK THE X-MEN ARE GOING TO BE PUSH-OVERS, THINK AGAIN! FAR BETTER MEN THAN YOU HAVE PLEDGED THEIR DESTRUCTION...

... YET THE X-MEN ARE STILL HERE. THEY ARE DANGEROUS!

SO ARE WE, WYNGARDE...

... AS THE X-MEN WILL SOON DISCOVER! WON'T THEY, MY DEAR WHITE QUEEN?

AS YOU SAY, SHAW!

CHICAGO -- THE WINDY CITY, CELEBRATED IN VERSE BY SANDBURG, IN SONG BY SINATRA. HOME OF THE WORLD'S TALLEST BUILDING AND -- SO THEY SAY -- BEST PIZZA.

THREE MILLION-PLUS PEOPLE LIVE IN THIS SPRAWLING, TOUGH, PASSIONATE, OLD-NEW METROPOLIS. OUR CONCERN, HOWEVER, IS NOT WITH THE CITY PROPER BUT WITH ONE OF ITS SUBURBS.

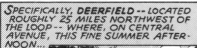

SPECIFICALLY, DEERFIELD -- LOCATED ROUGHLY 25 MILES NORTHWEST OF THE LOOP -- WHERE, ON CENTRAL AVENUE, THIS FINE SUMMER AFTER-NOON...

... KATHERINE PRYDE IS HEAD-ING HOME FROM DANCE CLASS. SHE'S 13 YEARS OLD, GOING ON FOURTEEN --

-- AND HER WORLD IS SLOWLY FALLING APART.

HI, MOM! HI, DAD!

KITTY, COME IN HERE A MOMENT, WILL YOU?

KITTY, THIS IS **Ms. FROST.** SHE REPRESENTS A VERY GOOD SCHOOL IN MASSACHUSETTS...

HELLO, KATHERINE. I'M SURE WE'RE GOING TO BE GREAT FRIENDS.

HI.

ARE YOU ALL RIGHT, PRECIOUS? YOU'RE HOME AWFULLY EARLY.

I HAD ANOTHER ONE OF THOSE DARN HEADACHES.

YOU GO UP-STAIRS AND LIE DOWN. I'LL BRING YOU SOME ASPIRIN IN A MINUTE.

I DON'T NEED ASPIRIN, MOM. I NEED A NEW HEAD -- THIS ONE'S ABOUT TO BUST WIDE OPEN!

I GUESS MOM AN' DAD ARE SERIOUS ABOUT SPLITTIN' UP, IF THEY'RE TALKIN' ABOUT SENDIN' ME AWAY TO SCHOOL. I'VE TOLD 'EM I DIDN'T WANT TO GO-- I LIKE IT IN DEERFIELD, ALL MY FRIENDS ARE HERE -- BUT WHAT I WANT DOESN'T COUNT.

WHERE'D THEY DREDGE UP THAT "Ms. FROST", ANYWAY? SHE LOOKED AT ME LIKE I WAS SOME-THING GOOD TO EAT. ЗICKE SHE GIVES ME THE CREEPS.

≥OWW!!!≤ C'MON, HEAD, GIMME A BREAK-- WHAT'D I EVER DO TO YOU?!

Ah, GEEZ-- IT... HURTS!

SHE CAN'T HELP CRYING AS SHE SPRAWLS ON HER BED, THE THROBBING PAIN GOUGING DEEP LINES AROUND HER TIGHT-CLENCHED EYES. SHE'S BEEN HAVING THESE HEADACHES FOR WEEKS NOW-- THE ATTACKS STEADILY INCREASING IN FREQUENCY, DURATION AND INTENSITY.

THIS ONE'S... THE WORST... EVER.

PLEASE, GOD-- I'M ONLY 13½... I CAN'T BE DYING!

SOMEBODY STOP THE HURTING!

PLEASE-- MAKE IT STOP!!

IT STOPS.

JUST LIKE THAT.

SLOWLY, GINGERLY, KITTY OPENS HER EYES.

Huh?! I'M IN THE LIVING ROOM!

HOW'D I GET HERE?! LAST THING I REMEMBER, I WAS LYING ON MY BED!

KITTY? I THOUGHT YOU WERE GOING UP TO YOUR ROOM. AND WHY ARE YOU LYING ON THE FLOOR, FOR GOODNESS' SAKES?

MOM! Oh... ah...

... I CAME DOWN FOR A GLASS OF WATER AND, ah, SNAGGED MY SNEAKER ON THE CARPET. I FELL.

ARE YOU OKAY, KITTEN? HEY, WHAT'S THE RUSH?! WHAT ABOUT YOUR WATER?

I'M FINE, DAD. I'LL GET IT LATER.

I, ah, GOTTA DO SOME HOMEWORK.

I DON'T KNOW WHAT'S GOTTEN INTO THAT GIRL, Ms. FROST. I APOLOGIZE FOR HER BEHAVIOR.

YOU NEEDN'T, Mr. PRYDE.

I UNDERSTAND PERFECTLY-- KITTY'S AT THAT... AWKWARD AGE. YOU HAVE MY SCHOOL'S BROCHURES. I'LL BE IN TOUCH.

THE FATHER LIKES MY SCHOOL--THE MOTHER DOES NOT. I'LL HAVE TO MAKE SURE HIS VIEW PREVAILS.

WELL, LOOK WHO'S HERE-- XAVIER AND THREE X-MEN. RIGHT ON SCHEDULE.

NICE LOOKIN' FRAIL. SOMETHIN' ABOUT HER SCENT, THOUGH-- RAISES THE HACKLES ON MY NECK. WONDER WHY?

MR. PRYDE, I'M CHARLES XAVIER...

OH, YES-- FROM THE "SCHOOL FOR GIFTED YOUNGSTERS." PLEASED TO MEET YOU, PROFESSOR.

I'M CARMEN PRYDE, FOLKS. COME ON IN.

THIS IS MY WIFE, TERRI.

AND, UNLESS I'M MISTAKEN, THAT YOUNG LADY IS THE ONE WE'VE HEARD SO MUCH ABOUT.

HOW DO YOU DO, KITTY?

UH, HI.

THESE PEOPLE ARE WEEEEEIRD. THAT GUY PUSHING THE WHEELCHAIR IS SO HUGE...KINDA NEAT-LOOKING, TOO.

KITTY, YOUR MOM AND I HAVE... BUSINESS TO DISCUSS WITH PROFESSOR XAVIER. SINCE YOU SEEM TO BE FEELING A LOT BETTER...

...YOU INTERESTED IN A TRIP TO THE "MALT SHOPPE" WITH HIS STUDENTS HERE? MY TREAT?

AND SO, A REAL QUICK CHANGE, AN EIGHT-BLOCK WALK AND A TRIPLE-SCOOP, "SOOPER-DOOPER" ICE CREAM SODA LATER, A KID FROM MIDDLE AMERICA AND AN AFRICAN "GODDESS" ARE WELL ON THE WAY TO BECOMING FAST FRIENDS.

WE GOT BLACK KIDS IN MY SCHOOL, ORORO, BUT NONE OF 'EM LOOK LIKE YOU. I MEAN, Y'KNOW-- WHITE HAIR AN' BLUE EYES??

SO FAR AS I KNOW, KITTY, I AM ONE OF A KIND. AND SO ARE YOU.

YOU MEAN, 'CAUSE I'M SO SMART?

NO--SOMETHING ELSE. KITTY, HAVE YOU EVER HEARD OF THE X-MEN?

SODA $1.25

Coca-Cola

20

SURE. THEY'RE SUPER HEROES OR SOMETHIN', LIKE THE AVENGERS. THEY WERE JUST IN A BIG FIGHT IN SCOTLAND.

HEY -- ARE YOU THEM???

WE ARE. PROFESSOR XAVIER SAID IT WAS ALL RIGHT TO TELL YOU.

GOSH. CAN I HAVE YOUR AUTOGRAPH?

SO MUCH ENERGY AND LIFE -- AND JOY. IF NOT FOR AN ACCIDENT OF WAR, I MIGHT HAVE BEEN LIKE THIS AT KITTY'S AGE.

INSTEAD, I WAS WALKING ALONE ACROSS THE SUDAN. I HADN'T YET LEARNED I COULD SOAR ON THE WINDS.

IN THAT DESERT, I ALMOST DIED.

MEANWHILE...

THIS AIN'T NO LIBERRY, FELLA. YOU WANNA READ THE MAGAZINE, BUY THE MAGAZINE.

I DON'T LIKE BEIN' TAPPED, BUB. OR ORDERED AROUND.

WOLVERINE... NO!

I DON'T LIKE PEOPLE READIN' WITHOUT PAYIN'. WANNA MAKE SOMETHIN' OF IT?

I THOUGHT YOU'D NEVER ASK.

WOLVERINE-- BEHIND YOU!

Eh?

SKA-RASSH

HOLEE--!!

WHAT THE FLAMIN'--?!

WE'VE FOUND THE X-MEN -- TAKE 'EM!

BY THE WHITE WOLF, A FLAME-THROWER! I BARELY MANAGED TO CHANGE INTO MY ARMORED FORM--

--AND SHIELD THE STORE-OWNER FROM THE BLAST-- IN TIME.

EVEN SO -- THE HEAT IS INCREDIBLE. I CAN ACTUALLY FEEL IT!

FELLAS -- I DUNNO WHO YOU ARE, AN', FRANKLY, I COULDN'T CARE LESS --

--BUT RIGHT NOW, YOU'RE THE ANSWER TO THE WOLVERINE'S PRAYERS!

AND, AT WOLVERINE'S COMMAND, GLEAMING ADAMANTIUM CLAWS POP OUT OF THE BACK OF HIS HANDS.

I'VE BEEN SPOILIN' FER A DECENT ROUGHHOUSE. I'M OBLIGED TO YOU CLOWNS FOR -- HEY!

MY CLAWS -- I DIDN'T EVEN TOUCH THE CREEP!

HE'S PROTECTED BY SOME SORT'A FORCE-FIELD --

UNNNGNH!!

THE BLOW HURLS WOLVERINE THE LENGTH OF THE SHOP. INSTINCTIVELY -- AND WITH A YELP OF MINGLED SURPRISE AND FEAR -- KITTY PRYDE KICKS HERSELF BACKWARDS TO GET OUT OF THE WAY.

THAT KICK SENDS HER A LOT FARTHER THAN SHE'D ANTICIPATED.

YYIIII--!!

POST NO BILLS

I ... I'M OUTSIDE. I ... PUSHED MYSELF ... RIGHT THROUGH THE WALL. BUT -- THAT'S IMPOSSIBLE!

FEEL SO ... TIRED ... DIZZY -- NEVER FELT THIS WAY BEFORE. WANT TO STAY ... AWAKE ...

... BUT ... CANNNNN'T ... ✷

AND, INSIDE WHAT'S LEFT OF THE "MALT SHOPPE"...

KITTY'S GONE! SHE MUST HAVE SLIPPED AWAY WITH THE STORE-OWNER AND THE OTHER CHILDREN. GOOD-- I'M GLAD SHE'S SAFE.

I WISH I COULD SAY THE SAME FOR ME. I'M HITTING THIS VILLAIN WITH ALL MY ELEMENTAL POWERS--WIND, RAIN, LIGHTNING-- YET, FOR EVERY ATTACK, HE HAS A DEFENSE.

WOLVERINE AND COLOSSUS DON'T SEEM MUCH BETTER OFF.

STORM-- LISTEN UP! EACH O' THESE GONZOS SEEMS EQUIPPED TO COUNTER OUR SPECIFIC POWERS.

LET'S SEE WHAT HAPPENS IF WE SWITCH PARTNERS!

AHHRRR--!!

WOLVERINE'S IDEA WORKED! I'LL HANDLE COLOSSUS' FOE, THEN SEE IF MY LIGHTNING BOLTS CAN AFFECT THE LAST MAN'S FORCE FIELD.

THEY CAN. THEY DO.

COLOSSUS FINISHES THE JOB.

PLEASANT DREAMS, TOVARISCH.

KANG

WE HAVE DONE WELL, MY FRIENDS. I THINK EVEN PROFESSOR XAVIER WOULD HAVE APPRECIATED OUR SKILL IN THIS BATTLE.

PERHAPS. I WISH SCOTT WERE HERE. THESE MEN KNEW OUR POWERS, AND HOW TO DEFEAT THEM-- BUT HOW ?!

LET'S WAKE THE SUCKERS UP AN' ASK 'EM. I THINK I CAN... PERSUADE 'EM TO TELL US ALL THEY KNOW.

SUDDENLY... TELEPATHIC FORCE BOLT-- ASSAULTING OUR MINDS! SO... POWERFUL!

THEY FIGHT THE MENTAL AMBUSH USING PSYCHIC TECHNIQUES TAUGHT THEM BY PROFESSOR X AND PHOENIX...

... BUT THE OUTCOME IS NEVER IN DOUBT. WITH A SMILE, EMMA FROST -- THE WHITE QUEEN -- WATCHES THEM FALL.

THEY'RE UNCONSCIOUS. LOAD THEM ABOARD THE HOVERCRAFT.

YES, MA'AM.

WYNGARDE WAS RIGHT -- THESE YOUNG PEOPLE KNOW THEIR BUSINESS.

BUT THE HELLFIRE CLUB KNOWS EVERY FACET, EVERY PARAMETER, OF THEIR MUTANT POWERS: THEIR STRENGTHS, THEIR WEAKNESSES. HOW THEY FIGHT, HOW THEY THINK. THAT GIVES US AN UNBEATABLE EDGE.

LET'S GO. AFTER WE TURN THESE PRISONERS OVER TO THE LAB, WE'LL GO AFTER XAVIER HIMSELF, AND SEE IF WE CAN'T MAKE THIS A CLEAN SWEEP OF THE X-MEN.

YES, MA'AM. BUT WHAT ABOUT OUR THREE ARMORED UNITS? WE LEFT THEM INSIDE, AND--!

OH, DON'T WORRY ABOUT THEM, CUTLER--

-- THE HELLFIRE CLUB HAS WAYS OF DEALING WITH FAILURES!

BSHRAM

THOSE MEN HAD POWER AND TRAINING SUFFICIENT TO DEFEAT THE X-MEN WITHOUT MY HELP. THEY BOTCHED THEIR JOB, AND NOW THE EXPLOSIVE CHARGES IN THEIR ARMOR HAVE REWARDED THEM FOR THEIR... "HANDY WORK".

DON'T ACT SO SHOCKED, CUTLER! WE PAY GOOD WAGES, WE EXPECT OUR MONEY'S WORTH.

STAYING ON BACK ROADS TO AVOID DETECTION, THE HOVERCRAFT MAKES ITS WAY SWIFTLY DOWN THE LAKE SHORE TOWARDS ITS BASE -- A MASSIVE INDUSTRIAL PARK ON THE OUTSKIRTS OF CHICAGO.

AND WITHIN THE CRAFT...

STRIP THEM -- SEARCH THEIR UNIFORMS AND THEIR PERSONS. CAREFULLY. REMOVE ANYTHING THAT MIGHT BE USED AS A WEAPON OR SIGNALLING DEVICE.

TAKE SPECIAL CARE WITH STORM. WE KNOW ABOUT THE LOCK-PICKS IN HER HEAD-DRESS -- MAKE SURE SHE HASN'T ANY OTHER SURPRISES. I'LL KEEP THEM TELEPATHICALLY SEDATED UNTIL WE REACH THE LAB.

WHAT ABOUT THE GIRL -- THE PRYDE KID?

SHE ESCAPED IN THE CONFUSION. THE X-MEN WERE ALWAYS OUR PRIMARY TARGET. NOW THAT WE HAVE THEM, SHE'LL KEEP.

WHEN WE WANT HER, WE KNOW WHERE TO FIND HER.

ACTUALLY, TO FIND KITTY, ALL THE WHITE QUEEN NEEDS TO DO IS TURN AROUND.

I DID IT! I CONCENTRATED -- AN' I'M WALKIN' RIGHT THROUGH THIS WALL FROM THE REAR COMPARTMENT!

I FEEL TINGLY ALL OVER -- BUT NOT AS TIRED AS THE LAST TIME. AN' MY HEADACHES ARE ALL GONE!

OH, NO! THAT CREEPY MISS FROST AND HER GOON SQUAD ARE HOLDING THE X-MEN PRISONERS. WHY... WHY DID I DECIDE TO SNOOP AROUND IN HERE?!

I... I GOTTA HELP 'EM, BUT HOW??? THESE GUYS HAVE GUNS -- AND SUPER-POWERS.

AN' I'M... ALL ALONE.

 NEXT

DEBUT OF THE *Dazzler!*

Cyclops. Storm. Nightcrawler. Wolverine. Colossus. Children of the atom, students of Charles Xavier, MUTANTS — feared and hated by the world they have sworn to protect. These are the STRANGEST heroes of all!

STAN LEE PRESENTS: THE UNCANNY X-MEN! ™

Dazzler

CHRIS CLAREMONT WRITER

JOHN BYRNE PENCILER/ CO-PLOTTER

TERRY AUSTIN INKER

TOM ORZECHOWSKI LETTERER

GLYNIS WEIN COLORIST

ROGER STERN EDITOR

JIM SHOOTER EDITOR-IN-CHIEF

DELANO STREET, IN LOWER MANHATTAN-- IN ITS HEYDAY, THIS WAS ONE OF THE BUSIEST MANUFACTURING CENTERS IN NEW YORK. THE BUSINESSES ARE CLOSED NOW, CRUMBLING. ONLY JUNKIES AND DERELICTS LIVE HERE FULL TIME.

IT'S HARDLY THE SORT OF NEIGHBORHOOD WHERE YOU'D EXPECT TO SEE A ROLLS-ROYCE AT MIDNIGHT. EVEN ONE OWNED BY THE UNCANNY X-MEN.

WELL, FOR BETTER OR WORSE, WE'VE ARRIVED.

ARE YOU SURE, SCOTT?

27

CONSIDERING THAT THEY THEMSELVES DIDN'T KNOW THEY'D BE COMING TO DELANO STREET UNTIL *LATE THIS AFTERNOON*, IT'S MORE THAN A LITTLE DISTURBING TO DISCOVER THAT THESE X-MEN *ARE BEING WATCHED.*

ALL RIGHT. AS YOU KNOW, OUR MUTANT DETECTOR, *CEREBRO*, PICKED UP TWO STRONG CONTACTS. PROFESSOR XAVIER AND THE OTHER X-MEN WENT TO CHECK OUT THE ONE IN CHICAGO, LEAVING US THE ONE IN NEW YORK.

CEREBRO INDICATED OUR MUTANT WAS ON THE MOVE ALL DAY... UNTIL A COUPLE OF HOURS AGO, WHEN HE FINALLY SETTLED DOWN. HERE.

I DON'T SEE WHY YOU TWO ARE SO NERVOUS. THIS IS MY KIND OF NEIGHBORHOOD: LOTS OF SHADOWS, AND LOTS OF THINGS TO CLIMB ON.

CONTACT CONFIRMED -- SPECIFIC DATA TO FOLLOW. SENSORS ON, ALL SYSTEMS ACTIVE. WE MARK THREE X-MEN -- *SCOTT SUMMERS*, A.K.A. *CYCLOPS.* TEAM LEADER. MUTANT ABILITY: SOLAR-CHARGED "*OPTIC BEAM*" FIRED FROM HIS EYES, CONTROLLED IN PART BY HIS RUBY QUARTZ VISOR.

HE37491-26143 "CYCLOPS"

JEAN GREY, A.K.A. MARVEL GIRL, A.K.A. *PHOENIX.* EXTREMELY HIGH-RANGE TELEPATH / TELEKINETIC. FULL POTENTIAL UNKNOWN. HANDLE WITH EXTREME CARE.

HE 37491-26144 "PHOENIX"

KURT WAGNER, A.K.A. *NIGHT-CRAWLER.*

HE 37491-26146 "NIGHTCRAWLER"

EXTRAORDINARY ATHLETIC ABILITIES -- AIDED BY UNUSUALLY DEXTROUS HANDS AND FEET, AND A PREHENSILE TAIL. ALSO, SUBJECT CAN TELEPORT OVER SMALL DISTANCES, AND BECOMES NEARLY INVISIBLE IN DEEP SHADOW.

ALERT THE ATTACK FORCE. WE'LL STRIKE AS SOON AS WE GET THE WORD FROM BASE. THOSE POOR FOOLS WON'T KNOW WHAT HIT 'EM.

MEANWHILE, BLISSFULLY UNAWARE OF THE DANGER...

NIGHTCRAWLER, FOR OBVIOUS REASONS, THIS IS AS FAR AS YOU GO.

STAY OUT HERE AND KEEP AN EYE ON THE ROLLS. YOU SEE OR HEAR ANYTHING FUNNY, LET ME KNOW-- FAST!

EXPECTING TROUBLE, SCOTT ?

JUST GETTING CAREFUL IN MY OLD AGE, JEAN. WE GO THIS WAY.

YOU'VE BEEN ON EDGE EVER SINCE PROFESSOR X RETURNED.

I KNOW. I GUESS I'D... GOTTEN USED TO BEING ON MY OWN, TO RUNNING THE X-MEN MY OWN WAY. SURE, I'VE MADE MISTAKES... BUT TO XAVIER, EVERYTHING I'VE DONE IS WRONG... UH-OH.

THOSE PEOPLE SEEM TO BE GOING WHERE WE'RE GOING.

SHORTLY, INSIDE...

≶PHEW!≷ WHAT A STENCH! I'LL BET THIS PLACE HASN'T BEEN CLEANED SINCE IT WAS BUILT!

DO YOU HAVE ANY IDEA WHAT WE'RE LOOKING FOR ?

NOT REALLY. OUR MUTANT COULD BE MALE OR FEMALE, YOUNG OR OLD. WE HAVEN'T A CLUE TO ITS ABILITIES. ALL WE'RE SURE OF IS THAT IT'S A SINGLE PERSON, VERY POWERFUL, AND SOMEWHERE IN THIS... CLUB.

SOUND AND LIGHT HIT WITH EQUAL FORCE IN AN AUDIO-VISUAL BLITZ-KRIEG THAT STUNS THE SENSES. EVEN AT THE DOOR, AS FAR AS POSSIBLE FROM THE DANCE FLOOR, IT'S IMPOSSIBLE TO TALK IN ANYTHING LESS THAN A SHOUT.

TELL ME, JEAN, IS THIS WHERE OLD DISCOS GO TO DIE ?

AUTOMATICALLY, JEAN SHIFTS INTO A TELEPATHIC RAPPORT WITH SCOTT, USING THE MIND-LINK TO COMMUNICATE WITH HIM IN COMPLETE PRIVACY.

FROM THE FIRST, BOTH X-MEN REALIZE THAT THE DISCO ISN'T A VERY NICE ONE.

WHAT KIND OF MUTANT ARE WE GOING TO FIND IN A PLACE LIKE THIS?!

OH, WELL -- WE WON'T KNOW TILL WE FIND HIM. OR HER. OR IT. I THINK WE'LL DO BETTER IF WE SPLIT UP, JEAN. YOU SCAN THE CROWD WITH YOUR PSI-POWERS.

I'LL USE MY WATCH. THERE'S A MICRO-CEREBRO BUILT INTO IT, PROGRAMMED WITH ALL THE DATA THE MAIN UNIT RECORDED ABOUT OUR MUTANT.

THE MOMENT I COME ANY-WHERE NEAR HIM, THE WATCH'S ALARM WILL START BEEPING.

"SCAN THE CROWD WITH YOUR PSI-POWERS." THAT'S EASIER SAID THAN DONE, SCOTT. I CAN'T SCREEN OUT EVERYONE'S THOUGHTS. SOME OF THE IMAGES I'M RECEIVING ARE SO... VILE.

BUT, I CAN HANDLE THAT. PART OF ME ALMOST FINDS THOSE THOUGHTS... ATTRACTIVE.

AND, WHILE SCOTT AND JEAN SLOWLY, CAREFULLY SEARCH THE DISCO, NIGHTCRAWLER YAWNS AND WISHES HE WERE SOMEWHERE ELSE.

HE'S NOTICED THE DELIVERY TRUCK PARKED ACROSS THE STREET, OF COURSE...

... AND FORGOTTEN IT A MOMENT LATER. AFTER ALL, HOW IS HE TO KNOW THAT, INSIDE THE VAN...

WE'RE READY TO GO, MR. SHAW-- WE CAN HIT 'EM ANYTIME.

EXCELLENT, RODI. THE HELLFIRE CLUB IS PROUD OF YOU.

ONLY A FEW BLOCKS DOWN FIFTH AVENUE FROM AVENGERS MANSION STANDS A BUILDING THAT -- LIKE THE VAN -- IS FAR LESS INNOCENT THAN IT APPEARS.

THIS IS THE LEGENDARY HELLFIRE CLUB.

FOR 150 YEARS, IT HAS BEEN ONE OF AMERICA'S OLDEST, MOST EXCLUSIVE GENTLEMEN'S CLUBS. ITS MEMBERSHIP LIST READS LIKE A "WHO'S WHO" OF THE NATION'S SOCIAL, POLITICAL, AND ECONOMIC ELITE.

BUT WITHIN THE CLUB IS AN *INNER CIRCLE* OPEN ONLY TO A SELECT FEW-- AN INNER CIRCLE WHO SEE THE CLUB AS AN AVENUE TO ACHIEVING *POWER.*

ONE MEMBER OF THIS INNER CIRCLE IS A MAN JEAN GREY HAS COME TO KNOW AS *JASON WYNGARDE.*

SHAW, TWO OF THE X-MEN WHO ROD! FACES ARE THE OLDEST, MOST EXPERIENCED-- MOST DANGEROUS-- MEMBERS OF THE TEAM. THEY'RE NOT TO BE TAKEN LIGHTLY.

NEITHER IS *SEBASTIAN SHAW.*

I DIDN'T BUILD A BILLION-DOLLAR EMPIRE FROM NO-THING BY MAKING MISTAKES, WYNGARDE. OR BY UNDER-ESTIMATING MY OPPONENTS.

WE'VE DONE PRETTY WELL AGAINST THE X-MEN SO FAR.

YES, BUT TO CAPTURE THEM ALL ?! I'LL BELIEVE IT, SHAW, WHEN I SEE IT.

IN THE MEANTIME, I'LL CONTINUE TO WORK ON SUBVERTING MS. GREY...

...AND GATHERING HER-- OF HER OWN FREE WILL-- INTO OUR FOLD.

HOW IS YOUR PLAN PROGRESSING, BY THE WAY? DO YOU THINK YOU HAVE A CHANCE OF SUCCESS?

NOT THINK, SHAW-- I KNOW. THE YOUNG LADY HASN'T REALIZED IT YET, BUT SHE'S MINE-- BODY AND SOUL!

AS YOU SAID, I'LL BELIEVE IT WHEN I SEE IT.

NO SOONER HAS WYNGARDE DEPARTED, THAN...

GOOD EVENING, SHAW.

FROST! HOW FARES MY DARLING WHITE QUEEN? IS ALL WELL IN CHICAGO?

31

EIGHT HUNDRED MILES TO THE WEST, IN A MASSIVE INDUSTRIAL COMPLEX ON THE OUTSKIRTS OF THE WINDY CITY, EMMA FROST-- THE WHITE QUEEN -- THROWS BACK HER HEAD AND LAUGHS.

IT COULDN'T BE BETTER. AS YOU CAN SEE, *COLOSSUS*, *WOLVERINE*, *STORM*, AND THE X-MEN'S MENTOR, *CHARLES XAVIER* HIMSELF, ARE ALL QUITE HELPLESS.

XAVIER IS UNDER ELECTRO-SLEEP SEDATION, WHILE THE INHIBITOR FIELDS BUILT INTO THEIR CAGES KEEP THE OTHERS FROM USING THEIR POWERS.

VERY GOOD. WHAT ABOUT THE *NEO-MUTANT* THEY SOUGHT?

SHE... WAS THE ONE THAT GOT AWAY. HER NAME IS KATHERINE PRYDE. SHE'S A CHILD. WE DON'T YET KNOW HER POWERS.

WE NEEDN'T WORRY ABOUT HER, THOUGH. I THINK I CAN... PERSUADE HER FATHER TO ENROLL HER IN MY MASSACHUSETTS ACADEMY. AFTER ALL, IT IS ONE OF THE MOST PRESTIGIOUS PRIVATE SCHOOLS IN THE COUNTRY.

AND ONCE SHE'S THERE, SHE'S OURS FOR THE TAKING!

AS THE TWO VILLAINS TALK, NO ONE IN THE VAST HOLDING CHAMBER NOTICES A SUDDEN, SLIGHT STIR IN THE AIR...

...THAT HERALDS THE UNORTHODOX ENTRANCE OF KITTY PRYDE.

I DID IT AGAIN!

I THOUGHT REAL HARD -- AN' I WALKED RIGHT THROUGH THAT WALL, LIKE IT WASN'T EVEN THERE! IT GETS EASIER EACH TIME I DO IT, TOO!

OKAY, I'VE SNUCK MY WAY INTO HERE --

-- WHAT THE HECK DO I DO *NOW*???

ONLY HOURS AGO, IT HAD SEEMED LIKE JUST ANOTHER ORDINARY DAY IN THE LIFE OF A KID WHOSE WORLD WAS FALLING APART. HER PARENTS WERE SPLITTING UP, AND KITTY HERSELF WAS BEING PLAGUED BY A SERIES OF STEADILY WORSENING, SKULL CRUSHING HEADACHES.

SHE CAME HOME FROM DANCE CLASS IN TIME TO BE INTRODUCED TO EMMA FROST-- IT WAS DISLIKE AT FIRST SIGHT.

HER REACTION TO THE X-MEN -- WHEN PROFESSOR XAVIER ARRIVED TO TRY TO RECRUIT HER FOR HIS "SCHOOL FOR GIFTED YOUNGSTERS" -- WAS QUITE THE OPPOSITE. WOLVERINE WAS SPOOKY, COLOSSUS A REAL HUNK...

... AND SHE AND STORM BECAME INSTANT FRIENDS.

THE FOUR YOUNG PEOPLE WERE ENJOYING ICE CREAM SODAS AT A NEARBY MALT SHOP -- WHILE THE PROFESSOR TALKED WITH KITTY'S PARENTS -- WHEN THEY WERE ATTACKED BY GOONS IN BATTLE ARMOR.

THE FIGHT WAS BRIEF AND FIERCE. THE X-MEN THOUGHT THEY'D WON...

...UNTIL, WITHOUT WARNING, THE WHITE QUEEN'S TELEPATHIC ATTACK TURNED THEIR MINDS INSIDE OUT. WHEN MORE GOONS CARRIED THE UNCONSCIOUS X-MEN ABOARD A WAITING HOVERCRAFT...

... KITTY FOLLOWED THEM. *

* LAST ISSUE--ROG.

I OUGHTTA HAVE MY HEAD EXAMINED, THINKING I CAN FREE THE X-MEN ALL BY MYSELF. BUT I'VE GOT TO DO SOMETHING.

STORM IS MY FRIEND. I CAN'T DESERT HER-- OR THE OTHERS.

'SIDES, FROM WHAT I'VE HEARD, ONCE THESE CREEPS ARE DONE WITH THE X-MEN, THEY'LL BE COMING AFTER ME!

CAN'T MAKE A SOUND--!

≥PSSST!≤ ORORO, IT'S ME, KITTY! KITTY PRYDE!

Uhnnn?

OH, CRIPES, SHE REALLY LOOKS OUT OF IT! ORORO!

WHO--? KITTY!

SSSHHHH! KEEP IT DOWN, FOR CRYIN' OUT LOUD! SOME-ONE'LL HEAR YOU! I CAME TO HELP. WHAT CAN I DO?

I... I... DON'T KNOW... IT'S SO HARD TO THINK!

THE INHIBITOR FIELD MUST BE AFFECTING MY MIND... AS WELL AS MY POWERS.

WHEN WE WERE CAPTURED, WE WERE SEARCHED TO THE SKIN. THEY TOOK MY LOCKPICKS, BUT...

...ah-HA! THEY MISSED THIS TAG, WORKED INTO THE FABRIC OF MY COSTUME!

MS. FROST-- THERE'S SOMEONE BY THE CAGES! IT'S A KID!

KITTY, TAKE THIS! FIND A TELEPHONE AND CALL THE NUMBER I'M GIVING YOU. TELL WHOEVER ANSWERS WHAT'S HAPPENED.

RUN FOR IT, LITTLE ONE! GET OUT OF HERE!

KITTY BOLTS FOR THE BACK OF THE ROOM, HEADING AWAY FROM THE EXIT DOORS, THE WHITE QUEEN'S AGENTS IN HOT PURSUIT.

YOU'RE WASTING YOUR TIME, KID. YOU'RE CHARGING INTO A DEAD END!

THEN, WITHOUT BREAKING STRIDE, KITTY TAKES AN INSTINCTIVE DEEP BREATH-- AND DIVES THROUGH THE FLOOR!

HUH?!?

THAT'S WHY SHE RAN BACK HERE-- SHE SUCKERED US AWAY FROM THE DOORS!

CRETINS! BY THE TIME THEY REACH THE LEVEL BELOW THIS, THE GIRL COULD BE ANYWHERE.

SEAL THE COMPLEX! ORGANIZE SEARCH TEAMS! I WANT KITTY PRYDE FOUND-- AT ONCE!

AT THAT MOMENT, BACK IN THE DISCO, JEAN GREY HAS JUST FINISHED HER SECOND CIRCUIT OF THE CROWDED DANCE FLOOR.

SHE'S NOT EVEN A QUARTER-CENTURY OLD, YET SHE'S FALLEN IN LOVE, DIED, RESURRECTED HERSELF AND SAVED THE UNIVERSE. SHE KNOWS SHE ONCE POSSESSED THE POWER OF... A GOD.

THAT MEMORY STILL TERRIFIES-- AND TANTALIZES-- HER.

SO FAR, I'VE NOTHING TO SHOW FOR TONIGHT BUT THREE DRUNKEN PASSES AND A COMMENT THAT MY DRESS IS TACKY. SCOTT ISN'T DOING ANY BETTER.

I WONDER IF CEREBRO COULD HAVE MADE A MISTAKE.

EXCUSE ME, MISS, I-- I WAS RIGHT! IT IS YOU! HULLO, AGAIN.

DO YOU REMEMBER ME? I'M JASON WYN-GARDE. WE MET IN STORNOWAY.

OH! YES, I...

THEIR EYES MEET--

-- AND SUDDENLY, REALITY... CHANGES AROUND JEAN.

THE 20th CENTURY GIVES WAY TO THE 18th, A LOWER-MANHATTAN DISCO...

..., TO A BURNED-OUT CHURCH IN A WOODLAND GLADE THAT WILL ONE DAY BECOME PART OF FIFTH AVENUE.

UNLIKE THE PREVIOUS TIME-SLIPS, JEAN DOESN'T TRY TO FIGHT HER WAY OUT OF THE PAST. THIS TIME, SHE ACCEPTS WHAT'S HAPPENING...

... AS SHE'S LED TO THE ALTAR AND HER WAITING HUSBAND-TO-BE. AS ALWAYS, HIS MANLY BEAUTY TAKES HER BREATH AWAY.

DEARLY BELOVED, WE ARE GATHERED TOGETHER IN THE FACE OF THIS CONGRE-GATION, TO JOIN TOGETHER THIS MAN AND THIS WOMAN IN HOLY MATRIMONY.

IT TAKES ALL HER STRENGTH OF WILL TO STAND DEMURELY AND LISTEN TO THE VICAR'S SERVICE...

...WHEN SHE WOULD RATHER BE IN SIR JASON WYNGARDE'S ARMS.

WILT THOU, JASON, HAVE THIS WOMAN TO BE THY WEDDED WIFE? WILT THOU LOVE HER, COMFORT HER, HONOUR AND KEEP HER IN SICKNESS AND IN HEALTH AND, FORSAKING ALL OTHERS, KEEP THEE ONLY UNTO HER, SO LONG AS YE BOTH SHALL LIVE?

I WILL.

WILT THOU, LADY JEAN, HAVE THIS MAN...?

OH, YES! YES!!

SMILING, HIS OBSIDIAN EYES GLOWING WITH AN EERIE, DARKLING LIGHT, THE MINISTER FINISHES THE CEREMONY...

... I PRONOUNCE THAT THEY BE MAN AND WIFE! SIR, YOU MAY KISS THE BRIDE.

YOU'RE MINE NOW, MILADY. BOUND TO ME TILL THE END OF TIME!

MILORD, I WOULD NOT HAVE IT ANY OTHER WAY!

MILORDS, GENTLEMEN -- LADIES -- OF THE HELLFIRE CLUB -- I GIVE YOU JEAN GREY, OUR BLACK QUEEN!

"LONG MAY SHE REIGN!!"

THE RUINED, DESECRATED CHURCH-YARD EXPLODES WITH CHEERS, BUT JEAN HEARS NONE OF THEM...

...AS EVERY FACET OF HER BEING IS OVERWHELMED BY A PHYSICAL AND EMOTIONAL TIDAL WAVE, THE LIKE OF WHICH SHE HAS NEVER KNOWN.

THEN, AS ABRUPTLY AS IT BEGAN, THE TIMESLIP ENDS...

!?!

?!?

SCOTT! LET ME EXPLAIN--!

BUT HOW DO I EXPLAIN? I'M NOT EVEN SURE WHAT HAPPENED MYSELF! DID AN ANCESTOR OF MINE MARRY AN ANCESTOR OF WYNGARDE'S? AND THAT CEREMONY--THOSE CLOTHES?! WHAT KIND OF WOMAN *WAS* SHE?!?

SCOTT?

I'VE NEVER SEEN HER ACT LIKE THAT--IT WAS AS IF SHE WASN'T JEAN AT ALL, ONLY SOMEONE WHO LOOKED LIKE HER.

Eh?! THE ANNOUNCER--!

LADEEZ AN' GENNELMEN-- HERE'S THE HONEY YOU ALL BEEN WAITIN' FOR--

--DAZZLER!

THE ROOM GOES BLACK AND DEATHLY STILL. THEN, THE HOUSE BAND STARTS A POUNDING, RHYTHMIC INTRO--

--AND SHE IS THERE!

A VISION IN SKINTIGHT SILVER, SILHOUETTED IN AN AWESOME LIGHTSHOW THAT SHIFTS IN COLOR, INTENSITY AND POSITION TO MATCH HER EMOTIONS AS SHE SINGS.

IT'S A SIGHT, A PERFORMANCE, THAT NO ONE WATCHING WILL EVER FORGET.

WOW! I KNOW ZILCH ABOUT DISCO, BUT THIS LADY IS GOOD!

MY WATCH--THE ALARM'S BUZZING! THE MICRO-CEREBRO SCANNER HAS FINALLY FOUND OUR NEO-MUTANT.

AND--IT'S DAZZLER!

OUTSIDE, THE NIGHT IS STILL QUIET, AND, FOR NIGHTCRAWLER, STILL DEADLY DULL. HE'S WONDERING HOW MUCH LONGER SCOTT AND JEAN ARE GOING TO TAKE...

BRRRINNG

... WHEN THE ROLLS' CAR-PHONE STARTS TO RING.

WE WEREN'T EXPECTING ANY CALLS. WONDER WHO IT COULD BE?

PROBABLY PROFESSOR X CHECKING UP ON US.

BOY, WAS HE MAD WHEN I TOLD HIM I WAS NO LONGER USING MY IMAGE INDUCER. * GOD--OR FATE--OR DUMB LUCK-- MADE ME WHAT I AM, AND I WON'T HIDE ANYMORE. NOT EVEN FOR THE X-MEN.

*GIVEN NIGHTCRAWLER TO ALTER HIS PHYSICAL APPEARANCE-- IN X-MEN #97 -- ROG.

THE MOMENT NIGHTCRAWLER HEARS THE STRAINED, SCARED -- YOUNG -- VOICE ON THE OTHER END, HE COMES FULLY ALERT, SHOVING HIS PERSONAL INTROSPECTIONS TO THE BACK OF HIS MIND.

H'LO? IS THIS THE X-MEN?! I'M KITTY PRYDE--ORORO TOLD ME TO CALL THIS NUMBER. SHE AN' HER FRIENDS AN' PROFESSOR XAVIER HAVE BEEN CAPTURED.

MACHINE PARTS

THEY NEED YOU GUYS TO COME RESCUE THEM. AN' ME, TOO. AN' PLEASE HURRY! THEY'RE SEARCHING ALL OVER FOR ME -- I GOTTA GO!

HIS NIGHT IS NO LONGER DULL. DEADLY, THOUGH, IS SOMETHING ELSE AGAIN.

WAIT! SLOW DOWN, GIRL. I NEED DETAILS.

WHO CAPTURED THE X-MEN? AND WHERE ARE THEY BEING HELD?

I WOULDN'T WORRY ABOUT THAT, FREAK, CONSIDERING YOU'LL BE JOINING YOUR MUTANT BUDDIES BEFORE TOO LONG.

YIKES!!

RAKT

NX -- 80 CHAS-X-1

IN AN INSTANT, THE ROLLS IS FILLED WITH A CLOUD OF BRIMSTONE, AS THE NIGHTCRAWLER IS SUDDENLY... ELSEWHERE!

IT MUST BE A TWO-PRONGED ATTACK-- ONE TEAM TO ZAP THE X-MEN IN CHICAGO, ANOTHER TO TAKE CARE OF US! I'D BETTER WARN SCOTT AND JEAN. IF THIS BRUISER'S OUT HERE AFTER ME, OTHERS LIKE HIM ARE PROBABLY AFTER THEM!

BAMF

TELEPORTING WON'T SAVE YOU THIS TIME, NIGHTCRAWLER!

WE KNOW ALL YOUR POWERS-- AND WE'RE EQUIPPED TO DEAL WITH THEM!

YEAHRRR!!

A SONIC BEAM--JUST LIKE THE ONE CYCLOPS USED DURING A TEST SEQUENCE IN THE DANGER ROOM!*

CAN'T CONCENTRATE... ENOUGH TO TELEPORT AGAIN. CAN... BARELY... EVEN THINK...

*SEE X-MEN #125--R.

YOU CAN'T EVEN RUN, MUTIE-- 'CAUSE ANYWHERE YOU CAN GO, I CAN FOLLOW!

WHAT?! SOMEHOW, HE'S... COMING UP THE WALL AFTER ME! THIS BRUISER SEEMS TO HAVE THOUGHT OF EVERYTHING!

THANKS TO THAT VERDAMMT SONIC AMBUSH, I'M IN NO DECENT SHAPE TO FIGHT. BUT, FOR ALL OUR SAKES, I'VE GOT TO FIGHT--

--AND WIN!

MEANWHILE...

SCOTT, I'D LIKE-- I NEED-- TO TALK TO YOU.

YEAH. BUT WHEN WE'RE FAR AWAY FROM THIS MADHOUSE--OKAY, JEAN? SOMEWHERE PRIVATE... PEACEFUL.

WE'LL LEAVE AFTER THIS SET, AFTER WE'VE INTRODUCED OURSELVES TO DAZZLER.

UNFORTUNATELY, JUST AS THE YOUNG WOMAN HAS THE AUDIENCE IN THE PALM OF HER HAND...

WHAT IN--?!

SCANNER MARKS THREE MUTANTS-- ONE ON STAGE, TWO IN THE CROWD. TAKE 'EM!

WHO IN BLAZES ARE-- HUH?!?

I DON'T KNOW, SCOTT. BUT THE SOONER PHOENIX AND CYCLOPS DEAL WITH IT, THE SOONER WE'LL LEARN.

SHE TRANSFORMED MY STREET CLOTHES INTO MY COSTUME, JUST LIKE THAT!

I'M BEGINNING TO WONDER IF THERE'S ANY LIMIT TO PHOENIX'S POWER.

AND IF THERE ISN'T, HOW MUCH LONGER CAN JEAN KEEP IT UNDER *CONTROL?!*

STILL, IT'S NICE TO HAVE THAT KIND OF MUSCLE ON OUR SIDE IN A FIGHT.

KNOCK 'EM OFF-BALANCE, PHOENIX! LET'S CLOBBER THESE CLOWNS AS FAST AS POSSIBLE, TO AVOID PANICKING THE PEOPLE IN HERE.

FRAK

IT'S A NICE, SENSIBLE PLAN, BUT THE MEN IN ARMOR HAVE OTHER IDEAS.

A BALL OF ENERGY ENVELOPS PHOENIX, AND SHE CRUMPLES.

THAT BEAM -- IT'S EXACTLY LIKE A TRAP THE PROFESSOR DEVISED FOR THE DANGER ROOM.

IT SCRAMBLES A PERSON'S BRAINWAVES -- THE EFFECT IS LIKE PSYCHIC EPILEPSY. BUT, TO BE EFFECTIVE, THE BEAM HAS TO BE ATTUNED TO ITS TARGET'S SPECIFIC BRAINWAVE PATTERN -- HOW COULD THEY HAVE KNOWN JEAN'S?!

HOLY--!

THIS GLOP -- IT CONTAINS SOME FORM OF RUBY QUARTZ. MY OPTIC BLASTS CAN'T PUNCH THROUGH IT!

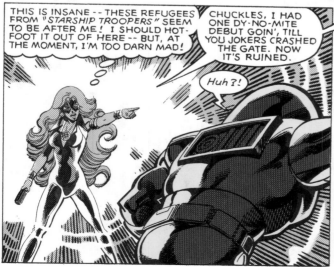

THIS IS INSANE -- THESE REFUGEES FROM *"STARSHIP TROOPERS"* SEEM TO BE AFTER ME! I SHOULD HOT-FOOT IT OUT OF HERE -- BUT, AT THE MOMENT, I'M TOO DARN MAD!

CHUCKLES, I HAD ONE DY-NO-MITE DEBUT GOIN', TILL YOU JOKERS CRASHED THE GATE. NOW IT'S RUINED.

Huh?!

AND FOR THAT, SUCKER, YOU GONNA PAY!

LIGHT -- IN ALL ITS INFINITE VARIETY -- BURSTS AROUND THE HAPLESS MAN, INSTANTLY FLOODING HIS EYES, HIS MIND, HIS SOUL. HIS BRAIN CAN'T COPE WITH THE SENSORY OVERLOAD. IT SHORT-CIRCUITS -- AND TURNS ITSELF COMPLETELY OFF.

HE'S CATATONIC! I... I DIDN'T MEAN TO "DAZZLE" HIM SO HARD -- I'VE NEVER INTENTIONALLY USED MY POWERS TO HURT ANYONE BEFORE. I DIDN'T KNOW...

THE COMPUTER DIDN'T LIE, BABE-- YOU ARE POWERFUL.

SHOOT -- THE OTHER ONE!

CONSIDER YOUR-SELF LUCKY MY EMPLOYERS WANT YOU ALIVE.

I FIGURED THE LIFE OF A DISCO QUEEN WOULD BE EXCITING -- BUT THIS IS RIDICULOUS.

GOT TO KEEP MOVING. I DON'T KNOW WHAT THAT ZAP BEAM IS AND I'D REALLY RATHER NOT FIND OUT!

DAZZLER'S ATTACK DECKED THE GOON WITH THE PSIONIC SCRAMBLER.

I'M FREE TO USE MY POWERS AGAIN!

THANKS, PHOENIX.

IT WAS GETTING A LITTLE HARD TO BREATHE IN THERE.

YOU TIN-PLATED TERRORS HAVE HAD YOUR CHANCE-- NOW IT'S THE X-MEN'S TURN!

AND WITH THE SUDDENNESS OF THOUGHT, CYKE CUTS LOOSE-- THE IRRESISTABLE HAMMER-BLOWS OF HIS OPTIC BLASTS SMASH-ING HIS TWO FOES OFF THEIR FEET.

AS I EXPECTED, THE ARMOR BLUNTED MOST OF THE FORCE OF MY SHOTS. BUT EVEN SO, I WAS CHANNELLING SO MUCH ENERGY INTO SO TIGHTLY FOCUSED A BEAM IT KNOCKED THEM SILLY.

THAT NOISE-- NIGHTCRAWLER!

SOMEBODY, ANYBODY-- GIVE ME A HAND!

THIS WHAT YOU HAD IN MIND?

LOOKS LIKE IT'S OPEN SEASON ON MUTANTS AGAIN. HOW DO YOU FEEL, NIGHTCRAWLER?

BLACK AND BLUE ALL OVER -- BUT I'M THAT, ANYWAY.

THINGS ARE WORSE THAN YOU THINK, CYCLOPS. THE X-MEN IN CHICAGO HAVE ALSO BEEN ATTACKED. AND THEY -- AND PROFESSOR X -- HAVE BEEN CAPTURED!

QUICKLY, NIGHTCRAWLER TELLS CYCLOPS WHAT KITTY PRYDE HAD TOLD HIM.

HOW DO WE KNOW THIS KID IS ON THE LEVEL? SHE COULD BE LURING US INTO AN AMBUSH.

HEY, HUNK -- YOU AVENGERS OR SOMETHIN'? YOU MIND CLUEIN' ME IN ON WHAT'S BEEN GOIN' DOWN HERE?

WE'RE, ah, X-MEN, MISS...?

CALL ME DAZZLER, DARLIN'. THAT'S MY NAME -- THAT'S WHAT I DO. DAZZLE PEOPLE.

HAVE YOU EVER WONDERED WHERE YOUR LIGHT POWERS CAME FROM?

NOPE.

YOU'RE A MUTANT, DAZZLER. YOU **HAVE** POWERS AND ABILITIES THAT SET YOU APART FROM THE REST OF HUMANITY. AND, AS YOU'VE JUST SEEN, THERE ARE PEOPLE WHO WILL STOP AT NOTHING TO CAPTURE -- OR KILL -- YOU.

ARE YOU SERIOUS?

LOOK AROUND, DAZZLER. YOU TELL ME.

FOR YOUR OWN SAFETY, I THINK YOU'D BETTER COME WITH US.

AS THEY REACH THE STREET, A SERIES OF EXPLOSIONS SHATTER THE TOP FLOOR OF THE BUILDING.

THE DISCO! INSIDE -- QUICK! I'LL PROTECT THE CAR FROM FALLING DEBRIS WITH A TELEPATHIC SHIELD.

CYCLOPS, I'M NOT PICKING UP OUR ATTACKERS' THOUGHTS ANYMORE. THEY JUST... CUT OUT.

I WAS PLANNING TO HAVE JEAN TELE-PATHICALLY INTERROGATE ONE OF THOSE GOONS.

I GUESS THEIR MASTERS WANTED TO MAKE SURE I COULDN'T. NICE PEOPLE.

THEY SEEM TO KNOW AN AWFUL LOT ABOUT THE X-MEN -- TOO MUCH. BUT HOW?! WHO ARE WE UP AGAINST?! WHAT ARE THEY AFTER?!

CYCLOPS -- A MAN, WAITING AT THE CORNER.

IT'S THE MAN JEAN KISSED IN THE DISCO.

IS HE PART OF THIS PUZZLE, TOO? OR SIMPLY MY RIVAL FOR JEAN'S AFFECTIONS? THE FIRST I CAN DEAL WITH. THE SECOND... I'M NOT SO SURE.

EITHER WAY, I DON'T LIKE HIM.

THE ROLLS' HEAD-LIGHTS TOUCH JASON WYNGARDE FOR A MOMENT, THROWING HIS SHADOW ACROSS THE WALL BEHIND HIM. CYCLOPS AUTOMATICALLY NOTES THE IMAGE...

...BUT HIS MIND -- PREOCCUPIED WITH A HOST OF FAR-MORE-PRESSING CONCERNS -- DOESN'T REGISTER IT. PERHAPS, ONE DAY, HE WILL REMEMBER -- AND RECOGNIZE -- WHO HE PASSED THIS NIGHT.

BY THEN, HOWEVER, IT MAY WELL BE FAR TOO LATE. FOR HIM, FOR THE X-MEN --

-- AND, MOST IMPORTANTLY, FOR THE WOMAN HE LOVES.

HA HA HA HA HA HA HA HA HA HA

NEXT ▷

IT'S CYCLOPS, PHOENIX, NIGHTCRAWLER AND DAZZLER TO THE RESCUE. BUT WILL THEY REACH CHICAGO IN TIME TO SAVE KITTY PRYDE? FIND OUT IN...

"RUN FOR YOUR LIFE!"

STAN LEE PRESENTS: THE UNCANNY X-MEN! ™

RUN FOR YOUR LIFE!

THE TIME IS VERY EARLY SUNDAY MORNING. THE PLACE, A BACK-ALLEY IN CHICAGO, JUST OFF THE LOOP.

LOTS OF TIMES TONIGHT, *KITTY PRYDE* THOUGHT SHE'D GIVEN HER PURSUERS THE SLIP-- BUT EACH TIME, THEY'D FOUND HER AGAIN.

CYCLOPS

PHOENIX

COLOSSUS

LF667

WOLVERINE

STORM

NIGHTCRAWLER

| A CLAREMONT * BYRNE * AUSTIN PRODUCTION | AIDED AND ABETTED BY | TOM ORZECHOWSKI, *letterer* * GLYNIS WEIN, *colorist* | ROGER STERN *editor* | JIM SHOOTER *ed.-in-chief* |

IN THE LAST FEW HOURS, SHE'S DISCOVERED RESERVOIRS OF STRENGTH WITHIN HERSELF SHE NEVER KNEW EXISTED. SHE'S TAPPED THEM ALL.

BKASH

BUT SHE'S ONLY 13½. SHE CAN'T KEEP UP THIS PACE FOREVER.

OH! MY-- ARM !!

THE KID AIN'T MOVIN'. I THINK WE GOT HER.

HEY! WHAT IN HEAVEN'S NAME IS THAT ?!!

IT'S PHOENIX-- ONE OF THE X-MEN! SHE DROPPED OUTTA NOWHERE, BETWEEN US AN' THE GIRL!

RUN HER DOWN!

SKRAMM

RUN ME DOWN, GENTLEMEN?

SOMEHOW, I DON'T THINK SO.

WHO...?

THAT WOMAN JUST WAVED HER ARMS, AN' THAT CAR STOPPED LIKE IT HAD HIT A BRICK WALL!

WHAT AM I GONNA DO NOW?!

OH, LORD, I'M SO SCARED. I'M TRYIN' TO DO WHAT'S RIGHT, BUT--!

YYIIII!!!

GUTEN ABEND. FRAULEIN PRYDE, I ASSUME?

DON'T BE FRIGHTENED BY MY TELEPORTING, LEIBCHEN. I'M ONE OF THE GOOD GUYS -- WE SPOKE ON THE PHONE!*

LET'S BE OFF, SHALL WE?

*LAST ISSUE --ROG.

46

AS NIGHTCRAWLER SCRAMBLES UP THE SIDE OF THE BUILDING, RUSHING HIS YOUNG CHARGE TO SAFETY, **CYCLOPS** AND THE WOMAN CALLED **DAZZLER** JOIN PHOENIX IN THE ALLEY BELOW.

I TRUST YOU'LL THINK TWICE ABOUT HOUNDING MUTANTS IN THE FUTURE.

PHOENIX, ARE YOU ALL RIGHT?!

NEVER FELT BETTER, CYCLOPS.

WOW! CYCLOPS SAID PHOENIX'S TELEKINETIC POWERS WERE IMPRESSIVE, BUT I NEVER DREAMED...

COMPARED TO THIS, MY MUTANT ABILITY TO CREATE FANCY LIGHTSHOWS IS NOTHING!

WHAT HAVE YOU DONE?! I TOLD YOU TO STOP THAT CAR, NOT TURN IT INTO INSTANT JUNK!

YOU DIDN'T FEEL THE GIRL'S STARK TERROR, SCOTT, OR THE THOUGHTS OF THE KILLERS CHASING HER. I'M A TELEPATH. I DID.

THESE... ANIMALS GOT NO MORE THAN THEY DESERVED.

I THOUGHT I'D SEEN JEAN IN EVERY CONCEIVABLE MOOD, BUT THIS IS NEW.

CYCLOPS, GET UP HERE! FAST!

HM?! IT'S NIGHTCRAWLER! JEAN, GIVE US A LIFT!

WITH A NOD AND A SMILE, PHOENIX WRAPS HER COMPANIONS IN A TELE-KINETIC ENERGY FIELD...

...AND TAKES OFF.

WHAT'S WRONG, NIGHTCRAWLER? WHERE'S THE GIRL?!

GOOD QUESTION. SHE BROKE AWAY FROM ME WHEN WE LANDED...

... AND DOVE RIGHT THROUGH THE ROOF!

47

WELL, THEN SHE'S DEFINITELY THE NEO-MUTANT PROFESSOR XAVIER AND THE OTHER X-MEN CAME TO CHICAGO TO FIND.

JEAN, CAN YOU TRACK HER TELE-PATHICALLY?

YES.

GOOD. YOU'RE THE MOST NORMAL-LOOKING OF US. YOU'LL HAVE TO HANDLE THE INITIAL CONTACT.

... JEAN BEGINS HER SEARCH OF THE WAREHOUSE LOFT.

SOMEONE'S COMING -- MUSTN'T MAKE A SOUND!

PSYCHOKINETICALLY REARRANGING THE MOLECULES OF HER PHOENIX COSTUME INTO A SET OF STREET CLOTHES...

THAT'S THE RIGHT IDEA, KITTEN -- EXCEPT AGAINST A MIND-READER LIKE ME YOUR THOUGHTS STAND OUT LIKE A BEACON.

TELL ME, WHAT'S A NICE KID LIKE YOU DOING IN A PLACE LIKE THIS?

OH!!

EASY, KITTY, EASY -- THERE'S NOTHING TO BE AFRAID OF. YOU'RE AMONG FRIENDS.

I'M JEAN GREY, ONE OF THE X-MEN. REMEMBER, YOU PHONED US FOR HELP.

X-MEN?

KITTY HESITATES FOR A MOMENT -- AND THEN, SHE COLLAPSES INTO JEAN'S ARMS, ALL OF THE ACCUMULATED TERRORS OF THE LAST TWELVE HOURS POURING OUT OF HER.

IT'S A WHILE BEFORE THE X-MEN, DAZZLER, KITTY AND THEIR PRISONERS RETURN TO THE MUTANTS' SKYSHIP, HIDDEN DEEP WITHIN A WOODLAND PARK LINING THE SHORE OF LAKE MICHIGAN.

THIS IS CRAZY--

-- I STARTED OUT LAST NIGHT TO BREAK INTO THE NEW YORK DISCO SCENE... AND NOW I'M SUDDENLY FIGHTING ALONGSIDE THE X-MEN.

MOST OF THESE ARE ONLY SCRAPES -- THEY LOOK A LOT WORSE THAN THEY REALLY ARE -- BUT SOME OF THESE CUTS ARE PRETTY DEEP. SING OUT IF I HURT YOU, KITTY.

OKAY.

ANYWAY, ORORO -- AN' COLOSSUS AN' WOLVERINE -- AN' I WERE AT THE MALT SHOP, WHEN THESE CREEPS BUSTED IN ON US. I GOT AWAY, BUT THE X-MEN AND PROFESSOR XAVIER GOT CAPTURED.

THEY WERE TAKEN TO THIS BIG INDUSTRIAL PARK JUST OUTSIDE THE CITY. I KIND'A TAGGED ALONG. *

I DON'T THINK THE LITTLE *FRAULEIN* LIKES ME.

*SEE X-MEN #129.--ROG.

ORORO GAVE ME YOUR PHONE NUMBER, TOLD ME TO CALL YOU GUYS TO COME RESCUE EVERY-ONE. I DID, AN' I'VE BEEN RUNNIN' EVER SINCE.

WE WERE ATTACKED, TOO, IN NEW YORK. *

*LAST ISSUE --R.

I'M THROUGH TANGLING WITH SHADOWS. MIND-SCAN OUR PRISONERS, JEAN, AND FIND OUT WHO WE'RE UP AGAINST.

AS GOOD AS DONE.

THE GOONS' MINDS ARE SHIELDED, BUT, WITH AN EASE THAT DEFIES DESCRIPTION, PHOENIX SLIPS PAST THEIR MENTAL DEFENSES.

... AND, IN THE BLINK OF AN EYE, LEARNS WHERE THE OTHER X-MEN ARE BEING HELD AND HOW WELL THAT COMPLEX IS DEFENDED. SHE LEARNS THAT THEY WERE STRUCK DOWN BY ANOTHER TELEPATH, A WOMAN NAMED EMMA FROST--

--ONE OF A GROUP OF WEALTHY INDUSTRIALISTS WHO SEEK PRE-EMINENT SOCIAL, POLITICAL AND ECONOMIC POWER IN THE WORLD.

THE HELLFIRE CLUB FOUNDED 1720

49

THE HELLFIRE CLUB?! BUT -- IN MY TIMESLIPS, THE PSYCHIC FLASH-BACKS I'VE EXPERIENCED LATELY,--

-- I'VE FOUND MYSELF LIVING THE LIFE OF AN ANCESTOR WHO WAS MARRIED TO A MEMBER OF THAT CLUB--A MAN NAMED *JASON WYNGARDE!*

B-BUT I'VE RECENTLY MET A MODERN-DAY JASON WYNGARDE WHO'S A DEAD RINGER FOR MY ANCESTOR'S HUSBAND. WHAT DOES IT ALL MEAN? IS IT COINCIDENCE, OR --?

ARE YOU OKAY, JEAN?

OH! Ah -- I'M FINE, SCOTT. I HAVE THE INFORMATION YOU NEED.

IT'S AN HOUR OR SO BEFORE DAWN -- THE SKY STILL DARK, THE CITY STREETS QUIET AND DESERTED ON THIS AVERAGE SUNDAY MORNING -- WHEN A NONDESCRIPT CAR PULLS UP TO THE MAIN GATE OF FROST ENTERPRISES.

THE VEHICLE IS AS UNREMARKABLE AS ANY PRODUCED BY DETROIT'S AUTOMAKERS, EXCEPT THAT EARLIER PHOENIX REDUCED IT TO SO MUCH SCRAP METAL.

HERE COMES SAL. I WONDER IF THEY FOUND THE KID?

PAYDIRT, M'MAN! THAT LITTLE BRAT GOT AWAY--BUT I FIGURE WHAT WE CAUGHT WILL MORE'N MAKE UP FOR THE LOSS.

THE X-MEN! HOW'D YOU DO IT, SALLY?

I'LL TELL YA LATER, ELTON, OVER A BREW. RIGHT NOW, ALL I WANNA DO IS GET THESE MUTIES UNDER LOCK AN' KEY.

THE REST OF THE X-MEN -- CAPTURED?! MOST IMPRESSIVE, ESPECIALLY SINCE SALVATORE'S TEAM WAS NOT EQUIPPED TO TANGLE WITH THEM.

EVERY-THING LOOKS NORMAL ENOUGH...

...BUT I'LL CALL OUT THE GUARD-- JUST IN CASE. IF YOUR FRIENDS ARE PLANNING ANY NASTY SURPRISES, STORM, THEY'LL FIND THE HELLFIRE CLUB READY FOR THEM.

IN THE MEANTIME, WE'LL CONTINUE WITH YOUR EXAMINATION.

YOU KNOW, ORORO, YOU REALLY MUSTN'T FIGHT MY PSYCHIC PROBES. THE HARDER YOU RESIST, THE MORE THIS WILL HURT.

I DON'T WANT TO HURT YOU, MY DEAR. I WANT US TO BE... FRIENDS.

HA!EARRRGH!!

BUT WHILE ALL EYES ARE ON THE X-MEN COMING IN THE FRONT OF THE COMPLEX, NO ONE NOTICES KITTY PRYDE SNEAKING IN THE BACK... IN A STYLE ALL HER OWN.

OH, MY GOSH! ORORO'S GONE!

GOT TO STAY COOL! CYCLOPS SAID IT'S OKAY TO BE SCARED, SO LONG AS I DON'T LET MY FEAR FOUL ME UP.

CYCLOPS ALSO GAVE ME A REAL IMPORTANT JOB TO DO, AN' HE'S TRUSTING ME TO DO IT RIGHT-- ON MY OWN.

I MUSTN'T LET HIM DOWN.

IF I COULDN'T FREE STORM, I'M S'POSED TO TRY WOLVERINE NEXT. GEE, EVEN ZONKED OUT, HE LOOKS SPOOKY.

I WONDER-- IF I REACH INTO THE LOCK...

...MAYBE I CAN GIMMICK IT-- YOW!

ALL I DID WAS TOUCH IT, AN' IT POPPED OPEN! WHAT'D I DO?!

BIK

I DON'T KNOW, AN' I'M NOT WASTIN' ANY TIME TRYIN' TO FIGURE IT OUT.

CRIMINEY! WOLVERINE'S NOT MUCH TALLER THAN ME, BUT HE WEIGHS A TON!

YOU'RE... THE KID.

KITTY PRYDE.

WHY'S IT... SO FLAMIN' HARD TO THINK?!

IT'S THE CAGES -- THEY MAKE YOU DOPEY. BUT YOU'RE OUTSIDE NOW. YOU SHOULD BE OKAY.

GIMME A MINUTE, WILLYA? WHAT'RE YOU DOIN' HERE?

I'M RESCUING YOU.

ALL BY YER LONESOME?

COURSE NOT. THE X-MEN ARE WITH ME--!

YEAAGKH!

KID!!

ZRIPT

OKAY, MUTIE, NOW CLIMB BACK INTO YOUR CAGE... NICE AND SLOW... UNLESS YOU WANT SOME OF THE SAME.

SUCKER, YOU JUST MADE THE BIGGEST MISTAKE OF YOUR LIFE.

AND THE LAST.

SNIKT

AND, WHILE RAZOR-SHARP ADAMANTIUM CLAWS SPRING FROM WOLVERINE'S HANDS, AT THE FRONT OF THE ADMINISTRATION BUILDING...

THERE'S SAL'S CAR. OUR BACK-UPS HAVEN'T ARRIVED YET, CAM -- THINK WE CAN HANDLE IT?

JACKO, YOU KEEP FRETTIN' LIKE THAT, YOU'LL GIVE YOURSELF AN ULCER. STAY ON YOUR TOES, AND FOLLOW MY LEAD.

ANY OF THOSE MUTIES SO MUCH AS TWITCHES, BLOW 'EM OUT OF THEIR SOCKS.

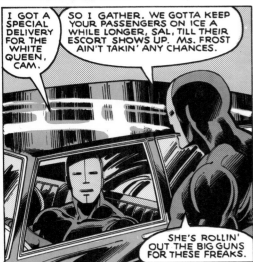

I GOT A SPECIAL DELIVERY FOR THE WHITE QUEEN, CAM.

SO I GATHER. WE GOTTA KEEP YOUR PASSENGERS ON ICE A WHILE LONGER, SAL, TILL THEIR ESCORT SHOWS UP. MS. FROST AIN'T TAKIN' ANY CHANCES.

SHE'S ROLLIN' OUT THE BIG GUNS FOR THESE FREAKS.

LOOKS LIKE WE'VE REACHED THE END OF THE LINE, JEAN.

I'M IN TELEPATHIC CONTACT WITH NIGHTCRAWLER AND DAZZLER, SCOTT -- AS I AM WITH YOU. EVERYONE'S READY.

GOOD -- 'CAUSE THE FIREWORKS ARE ABOUT TO START.

SUDDENLY, CYCLOPS LOOKS UP, OPENS HIS RUBY QUARTZ VISOR WIDE -- AND AN AWESOME, IRRESISTIBLE BEAM OF PURE FORCE BLASTS OUT FROM HIS EYES.

KRAKOW

THESE OPTIC BLASTS ARE BOTH SCOTT SUMMERS' MUTANT POWER AND HIS PRIVATE CURSE, FOR THEY CANNOT BE CONTROLLED -- SAVE BY HIS VISOR OR SPECIAL RUBY QUARTZ GLASSES.

STILL, THEY'RE VERY USEFUL IN A FIGHT.

BEFORE THE GUARDS HAVE RECOVERED FROM THE SHOCK OF CYCLOPS' BLAST, DAZZLER MOVES INTO ACTION, DRAWING ON ALL THE SOUNDS AROUND HER, AND CONVERTING THEM INTO RADIANT ENERGY...

...SHE CREATES A LIGHTSHOW, SO INTENSE AND BEAUTIFUL, THAT THE GUARDS' MINDS CAN'T COPE WITH IT! IN OTHER WORDS --

--THEY'RE DAZZLED!

TAKE OFF, X-MEN! YOU KNOW WHAT TO DO!

B A M F

AS SHE'S DONE BEFORE, PHOENIX MIND-LINKS CYCLOPS WITH THE REST OF THE TEAM, KEEPING THEM ALL IN CONSTANT TOUCH.

THIS TIME, STRANGELY ENOUGH, CYCLOPS FINDS THAT THE PROCESS MAKES HIM FEEL... UNCOMFORTABLE.

I CAN'T GET OVER HOW EASILY JEAN REASSEMBLED THAT CAR WITH HER *TK* POWERS...

ZRAP

... AND THEN MANIPULATED THAT UNCONSCIOUS DRIVER LIKE HE WAS NO MORE THAN HER PUPPET. EVERY WORD, EVERY MOVE, CAME FROM HER, AND SHE PULLED IT OFF WITHOUT A HITCH, WITHOUT STRAIN.

I SHOULD BE PROUD OF HER-- INSTEAD, I'M... FRIGHTENED.

WHAT --?! THE ALERT SIREN! WE'RE UNDER ATTACK!

IT'S THE X-MEN!

OBVIOUSLY, YOU FOOL!

DON'T JUST STAND THERE! YOU AND YOUR MEN ARE SUPPOSED TO BE THE BEST COMBAT TROOPS MONEY CAN BUY. HERE'S YOUR CHANCE TO PROVE IT.

USE ANY MEANS YOU HAVE TO--ONLY STOP THE X-MEN!

IT SEEMS YOUR FRIENDS' "TROJAN HORSE" GAMBIT HAS PAID OFF, STORM.

BUT CYCLOPS AND THE OTHERS HAVE A LONG WAY TO GO BEFORE THEY REACH THIS LAB. THAT'S MORE THAN ENOUGH TIME TO TEACH YOU-- AND THEM -- A LESSON THEY'LL NEVER FORGET.

ALL THEY'LL FIND WHEN THEY REACH THIS CHAMBER IS A MINDLESS THING, HUMAN ONLY IN PHYSICAL FORM-- YOU, STORM.

IS THAT SO?

WHO--?! PHOENIX!

THE ONE AND ONLY. AND YOU'RE EMMA FROST -- THE HELLFIRE CLUB'S WHITE QUEEN.

I UNDERSTAND YOU CALL YOURSELF SOMETHING OF A TELEPATH.

WELL, "YOUR MAJESTY," LET'S SEE HOW GOOD YOU REALLY ARE.

ELSEWHERE... I DON'T BELIEVE IT! THERE'S ONLY THREE OF THEM MUTIES, AND WE'RE HITTIN' THEM WITH EVERYTHING WE'VE GOT-- AN' THEY'RE CLOBBERIN' US!

MANCUSI, CALL FOR REINFORCEMENTS! GET A SQUAD ON THOSE UPPER LEVEL CATWALKS! TRY TO SET UP A CROSS-FIRE!

SKIPPER, I MARK ONLY TWO X-MEN. WHERE'S THE ONE WITH THE TAIL?!

KCHAM

FRAK

I'M RIGHT BEHIND YOU, MEIN HERR.

I'VE BEEN ACHING TO TRY THIS STUNT AGAIN.*

BY TELEPORTING AS FAST AS I CAN PUNCH...

...I CAN DECK ALL THESE MEN BEFORE THE FIRST ONE EVEN HITS THE GROUND!

B A M F

WOK

BOK

SOK

*LAST USED IN X-MEN #111 -- ROG.

55

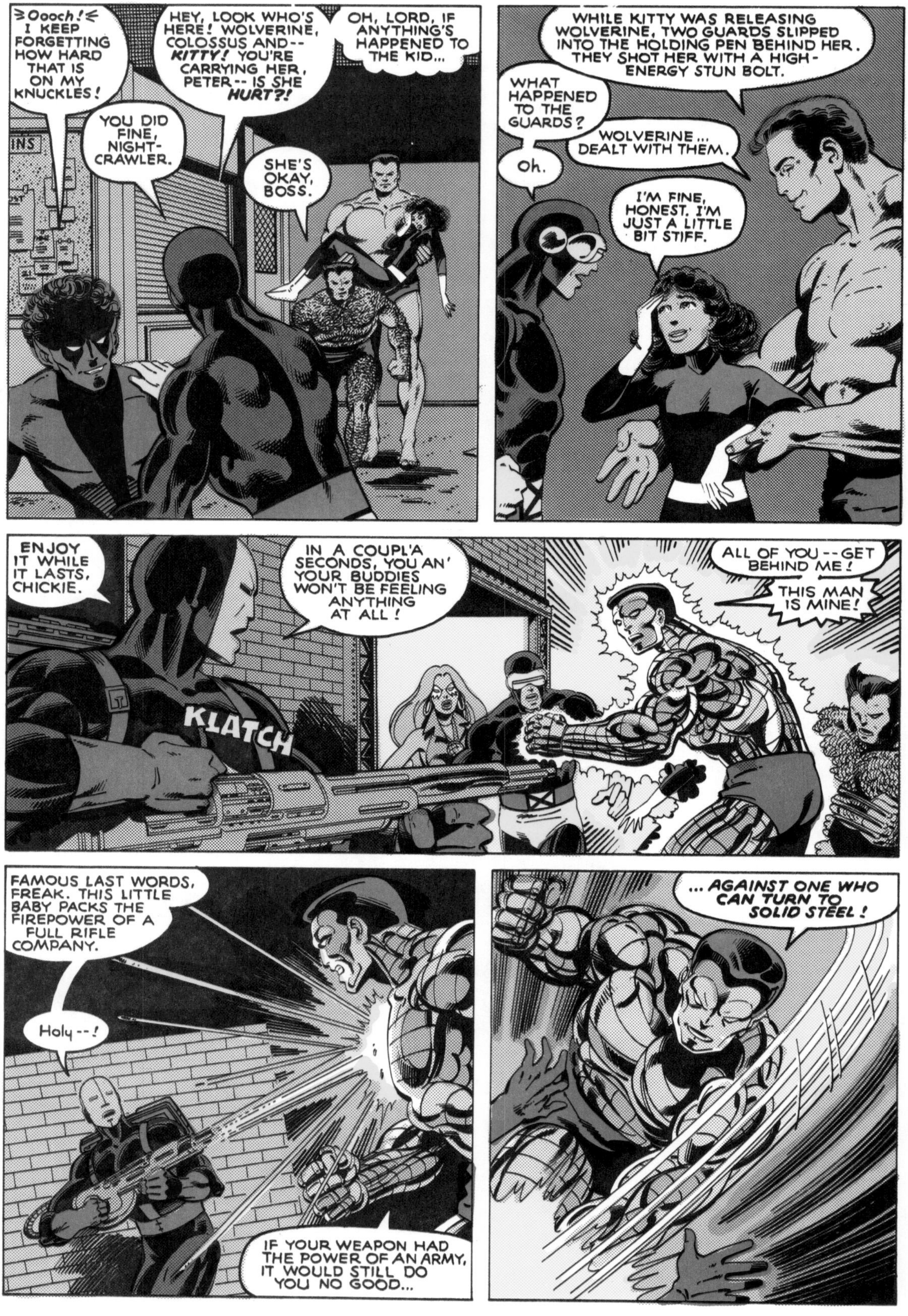

≽Oooch!≼ I KEEP FORGETTING HOW HARD THAT IS ON MY KNUCKLES!
HEY, LOOK WHO'S HERE! WOLVERINE, COLOSSUS AND-- KITTY! YOU'RE CARRYING HER, PETER-- IS SHE HURT?!
OH, LORD, IF ANYTHING'S HAPPENED TO THE KID...
YOU DID FINE, NIGHT-CRAWLER.
SHE'S OKAY, BOSS.
WHILE KITTY WAS RELEASING WOLVERINE, TWO GUARDS SLIPPED INTO THE HOLDING PEN BEHIND HER. THEY SHOT HER WITH A HIGH-ENERGY STUN BOLT.
WHAT HAPPENED TO THE GUARDS?
WOLVERINE... DEALT WITH THEM.
Oh.
I'M FINE, HONEST. I'M JUST A LITTLE BIT STIFF.
ENJOY IT WHILE IT LASTS, CHICKIE.
IN A COUPL'A SECONDS, YOU AN' YOUR BUDDIES WON'T BE FEELING ANYTHING AT ALL!
KLATCH
ALL OF YOU--GET BEHIND ME!
THIS MAN IS MINE!
FAMOUS LAST WORDS, FREAK. THIS LITTLE BABY PACKS THE FIREPOWER OF A FULL RIFLE COMPANY.
Holy--!
IF YOUR WEAPON HAD THE POWER OF AN ARMY, IT WOULD STILL DO YOU NO GOOD...
...AGAINST ONE WHO CAN TURN TO SOLID STEEL!

I AM ASHAMED. I LOST MY TEMPER. I KNOW I AM DIFFERENT, BUT THE WAY THAT MAN CALLED ME "FREAK"... EH? WHY IS KITTY STARING AT ME?

WOW, PETER-- YOU SAVED US ALL. THAT WAS NEAT!

IT WAS?

WE STILL HAVE TO FIND STORM AND PROFESSOR X.

THE PROF SPLIT ON HIS OWN-- WOULDN'T LET ME OR PETEY GO WITH 'IM. HE TOLD US TO GET 'RORO.

I'VE BEEN FOLLOWIN' HER SCENT.

LEAD ON, THEN.

LET'S MOVE IT, BEFORE THIS WHITE QUEEN'S PRIVATE ARMY REGROUPS.

I CAUGHT A TELEPATHIC FLASH FROM JEAN THAT SHE WAS GOING AFTER STORM. I HOPE SHE HASN'T RUN INTO TROUBLE.

TROUBLE? NOT QUITE.

AT FIRST, BOTH WOMEN SEEMED EVENLY MATCHED... BUT AS THE BATTLE PROGRESSED, IT BECAME EVIDENT THAT PHOENIX WAS MERELY TAKING THE WHITE QUEEN'S MEASURE.

NOW THAT SHE'S LEARNED HER FOE'S STRENGTHS AND WEAKNESSES, PHOENIX BEGINS TO ATTACK IN EARNEST.

IT'S AN ATTACK WHICH THE HELP-LESS STORM CAN ONLY WATCH... IN AWE AND FEAR!

THE PHOENIX-EFFECT IS SO BEAUTIFUL... YET SO TERRIBLE. LIKE JEAN HERSELF. I'VE SEEN HER LIKE THIS ONLY ONCE BEFORE, IN THE HEART OF THE ALIEN M'KRANN CRYSTAL--

--BEFORE SHE... SAVED THE UNIVERSE FROM DESTRUCTION.*

*X-MEN #108--ROG.

HER POWER IS A SONG WITHIN HER...

... A PASSION BEYOND HUMAN COMPREHENSION. SHE IS MORE ALIVE THAN SHE HAS EVER BEEN-- AS SHE SMASHES THROUGH THE WHITE QUEEN'S PSYCHIC DEFENSES WITH CONTEMPTUOUS EASE.

AND YET, SHE KNOWS THIS IS NOTHING COMPARED TO WHAT SHE FELT WITHIN THE GREAT M'KRANN CRYSTAL.

BIRD-- ENERGY CONSTRUCT-- IS DRAINING MY STRENGTH, MY VERY... LIFE-FORCE!

ONLY ONE CHANCE... MUST CHANNEL... ALL REMAINING POWER... INTO TELEPATHIC PSI-BOLT...

THE WHITE QUEEN STRIKES...

... WITH DEVASTATING EFFECT!

WHAT THE--?!

CYKE, THAT BUILDING IS WHERE 'RORO'S SCENT'S BEEN LEADIN' US!

I WAS HIT BY A FLASH OF PAIN FROM JEAN-- THROUGH THE MIND-LINK-- AN INSTANT BEFORE THE EXPLOSION. SHE MUST HAVE BEEN IN THERE WITH STORM! THE BLAST-- IT LEVELLED THE ENTIRE BUILDING!

DAZZLER, KEEP KITTY BACK! THE REST OF YOU, GIVE ME A HAND!

JEAN CAN'T BE DEAD-- I'D FEEL IT! I'M CALLING YOU, LADY-- ANSWER ME! JEAN! JEAN!

CYCLOPS' FRANTIC MENTAL CRY IS ANSWERED ALMOST IMMEDIATELY-- THOUGH NOT QUITE IN THE WAY HE EXPECTED.

Unglaublich.

GOOD LORD.

JEAN! STORM!

RELAX, CYCLOPS. WE'RE BOTH NONE THE WORSE FOR WEAR. I'M... AFRAID THE WHITE QUEEN WASN'T SO LUCKY.

IT'LL TAKE MORE THAN A COLLAPSING BUILDING TO DO ME IN. BUT IT WAS SWEET OF YOU TO BE SO CONCERNED!

WELL DONE, MY X-MEN!

PROFESSOR X!

I KNEW I WAS RIGHT IN HOLDING BACK AND PLAYING OBSERVER! NOW, LET'S BE ON OUR WAY BEFORE THE AUTHORITIES ARRIVE!

AND SO, QUICKLY, QUIETLY...

...NINE MUTANTS MAKE THEIR WAY OUT OF THE COMPLEX. SUNRISE FINDS THEM ON CENTRAL AVENUE, IN DEERFIELD, IN FRONT OF KITTY PRYDE'S HOUSE.

ALL IN ALL, MY X-MEN, I AM MOST PLEASED WITH THE WAY YOU HANDLED YOURSELVES.

NICE O' YOU TO SAY SO, CHUCK.

DAZZLER, YOU HAVE SEEN SOMETHING OF THE LIFE THE X-MEN LEAD. ARE YOU SURE YOU WON'T JOIN US?

I APPRECIATE THE OFFER, PROF--

--BUT WORLD-SAVIN' AIN'T MY STYLE. I PREFER THE EXCITEMENT I GET ON STAGE, SINGIN' MY HEART OUT TO AN AUDIENCE THAT REALLY DIGS ME.

SEE YA, FOLKS. KEEP IN TOUCH.

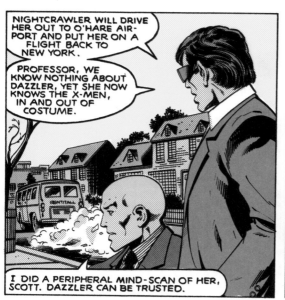

NIGHTCRAWLER WILL DRIVE HER OUT TO O'HARE AIRPORT AND PUT HER ON A FLIGHT BACK TO NEW YORK.

PROFESSOR, WE KNOW NOTHING ABOUT DAZZLER, YET SHE NOW KNOWS THE X-MEN, IN AND OUT OF COSTUME.

I DID A PERIPHERAL MIND-SCAN OF HER, SCOTT. DAZZLER CAN BE TRUSTED.

KITTY!

OH, BABY, WE WERE SO WORRIED! YOU WERE GONE ALL NIGHT-- WE DIDN'T KNOW WHAT HAD HAPPENED. WE CALLED THE POLICE...

WHERE HAVE YOU BEEN?!

HI, DAD. HI, MOM.

Uh-oh. IF THOSE ARE KITTY'S PARENTS, PROFESSOR, I THINK WE MAY HAVE A BIT OF EXPLAINING TO DO.

GOOD MORNING, Mr. PRYDE.

SHOVE IT, MISTER! WHAT HAVE YOU BEEN DOING WITH MY DAUGHTER?!

SHE GOES OFF WITH YOUR STUDENTS AND DISAPPEARS-- YOU DISAPPEAR-- THE MALT SHOP WAS BURNED TO THE GROUND! WE THOUGHT SHE'D BEEN KILLED-- TILL THE POLICE IDENTIFIED THE BODIES THEY FOUND!

GEE, MOM, THERE'S NO NEED TO MAKE A FUSS. I'M OKAY.

ENOUGH'S ENOUGH.

I DON'T KNOW WHAT YOUR GAME IS, MISTER, BUT...

... IT'S GOOD TO SEE YOU AGAIN.

MY WIFE AND I WERE VERY IMPRESSED BY YOUR PRESENTATION YESTERDAY. IN FACT, WE'VE BEEN DISCUSSING YOU AND YOUR *"SCHOOL FOR GIFTED YOUNGSTERS"* QUITE A LOT SINCE YOU LEFT.

THAT'S, *ah,* NICE TO HEAR, MR. PRYDE.

CALL ME CARMEN.

HUH?! SUDDENLY HE'S ALL SWEETNESS AND LIGHT-- AND THE PROFESSOR SEEMS AS SURPRISED AS ME! BUT IF HE DIDN'T "CHANGE" PRYDE'S MIND, WHO--?

JEAN, YOU DIDN'T--!

JUST DOING WHAT COMES NATURALLY.

I KNOW YOU DON'T APPROVE OF ME-- OR THE PROFESSOR-- USING OUR PSI-POWERS LIKE THIS SCOTT...

... BUT KITTY'S FATHER WASN'T ABOUT TO LISTEN TO REASON. SO, TO SPARE EVERYONE A LOT OF UNNECESSARY GRIEF, I MODIFIED HIS AND HIS WIFE'S MEMORIES A LITTLE.

NO HARM DONE-- AND THERE'S AN END TO IT.

WE HAVE BRUNCH-MAKINGS IN THE 'FRIDGE. YOU'RE ALL WELCOME TO JOIN US.

IT WILL BE OUR PLEASURE... CARMEN.

SCOTT, DID JEAN DO WHAT I THINK SHE DID?

SHE USED HER TELEPATHIC ABILITIES AGAINST AN INNOCENT PERSON'S MIND, SOMETHING THAT USED TO BE AN ANATHEMA TO HER.

ORORO, YOU WERE IN THAT LAB WHEN SHE FOUGHT THE WHITE QUEEN. WHAT WAS IT-- WHAT WAS SHE-- LIKE?

NOT HUMAN. WHEN SHE USES HER POWER-- AS PHOENIX-- THERE IS A FEROCITY ABOUT HER... AND A GRANDEUR... SHE HAS CHANGED SO MUCH.

YET... SHE HASN'T CHANGED AT ALL.

Ah, MAYBE WE'RE IMAGINING THINGS!

YOU DON'T BELIEVE THAT. WE BOTH SENSE A ... WRONGNESS ABOUT HER.

THERE IS A DARK SIDE TO THE PHOENIX THAT COULD CONSUME HER! IT'S ALMOST AS IF SOMETHING-- OR SOMEONE-- WAS MANIPULATING HER, HELPING THAT WRONGNESS TO GROW! IF THAT IS THE CASE, WE MUST FIND OUT WHO OR WHAT IS DOING THIS... BEFORE IT IS TOO LATE!

NEXT> AND HELLFIRE IS THEIR NAME!

Cyclops. Storm. Nightcrawler. Wolverine. Colossus. Children of the atom, students of Charles Xavier, MUTANTS — feared and hated by the world they have sworn to protect. These are the STRANGEST heroes of all!

STAN LEE PRESENTS: **THE UNCANNY X-MEN!** ™

| CHRIS CLAREMONT WRITER / CO-PLOTTERS | JOHN BYRNE PENCILER | TERRY AUSTIN INKER | TOM ORZECHOWSKI, *letterer* GLYNIS WEIN, *colorist* | JIM SALICRUP EDITOR | JIM SHOOTER Ed.-IN-CHIEF |

AND HELLFIRE IS THEIR NAME!

IN NEW MEXICO, ALONG THE CONTINENTAL DIVIDE-- LITERALLY MILES FROM ANYWHERE-- STANDS A VERY SPECIAL HOUSE, OWNED BY A VERY *SPECIAL* YOUNG MAN.

SCOTTY! LONG TIME, NO SEE, OL' BUDDY!

WELCOME TO ANGEL'S AERIE, X-MEN. MY HOME AWAY FROM HOME.

HE WAS CHRISTENED *WARREN WORTHINGTON III,* HEIR APPARENT TO ONE OF AMERICA'S LARGER PRIVATE FORTUNES.

IN LATER YEARS, HE BECAME SOMEWHAT BETTER KNOWN AS THE HIGH-FLYING *ANGEL,* ONE OF THE FOUNDING MEMBERS OF THE UNCANNY X-MEN.

HE'S SEEN LITTLE OF THE X-MEN SINCE HE LEFT THE TEAM-- HE HARDLY KNOWS *NIGHTCRAWLER, STORM, COLOSSUS* AND *WOLVERINE,* THE MUTANTS WHO REPLACED HIM-- YET THESE YOUNG PEOPLE AND THEIR MENTOR, *PROFESSOR CHARLES XAVIER,* ARE CLOSER AND MORE IMPORTANT TO HIM THAN HIS OWN FAMILY.

THANKS FOR TAKING US IN, WARREN-- ESPECIALLY ON SUCH SHORT NOTICE.

MY PLEASURE. BESIDES, IT'S GOOD TO SEE YOU AGAIN.

MAKE YOURSELVES COMFORTABLE, GROUP. MY HOME IS YOURS.

IT IS A BEAUTIFUL HOME, ANGEL. AND BEAUTIFUL COUNTRY.

COLOSSUS, THESE HILLS AIN'T NOTHIN' COMPARED TA THE *CANADIAN* ROCKIES-- NOW, THAT'S BEAUTIFUL COUNTRY!

YOU'RE LOOKING GOOD, BLONDIE.

YOU'RE NOT SO BAD YOURSELF, RED.

mmmMM-- WE KEEP THIS UP, JEAN, AND WE'RE LIABLE TO MAKE SCOTT JEALOUS.

KEEP IT UP, WINGS, AND "SCOTT" IS THE *LEAST* OF YOUR WORRIES.

≥ Ahem! ≤

X-MEN, MEET *CANDY SOUTHERN.* SHE AND I ARE WHAT "*PEOPLE*" MAGAZINE CALL AN *ITEM.*

HI.

OKAY, SCOTT-- WHAT BRINGS YOU TO THIS NECK OF THE WOODS? YOU SOUNDED PRETTY SERIOUS ON THE PHONE.

I WAS.

I DON'T MEAN TO BE RUDE, WARREN, BUT COULD WE TALK SOMEWHERE PRIVATE ...?

WHAT THE--?!

WARREN!?!

PRIVACY YOU WANT--

-- PRIVACY YOU *GOT!*

IF ANYONE'S HUNGRY, WE HAVE LUNCH FIXINGS INSIDE THE HOUSE, PROFESSOR?

THANK YOU, MISS SOUTHERN. GO WITH HER, X-MEN. I'LL BE ALONG DIRECTLY.

FIRST, SCOTT DISOBEYED MY INSTRUCTIONS BY BRINGING THE X-MEN HERE INSTEAD OF TO OUR NEW YORK HEADQUARTERS. AND NOW, HE FLIES OFF WITH ANGEL WITHOUT EVEN A WORD OF EXPLANATION.

I DO NOT UNDERSTAND WHY HE IS BEHAVING SO STRANGELY -- AND I DO NOT LIKE IT!

WINGS BEATING STRONGLY THROUGH THE STILL AFTERNOON AIR -- COVERING A HALF-DOZEN MILES IN TWICE AS MANY MINUTES -- ANGEL EFFORTLESSLY CARRIES CYCLOPS OUT ACROSS THE DESERT.

WARREN, IS THIS TRIP REALLY NECESSARY?

CAN'T GET MORE PRIVATE THAN THIS, SCOTT. NO ONE LISTENING AT THE KEYHOLE-- NO ONE EVEN IN SIGHT! AND NO HIDDEN MICROPHONES. AFTER ALL, WHO'S GOING TO BUG A BUTTE?

WE'RE ALONE, SCOTT. WHAT'S ON YOUR MIND?

SOMEONE'S AFTER THE X-MEN.

SO WHAT ELSE IS NEW? SOMEONE'S *ALWAYS* AFTER THE X-MEN.

THIS IS DIFFERENT.

"LAST WEEK, OUR MUTANT DETECTING COMPUTER -- *CEREBRO*-- PICKED UP TWO NEW CONTACTS. PROFESSOR X TOOK STORM, COLOSSUS AND WOLVERINE WITH HIM TO CHECK OUT THE ONE IN CHICAGO.

"THERE THEY WERE ATTACKED--AND CAPTURED-- BY A FOE WHO KNEW *EVERYTHING* ABOUT THEIR POWERS AND HOW TO DEFEAT THEM. SHE WAS A TELEPATH WHO CALLED HERSELF THE *WHITE QUEEN.*

"IN THE CONFUSION, THE CHICAGO NEO-MUTANT -- A TEENAGER NAMED *KITTY PRYDE* -- MANAGED TO SLIP AWAY LONG ENOUGH TO CALL THE REST OF US IN NEW YORK FOR HELP.

"UNFORTUNATELY, HER WARNING CAME JUST AS NIGHTCRAWLER, JEAN AND I -- AND OUR NEO-MUTANT, A DISCO SINGER CALLED *DAZZLER*-- WERE BEING AMBUSHED OURSELVES.

"IF IT HADN'T BEEN FOR DAZZLER, WE'D HAVE BEEN CAPTURED, TOO.

"WE HEADED FOR CHICAGO AND -- WITH KITTY AND DAZZLER'S AID -- RESCUED THE OTHERS.

"JEAN -- *PHOENIX* -- FOUGHT THE WHITE QUEEN IN A PSYCHIC DUEL. I WANTED THE WOMAN TAKEN ALIVE, FOR QUESTIONING. BUT, IN THE END, SHE PREFERRED SUICIDE TO CAPTURE." *

*A VERY ABBREVIATED RECAP OF THE EVENTS OF X-MEN #129-131 -- JIM.

PHOENIX MIND-SCANNED A GUARD AND WE LEARNED THAT THE WHITE QUEEN BELONGED TO A GROUP OF INDUSTRIAL-ISTS OUT TO RULE THE WORLD. THEY SEE MUTANT-KIND -- AND THE X-MEN -- AS A MEANS TO ACHIEVING THAT GOAL.

THEY CALL THEMSELVES THE *HELLFIRE CLUB.*

ARE YOU SURE?! I'M A *MEMBER* OF THE HELLFIRE CLUB. SO'S CANDY.

I INHERITED THE MEMBERSHIP, ALONG WITH WORTHINGTON INDUSTRIES, WHEN MY FOLKS PASSED AWAY. IT'S AN OLD, VERY STUFFY -- YET RISQUÉ -- ESTABLISHMENT CLUB.

CANDY AND I VISITED IT ONCE...

... BEFORE *I* TOLD THE WORLD I WAS THE ANGEL. WE DIDN'T LIKE IT. WE NEVER WENT BACK.

WHATEVER YOUR WHITE QUEEN LEARNED ABOUT THE X-MEN, IT WASN'T FROM ME.

THERE HAS TO BE A LEAK SOMEWHERE. WARREN, THESE PEOPLE KNEW OUR POWERS, OUR PLANS, THE WAY WE FIGHT -- THE WAY WE THINK!

THAT'S WHY I BROUGHT THE X-MEN HERE INSTEAD OF HOME -- PARTLY TO THROW OUR FOES OFF-BALANCE AND BUY US SOME BREATHING SPACE, PARTLY BECAUSE I DON'T THINK THE MANSION'S SAFE ANYMORE.

AND, AS IF THAT WASN'T ENOUGH TO WORRY ABOUT, SOME-THING ODD HAS BEEN HAPPENING TO JEAN LATELY...

SOMEONE MENTION MY NAME?

YOU FELLAS HAVE BEEN TALKING FOR HOURS. TIME FOR A BREAK.

WHA--? *JEAN!*

NICE ENTRANCE, RED.

ALL OF A SUDDEN, I HAVE THE FEELING I'M NOT WANTED.

PERCEPTIVE LAD. YOU'LL GO FAR.

SURE THING, WARREN.

RUNNING A MULTI-MILLION DOLLAR BUSINESS HAS BEEN GOOD FOR ANGEL. HE'S LOST NONE OF HIS FIRE, HIS PASSION-- BUT HE'S STEADIER INSIDE, A LOT SURER OF HIMSELF. HE'S GROWN UP.

I AIM TO, JEANNIE. WE'LL FINISH OUR TALK LATER, SCOTT. BE SEEING YOU.

WE'VE **ALL** GROWN UP, SCOTT.

SHE DID IT AGAIN, CHANGED FROM COSTUME TO STREET CLOTHES BY TELEKINETICALLY REARRANGING THE MOLECULES OF HER OUTFIT. WHY DO I FIND THAT SO DISCONCERTING?

WHY SHOULDN'T JEAN USE HER PSI-POWERS TO MAKE HER LIFE EASIER?

YOU'RE BROODING.

IT'S WHAT I DO BEST. AND... I'VE GOT A LOT ON MY MIND.

DIDN'T YOU HEAR ME?! IT'S TIME FOR A **BREAK!** STOP BEING CYCLOPS, LEADER OF THE X-MEN, FOR AWHILE. TRY BEING SCOTT SUMMERS, LOVER OF JEAN GREY. WHO KNOWS, YOU MIGHT EVEN **ENJOY** YOURSELF.

JEAN-- **NO!** WHAT ARE YOU DOING?! PUT MY VISOR DOWN!

IF I OPEN MY EYES EVEN FRACTIONALLY WITHOUT THE VISOR'S RUBY QUARTZ SHIELD TO CONTAIN MY OPTIC BLASTS-- !

OPEN YOUR EYES, SCOTT. NOTHING WILL HAPPEN.

I'M TELEKINETICALLY KEEPING YOUR OPTIC BLASTS IN CHECK. I... WANTED TO SEE YOUR FACE, THAT'S ALL.

YOU HAVE A GOOD FACE.

I DON'T BELIEVE IT! MY EYES -- HOW CAN JEAN HOLD BACK ALL THAT POWER?!

JEAN...

HUSH. NO QUESTIONS NOW, MY LOVE. NO WORDS.

"THIS IS OUR MOMENT. LET'S NOT WASTE IT."

A WEEK PASSES...

... AND OUR SCENE SHIFTS EASTWARD TWO THOUSAND MILES, FROM THE NEW MEXICO DESERT TO THE MAN-MADE CANYONS OF MANHATTAN.

ON FIFTH AVENUE, FOUR BLOCKS DOWNTOWN FROM AVENGERS MANSION, NEW YORK'S LEGENDARY HELLFIRE CLUB IS CELEBRATING ITS LATEST "BIRTHDAY" WITH ONE OF THE MOST EXCLUSIVE PARTIES THE BIG APPLE HAS EVER SEEN.

THE GUEST LIST INCLUDES SOME OF THE RICHEST, MOST POWERFUL MEN AND WOMEN IN THE WORLD, PEOPLE WHOSE WEALTH OUTSTRIPS THAT OF MANY COUNTRIES. ALL ARE LOOKING FORWARD TO A PLEASANT, ENTERTAINING EVENING.

MEANWHILE, IN A STORM SEWER ROUGHLY TWENTY FEET BELOW THE STREET, A PAIR OF WOULD-BE GATE CRASHERS ARE MAKING THEIR WAY TOWARDS THE CLUB.

WATER'S RISIN', NIGHTCRAWLER.

WE GOT MUCH FARTHER TA GO?

MY SCANNER SAYS WE'RE ALMOST THERE, WOLVERINE.

THESE POWER AND COMMUNICATIONS CABLES ALL SERVICE THE HELLFIRE CLUB. THAT PLACE USES AS MUCH ELECTRICITY AS A SKYSCRAPER -- I WONDER WHY?

BEATS ME, ELF. BUT THESE CABLES GIVE ME AN IDEA.

EXTENDED BY MENTAL COMMAND FROM THE BACKS OF WOLVERINE'S HANDS, ADAMANTIUM CLAWS FLASH IN THE LIGHT OF HIS LANTERN.

WOLVERINE -- WHAT?!!

RELAX, ELF. ALL I DID WAS STRIP THE INSULATION OFF THESE POWER LINES. WHEN THE WATER HITS 'EM, THEY'LL SHORT OUT -- PROBABLY BLOW EVERY LIGHT IN THE CLUB.

IF SOMETHING GOES WRONG TONIGHT, A SURPRISE BLACK-OUT COULD COME IN HANDY.

VERY NICE, *MEIN FREUND.* VERY SNEAKY.

I DO MY BEST, BUB.

NIGHTCRAWLER TO CYCLOPS -- WE ARE IN POSITION AND READY TO MAKE OUR MOVE. OVER.

AND, IN A LIMOUSINE PARKED JUST AROUND THE CORNER...

ROGER, NIGHTCRAWLER.

THANKS TO ANGEL, WE FOUR HAVE INVITATIONS TO THIS BASH, UNDER FALSE NAMES. THE WHITE QUEEN'S ALLIES -- WHOEVER THEY ARE -- SHOULD HAVE NO IDEA WE'RE COMING.

PROFESSOR, IF YOU HAVEN'T HEARD FROM US BY MIDNIGHT, WE'VE RUN INTO TROUBLE.

SCOTT, I DO NOT LIKE THE IDEA OF YOU AND THE X-MEN BLITHELY WALKING INTO A POTENTIAL DEATHTRAP.

NEITHER DO I, REALLY. BUT I CAN'T SEE ANY ALTERNATIVE.

WE HAVE NO HARD EVIDENCE CONNECTING THE WHITE QUEEN'S OUTFIT WITH THIS HELLFIRE CLUB -- OTHER THAN THE NAME. AND WE CAN'T AFFORD TO MAKE A MISTAKE. WE NEED PROOF, ONE WAY OR THE OTHER.

IF THEY DO TURN OUT TO BE THE SAME GANG -- AND IF THEY'RE READY FOR US -- AT LEAST YOU'LL BE SAFE IN NEW MEXICO. YOU AND ANGEL WILL BE FREE, AND ABLE TO DEAL WITH THEM.

WISH US LUCK, PROFESSOR. CYCLOPS OUT.

YOU DON'T APPROVE OF SCOTT'S PLAN, PROFESSOR?

IT'S NOT THAT. I... I'M STILL UNABLE TO RE-ESTABLISH MY PSYCHIC RAPPORT WITH THE X-MEN. THEY'RE GOING INTO ACTION AND I WON'T BE ABLE TO HELP, OR GUIDE, THEM.

BY HEAVEN, ANGEL, I WON'T EVEN KNOW WHAT'S HAPPENING UNTIL IT'S TOO LATE!

AT THAT MOMENT, INSIDE THE FOYER OF THE HELLFIRE CLUB...

I HAVE NEVER WORN CLOTHES AS FINE AS THIS. THEY FEEL MARVELOUS.

YET, IT DOES NOT FEEL... RIGHT TO WEAR A SUIT THAT COST MORE THAN MY FATHER EARNS IN AN ENTIRE YEAR.

IT HAS BEEN TOO LONG SINCE I HAVE BEEN HOME. I MISS IT MORE AND MORE EACH DAY.

SENSES FULLY ALERT FOR THE SLIGHTEST HINT OF DANGER, COLOSSUS AND STORM MOVE INTO THE CLUB'S MAIN HALL.

ORORO, EVEN I HAVE HEARD OF SOME OF THE PEOPLE HERE -- SOME OF THEM ARE MY COUNTRYMEN! HOW COULD SUCH AS THEY PLOT THE DESTRUCTION OF THE X-MEN?

THAT'S WHAT WE'RE HERE TO FIND OUT, PETER. WE'RE BOTH BAIT AND TRAP.

LUCKY US.

OUTSIDE, THE FINAL TWO X-MEN MAKE THEIR ENTRANCE, JEAN USING HER TELEPATHIC POWER TO KEEP SCOTT IN CONSTANT TOUCH WITH HIS TEAM-MATES.

ORORO AND PETER ARE INSIDE, SCOTT. THEY SAY ALL IS WELL.

I WONDER HOW LONG THAT WILL LAST?

NOT LONG AT ALL, ACTUALLY -- FOR, IN A HIDDEN SUB-BASEMENT BELOW THE CLUB...

SHAW, ALL OF YOU -- THE MONITOR SCREEN!

LOOK WHO'S HERE! HIS NAME IS PIERCE.

HIS COMPANIONS ARE SHAW, LELAND, AND WYNGARDE. TOGETHER, THEY FORM THE NUCLEUS OF THE HELLFIRE CLUB'S INNER CIRCLE -- A SECRET SOCIETY DEDICATED TO THE ACQUISITION OF POWER, IN ALL ITS MYRIAD FORMS.

WHAT A PLEASANT SURPRISE. JEAN GREY AND SCOTT SUMMERS -- PHOENIX AND CYCLOPS OF THE X-MEN.

PIERCE, SEARCH THE CLUB. IF THEY'RE HERE, THE OTHER X-MEN CAN'T BE FAR AWAY.

WYNGARDE! FOR WEEKS NOW, YOU'VE BEEN BOASTING THAT MISS GREY IS YOURS -- "BODY AND SOUL." TONIGHT IS YOUR CHANCE TO PROVE IT.

SHE CAN LEAD OUR ATTACK ON THE X-MEN.

FOR YOUR SAKE, I HOPE SHE SUCCEEDS.

MEANWHILE, IN THE MAIN FLOOR BALLROOM...

I'VE MIND-SCANNED EVERYONE IN THIS ROOM. THEY'RE ALL PERFECTLY NORMAL.

IT'S EARLY YET. BY THE WAY, I LIKE YOUR DRESS.

I THOUGHT YOU WOULD-- EH?

PARDON ME, SIRRAH. MAY I CUT IN?

BEFORE EITHER X-MAN CAN PROTEST...

... JASON WYNGARDE GATHERS JEAN IN HIS ARMS AND SWEEPS HER AWAY. AND AS HE DOES, HE REACHES INTO JEAN'S MIND...

... AND ONCE MORE TURNS THE CLOCK BACK TWO HUNDRED YEARS.

SO FAR AS JEAN IS NOW CONCERNED, SHE IS LADY JEAN GREY, AND SHE IS DANCING WITH A MAN SHE LOVES MORE THAN LIFE ITSELF.

HER HUSBAND.

WHAT THE--?!?

THAT'S JASON WYNGARDE!

THIS IS A LOT LIKE WHAT HAPPENED THE NIGHT JEAN AND I FIRST MET DAZZLER. * HE MOVED IN, SAID HELLO, AND THE NEXT INSTANT, HE AND JEAN WERE KISSING LIKE LONG LOST LOVERS.

AND NOW-- ONE LOOK AT HIM AND IT'S AS IF I DON'T EXIST ANYMORE.

*X-MEN #129 -- JIM.

I DON'T LIKE WYNGARDE-- AND THERE'S MORE TO MY FEELING THAN JEALOUSY.

IN NEW MEXICO, JEAN TOLD ME ABOUT HER "TIMESLIPS"-- RANDOM EPISODES WHERE SHE FOUND HERSELF PHYSICALLY SHIFTING IN TIME, RELIVING THE LIFE OF AN ANCESTOR. A WOMAN MARRIED TO JASON WYNGARDE AND HAILED AS THE BLACK QUEEN OF THAT ERA'S HELLFIRE CLUB.

I CAN'T BELIEVE THAT THESE TIMESLIPS AND JEAN'S TOTAL FASCINATION WITH THIS WYNGARDE CREEP ARE A COINCIDENCE.

Uh-oh -- WYNGARDE'S TAKING JEAN UPSTAIRS.

JEAN?! WAIT UP-- JEAN!

SHE'S IGNORING ME! WHAT KIND OF HOLD DOES WYNGARDE HAVE OVER HER?!

HOW CHARMING -- THE STALWART HERO OUT TO RESCUE HIS DAMSEL FAIR.

NOT THIS TIME, CYCLOPS!

WHA--?! THAT FACE!

MASTERMIND!

THE NIGHT THE X-MEN MET DAZZLER, SCOTT SAW JASON WYNGARDE MOMEN-TARILY SILHOUETTED IN THE HEADLIGHTS OF THE X-MEN'S ROLLS-ROYCE...

... THROWING A SHADOW ON THE WALL BEHIND HIM THAT DIDN'T MATCH HIS FACE. SCOTT SHOULD HAVE RECOGNIZED THE MASTER OF ILLUSION. *

BUT HE WAS IN A HURRY, WITH FAR MORE IMMEDIATE WORRIES ON HIS MIND. AND SO, HE MADE A MISTAKE.

I'D BETTER GET TO JEAN FAST! IF SHE'S UNDER MASTERMIND'S INFLUENCE...

* IN X-MEN #130, PAGE 31, PANEL 3 -- SNEAKY SALICRUP.

TOO LATE, CYCLOPS!

AARRRGH!

SPLOW!

MAGNIFICENT, MY LOVE.

BUT-- THE HELLFIRE CLUB WANTS THE X-MEN ALIVE. IS CYCLOPS--?

WORRY NOT, JASON.

HAD THE BLACK QUEEN STRUCK TO KILL, THERE WOULD BE NOTHING LEFT OF THE LAD BUT ASHES.

ORORO, DID YOU HEAR? THAT SOUND -- AND WAS THAT A MAN'S *SCREAM* AS WELL?

IT IS SO HARD TO BE SURE OVER THE NOISE OF THIS PARTY.

I AM SURE, PETER -- MY HEARING IS ALMOST AS SHARP AS WOLVERINE'S. IT WAS A MAN'S SCREAM-- *CYCLOPS'* SCREAM.

AND THAT SOUND WAS ONE OF PHOENIX' ENERGY BLASTS!

UPSTAIRS, COLOSSUS -- *QUICKLY!* OUR FRIENDS MUST BE IN DANGER!

YYIIII--!

GOOD HEAVENS!

OUR TRAP HAS SPRUNG. GODDESS GRANT THAT OUR POWERS ARE SUFFICIENT...

...TO DEAL WITH WHATEVER WE'VE SNARED.

GREETINGS, X-MEN. I AM *SEBASTIAN SHAW.* I ADVISE YOU TO SURRENDER...

...OR YOU WILL BE *HURT.*

BY WHOM, LITTLE MAN -- BY *YOU?* DO NOT MAKE ME LAUGH.

I MUST TAKE CARE TO HIT HIM LIGHTLY. I ONLY WISH TO KNOCK HIM UNCONSCIOUS, BUT WITH MY STRENGTH AND ARMORED FORM, I COULD EASILY KILL.

BRAK!

LENIN'S GHOST-- MY BLOW HAD *NO EFFECT!*

KRAKOW!

WRONG, MY TIN-PLATED COMRADE.

IF ANY-THING, YOUR PUNCH HAS MADE ME *STRONGER* THAN EVER!

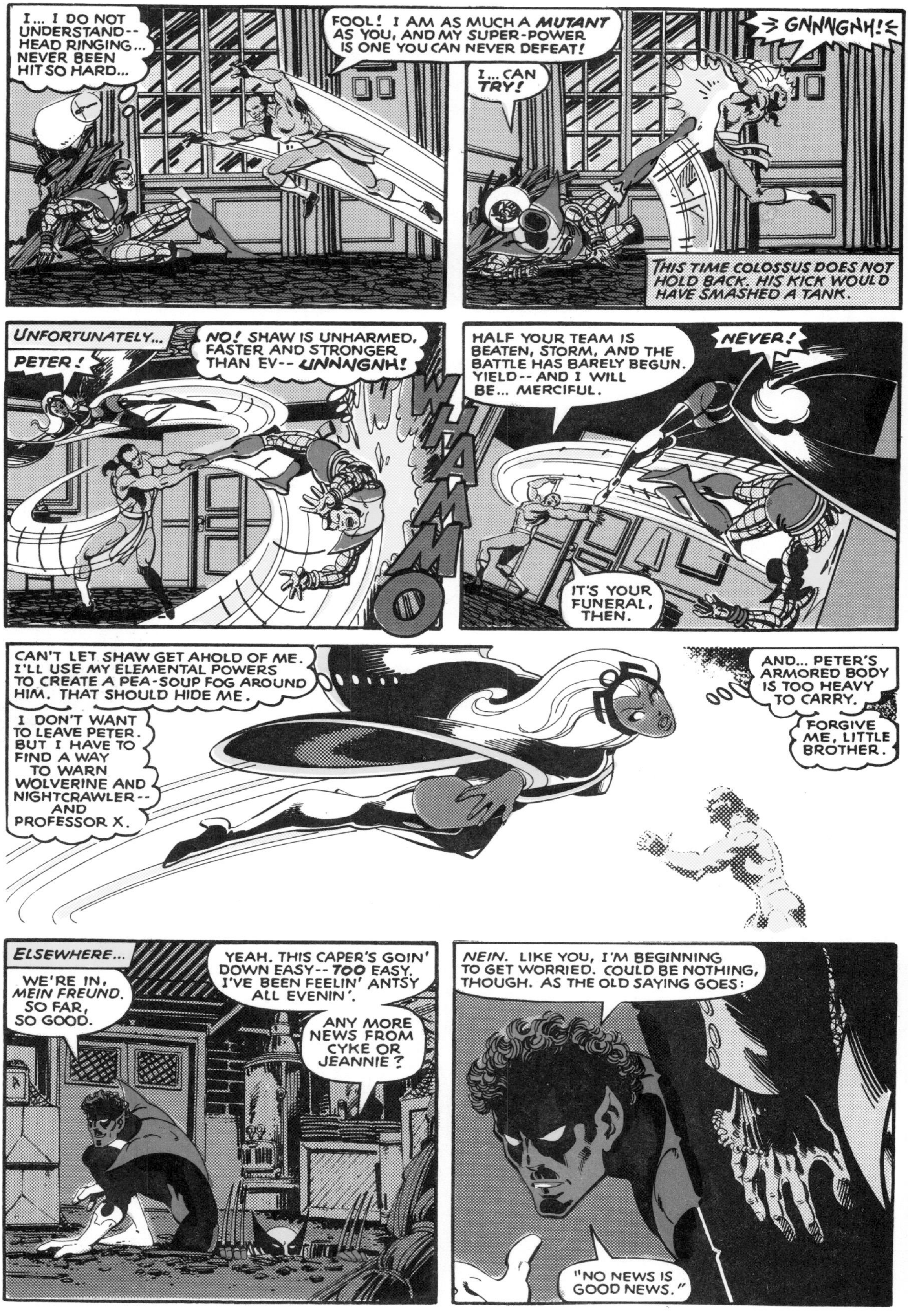
I... I DO NOT UNDERSTAND-- HEAD RINGING... NEVER BEEN HIT SO HARD...
FOOL! I AM AS MUCH A MUTANT AS YOU, AND MY SUPER-POWER IS ONE YOU CAN NEVER DEFEAT!
I... CAN TRY!
GNNNGNH!
THIS TIME COLOSSUS DOES NOT HOLD BACK. HIS KICK WOULD HAVE SMASHED A TANK.
UNFORTUNATELY...
PETER!
NO! SHAW IS UNHARMED, FASTER AND STRONGER THAN EV-- UNNNGNH!
WHAMMO
HALF YOUR TEAM IS BEATEN, STORM, AND THE BATTLE HAS BARELY BEGUN. YIELD-- AND I WILL BE... MERCIFUL.
NEVER!
IT'S YOUR FUNERAL, THEN.
CAN'T LET SHAW GET AHOLD OF ME. I'LL USE MY ELEMENTAL POWERS TO CREATE A PEA-SOUP FOG AROUND HIM. THAT SHOULD HIDE ME.
I DON'T WANT TO LEAVE PETER. BUT I HAVE TO FIND A WAY TO WARN WOLVERINE AND NIGHTCRAWLER-- AND PROFESSOR X.
AND... PETER'S ARMORED BODY IS TOO HEAVY TO CARRY.
FORGIVE ME, LITTLE BROTHER.
ELSEWHERE...
WE'RE IN, MEIN FREUND. SO FAR, SO GOOD.
YEAH. THIS CAPER'S GOIN' DOWN EASY-- TOO EASY. I'VE BEEN FEELIN' ANTSY ALL EVENIN'.
ANY MORE NEWS FROM CYKE OR JEANNIE?
NEIN. LIKE YOU, I'M BEGINNING TO GET WORRIED. COULD BE NOTHING, THOUGH. AS THE OLD SAYING GOES:
"NO NEWS IS GOOD NEWS."

>URRRGKH!<

GRIP-- LIKE STEEL VISE--CAN'T BREATHE! AND... SOME SORT OF ELECTRICAL FIELD SHOOTING THROUGH MY BODY-- CAN'T CONCENTRATE ENOUGH... TO *TELEPORT* TO SAFETY.

IN YOUR CASE, GOBLIN, YOUR LACK OF NEWS COULD HAVE *FATAL* CONSE-QUENCES.

THAT'S THE TRUTH, SKINNY-- FATAL FER *YOU!*

HUH?! YER ARM-- *WIRES!*

CURSE YOU! WHAT HAVE YOU DONE?!

CRIPES! YOU'RE A FLAMIN' *ROBOT!*

NOT QUITE, WOLVERINE.

DONALD PIERCE IS A *CYBORG!*

A CYBERNETIC ORGANISM-- PART MAN, PART MACHINE. A LIVING BEING, WITH THE POWER OF A *JUGGERNAUT!*

YEAH, I KNOW ALL ABOUT CYBORGS-- I ALMOST BECAME ONE MYSELF.

YOU MAY BE A *"SIX MILLION DOLLAR MAN,"* BUB -- BUT WHEN I'M DONE WITH YOU...

...SIX *BILLION* BUCKS WON'T BE ENOUGH TA PUT YA BACK TOGETHER AGAIN.

I'M AFRAID I CAN'T ALLOW THAT, DEAR BOY.

YOU'RE WELCOME TA TRY AN' STOP ME, TUBBY. AT YER OWN RISK.

THE NAME IS LELAND, *HARRY LELAND.*

AND YOUR CHALLENGE IS ACCEPTED, DEAR BOY. STOP YOU I SHALL.

WHAT --!?? I'M GETTIN' *HEAVIER!* CAN'T MOVE -- CAN BARELY... STAND! WHAT'S FATSO DOIN' TA ME?!

DEAR BOY, YOU X-MEN ARE NOT THE ONLY MUTANTS IN THE WORLD SKILLED IN THE USE OF THEIR SPECIAL, UNIQUE ABILITIES.

MY OWN TALENT INVOLVES *MASS.*

SIMPLY BY CONCENTRATING, I CAN *INCREASE* THE MASS OF OBJECTS -- AND PEOPLE -- AROUND ME.

MUST WEIGH... TONS -- AN' HE'S MAKIN' ME HEAVIER... ALL THE TIME...

STRAIN... KILLIN' ME... BUT I CAN'T -- I *WON'T* -- GIVE UP!

IN THE END, HOWEVER, IT'S NOT WOLVERINE WHO YIELDS...

MY GOODNESS!

...BUT THE FLOOR BENEATH HIM.

HE DROPS LIKE A RUNAWAY ROCKET INTO A STORM SEWER BURIED DEEP BENEATH THE CLUB AND THE IMPACT WHEN HE FINALLY HITS THE WATER IS MORE AKIN TO SLAMMING FULL TILT INTO A STEEL WALL.

IT LEAVES HIM STUNNED, BARELY CONSCIOUS. AND IN THE BLINK OF AN EYE, HE'S SWEPT AWAY.

I CAN'T RAISE NIGHTCRAWLER OR WOLVERINE ON MY RADIO COMLINK. HAVE THEY BEEN ATTACKED, TOO? AM I THE ONLY X-MAN LEFT?!

THE HELLFIRE CLUB BEAT US SO QUICKLY, SO EASILY! IN THE GODDESS' NAME -- HOW?! *HOW?!?*

I TRIED BLASTING THROUGH THESE WINDOWS WITH MY LIGHTNING BOLTS, BUT THEY HAD NO EFFECT. SOME DEFENSIVE SYSTEM NEUTRALIZED THEIR POWER.

ONLY ONE ROUTE LEFT, DOWN-STAIRS AND OUT THE FRONT DOOR, USING THE PARTY GUESTS TO COVER MY ESCAPE -- *OH!!*

SURPRISE!

I KNOW EVERY INCH OF THIS HOUSE, STORM. THERE'S NO WAY YOU CAN ELUDE ME FOR VERY LONG.

MY ANKLE -- IF SHAW TIGHTENS HIS GRIP, HE'LL CRUSH IT!

THESE VILLAINS SEEM TO KNOW ALL ABOUT THE X-MEN. SHAW WILL ASSUME I'LL FIGHT HIM WITH MY ELEMENTAL POWERS. INSTEAD, I'LL DO SOMETHING UNEXPECTED...

KRAK!

OWW!

IF I CAN BREAK FREE FOR ONLY A MOMENT--!

DONE IT -- NO!

SHAW GRABBED MY CAPE! I'VE NEVER SEEN ANYONE MOVE SO FAST!

I LIKE A WOMAN WITH SPIRIT, STORM, BUT NOT TOO MUCH SPIRIT. YOU SHOULD HAVE LEARNED FROM COLOSSUS' DEFEAT-- I ABSORB KINETIC ENERGY.

THE HARDER ANYONE STRIKES ME, THE MORE POWERFUL I GET!

I TOLD YOU BEFORE, THAT IF YOU YIELDED TO ME, I WOULD BE MERCIFUL.

BUT YOU RESISTED.

NOW PAY THE PRICE!

KROM

WE'VE DONE WELL TONIGHT. WE'VE TROUNCED THE X-MEN, WITH NO LOSS TO OURSELVES. AND NONE OF THE CLUB'S GUESTS ARE THE WISER.

IT'S BEEN A LONG TIME SINCE I EXERCISED MY MUTANT ABILITY.

I'D FORGOTTEN HOW GOOD IT FELT.

PERHAPS THE HELLFIRE CLUB SHOULD SET ITS SIGHTS HIGHER -- TODAY, THE X-MEN; TOMORROW... THE AVENGERS? I WONDER -- DARE I MATCH MY POWER AGAINST THAT OF IRON MAN? OR THOR?

HOW'S YOUR ARM, PIERCE?

IT WAS JUST A SCRATCH, SHAW. EASILY REPAIRED. I'M FINE NOW.

SCRATCH--HAH! WOLVERINE CUT THROUGH YOUR PRECIOUS BIONIC ARM LIKE IT WAS MADE OF BUTTER.

JASON, WE'VE JUST WON A SPLENDID VICTORY.

WHY SPOIL IT WITH HARSH WORDS?

THE BLACK QUEEN SPEAKS TRUE, WYNGARDE. BE OF GOOD CHEER, OR BE SILENT.

THIS COULD BE TROUBLE. WYNGARDE IS DELIBERATELY PROVOKING PIERCE-- BUT HE'S REALLY CHALLENGING ME.

WYNGARDE IS AS MUCH A NATURAL LEADER AS I. SOONER OR LATER, HE'LL MAKE HIS BID TO TAKE OVER THE INNER CIRCLE...

...POSITIVE THAT-- SO LONG AS HE CONTROLS PHOENIX, OUR BLACK QUEEN -- NONE OF US WILL OPPOSE HIM.

OURS WAS A GROUP EFFORT, WYNGARDE -- A GROUP VICTORY. WE ALL DID OUR PART.

OF COURSE, SHAW. BUT JUST REMEMBER THAT IT WAS MY PSYCHIC SEDUCTION OF JEAN GREY THAT PROVIDED THE KEY TO OUR VICTORY.

WE COULD HAVE WON WITH-OUT HER.

IS THAT SO? VERY WELL THEN, PIERCE-- I'LL SIMPLY RELEASE MY "HOLD" ON HER.

SEE HOW LONG YOU LAST.

PIERCE, WYNGARDE -- THAT'S ENOUGH, BOTH OF YOU! AS CHAIRMAN OF THE INNER CIRCLE, I, SEBASTIAN SHAW, PROPOSE A TOAST:

TO THE *HELLFIRE CLUB* -- AND OUR *BLACK QUEEN* --

LONG MAY SHE REIGN!

"AS FOR OUR CAPTURED MUTANTS -- BY THE TIME WE'VE FINISHED WITH THEM, THE X-MEN MAY WELL WISH THEY'D PERISHED WITH WOLVERINE."

RNNCH!

OKAY, SUCKERS -- YOU'VE TAKEN YER *BEST* SHOT!

NOW IT'S MY TURN!

NEXT

WOLVERINE -- ALONE!

'NUFF SAID!

79

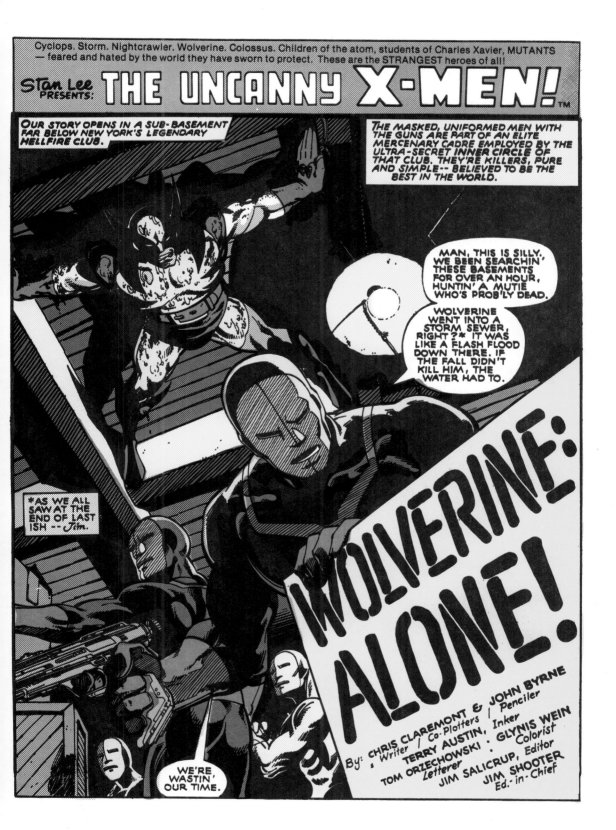

Cyclops. Storm. Nightcrawler. Wolverine. Colossus. Children of the atom, students of Charles Xavier, MUTANTS — feared and hated by the world they have sworn to protect. These are the STRANGEST heroes of all!

STAN LEE PRESENTS: THE UNCANNY X-MEN! ™

OUR STORY OPENS IN A SUB-BASEMENT FAR BELOW NEW YORK'S LEGENDARY HELLFIRE CLUB.

THE MASKED, UNIFORMED MEN WITH THE GUNS ARE PART OF AN ELITE MERCENARY CADRE EMPLOYED BY THE ULTRA-SECRET INNER CIRCLE OF THAT CLUB. THEY'RE KILLERS, PURE AND SIMPLE -- BELIEVED TO BE THE BEST IN THE WORLD.

MAN, THIS IS SILLY. WE BEEN SEARCHIN' THESE BASEMENTS FOR OVER AN HOUR, HUNTIN' A MUTIE WHO'S PROB'LY DEAD.

WOLVERINE WENT INTO A STORM SEWER, RIGHT?* IT WAS LIKE A FLASH FLOOD DOWN THERE. IF THE FALL DIDN'T KILL HIM, THE WATER HAD TO.

*AS WE ALL SAW AT THE END OF LAST ISH -- Jim.

WE'RE WASTIN' OUR TIME.

WOLVERINE: ALONE!

By: CHRIS CLAREMONT & JOHN BYRNE
Writer / Co-Plotters / Penciler
TERRY AUSTIN, Inker
TOM ORZECHOWSKI · GLYNIS WEIN
Letterer · Colorist
JIM SALICRUP, Editor
JIM SHOOTER
Ed.-in-Chief

81

AN' EVEN IF HE DID SURVIVE -- SO WHAT?! THE INNER CIRCLE'S CAPTURED THE REST OF THE X-MEN. WOLVERINE'S JUST ONE MAN.

HOW MUCH DAMAGE CAN HE DO?

HUH?! WATER --?!?

THERE AIN'T NO PIPES IN HERE -- HOW COME WE GOT A LEAK?

MURRAY -- ALL OF YOU -- THE *CEILING!*

SURPRISE!!

THE MERCENARIES REACT WITH DESPERATE, DEADLY SPEED.

ANGELO -- HE'S COMING FOR *YOU!*

IT DOESN'T SAVE THEM.

NEITHER DOES THEIR SKILL.

YAHHRR

WOLVERINE NEVER STOPS, NEVER SLOWS, EACH MOVE BLENDING INTO THE NEXT IN A FRIGHTENING DISPLAY OF DESTRUCTION. HE'S DOING WHAT HE DOES BEST...

...AND HAVING THE TIME OF HIS LIFE.

WAY-TA-GO!

I'VE BEEN IN BETTER ROUGH-HOUSES. THE ODDS HERE ARE ONLY THREE-TA-ONE-- MAKE THAT *TWO*-TA-ONE--

--BUT I AIN'T COMPLAININ'.

THESE TWERPS ARE JUST SMALL FRY, THOUGH. THE ONES I WANT ARE THEIR BOSSES-- UH-OH!

WHOUFF!

GOT HIM!

BUDDABUDDA!

HE'S DOWN, COLE, AN' HE AIN'T MOVIN'! IS HE--?!

I DON'T KNOW! STAY BACK AND COVER ME!

I'M POSITIVE I HIT WOLVERINE DEAD CENTER, BUT AFTER WHAT I'VE SEEN TONIGHT, I'M TAKING NO CHANCES.

BLAST! I'LL HAVE TO SHIFT SOME OF THESE CRATES TO GET A CLEAR SHOT. THAT'S BRINGING ME A LOT CLOSER TO WOLVERINE THAN I HAD IN MIND.

STAY ALERT, ROSEN! IF HE BLINKS AN EYE-- KILL HIM!

HEY, *HEY!* YOU KNOW WHAT, BUDDY? I THINK THE LITTLE RUNT IS DEAD.

YOUR MISTAKE, BUB.

THE "LITTLE RUNT" *LIVES!*

NO!

SHO--

WHICH IS MORE'N I CAN SAY FER YOU.

THAT WAS CLOSE -- ALMOST *TOO* CLOSE. IF I HADN'T SPUN AWAY WHEN THIS GUY FIRED, HIS BURST WOULD'A CUT ME IN TWO 'STEAD O' SIMPLY CREASIN' MY SIDE!

. . . . . ONLY ONE GOON LEFT.

D-DON'T MOVE, FELLA!

HE'S SCARED -- CAN'T SAY AS I BLAME HIM, EITHER. LET'S SEE IF I CAN'T MAKE HIM FEEL WORSE!

HEY, BUB, I KNOW WHAT YOU'RE THINKIN'.

"HE'S HURT, AN' HE'S FIVE METERS AWAY FROM ME, AN' I GOT A FULL CLIP OF AMMO IN MY RIFLE."

"QUESTION IS! CAN I KILL WOLVERINE BEFORE HE CAN REACH ME AN' CUT ME INTO SHISH-KEBAB WITH THOSE FREAKY CLAWS OF HIS?"

WELL, BUB, WOLVERINE IS VIRTUALLY UNKILLABLE.

WOLVERINE'S CLAWS ARE *ADAMANTIUM*, THE STRONGEST METAL KNOWN -- CAPABLE OF SLICIN' THROUGH VANADIUM STEEL LIKE A HOT KNIFE THROUGH BUTTER.

AN' FIVE METERS O' FLOOR AIN'T MUCH DISTANCE AT ALL -- FER ME.

IT'S YOUR PLAY, HERO. I'M WAITIN'.

SHOOT, I WAS HOPIN' YOU'D GO FOR IT.

KLUNK!

WHAT ARE YOU DOING?! STAY BACK! I GIVE UP -- I SURRENDER!!

NO, PLEASE -- NO!!

I'VE MELLOWED SOME SINCE JOININ' THE X-MEN. IN THE OLD DAYS, I WOULDN'T HAVE GIVEN THIS PUNK A CHOICE.

BE COOL, BUB, I AIN'T GONNA KILL YA. I AIN'T EVEN GONNA HURT YA --

YYIIII--!!

SNIKT!

-- PROVIDED YA TELL ME ALL THERE IS TA KNOW ABOUT THE HELLFIRE CLUB HOTSHOTS WHO CLOBBERED THE X-MEN.

ON THAT NOTE, LET'S SHIFT OUR SCENE TO AN UPSTAIRS LIBRARY, WHERE WE FIND THOSE SELFSAME X-MEN -- COLOSSUS, NIGHTCRAWLER, STORM AND CYCLOPS -- CHAINED AND HELPLESS, THEIR MUTANT POWERS COMPLETELY NEUTRALIZED BY INHIBITOR FIELDS BUILT INTO THEIR MANACLES.

THEIR CAPTORS CALL THEMSELVES THE "INNER CIRCLE" OF THE HELLFIRE CLUB, AND THEY FORM THE ROTTEN CORE OF A PERFECTLY LEGITIMATE, RESPECTABLE, LEGENDARY NEW YORK INSTITUTION. THEY'RE AN EXCLUSIVE, ULTRA-SECRET CABAL (A CLUB WITHIN THE CLUB) DEDICATED TO THE ACQUISITION OF POWER FOR ITS MEMBERS.

AMONG THOSE MEMBERS: THE BLACK QUEEN -- JEAN GREY, ONCE AN X-MAN UNTIL SHE WAS PSYCHICALLY SEDUCED INTO THE ENEMY CAMP BY JASON WYNGARDE, A MAN BETTER KNOWN TO US AS MASTERMIND, MUTANT MASTER OF ILLUSION.

THE CHAIRMAN OF THE INNER CIRCLE IS SEBASTIAN SHAW -- ALSO A MUTANT. BESIDE HIM STAND LELAND AND PIERCE; ONE A MUTANT, THE OTHER A CYBORG -- PART HUMAN, PART ROBOT.

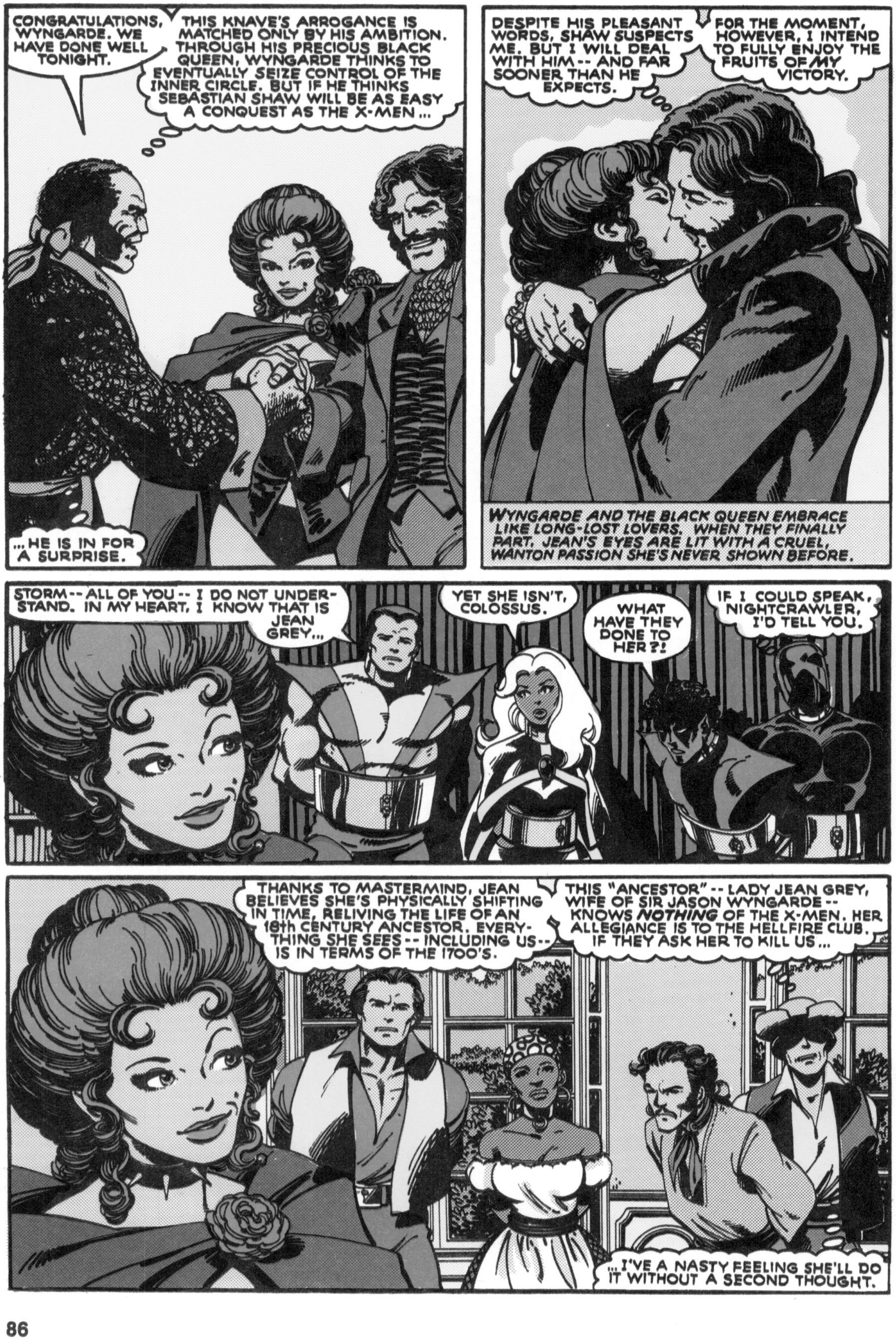
CONGRATULATIONS, WYNGARDE. WE HAVE DONE WELL TONIGHT.
THIS KNAVE'S ARROGANCE IS MATCHED ONLY BY HIS AMBITION. THROUGH HIS PRECIOUS BLACK QUEEN, WYNGARDE THINKS TO EVENTUALLY SEIZE CONTROL OF THE INNER CIRCLE. BUT IF HE THINKS SEBASTIAN SHAW WILL BE AS EASY A CONQUEST AS THE X-MEN...
...HE IS IN FOR A SURPRISE.
DESPITE HIS PLEASANT WORDS, SHAW SUSPECTS ME. BUT I WILL DEAL WITH HIM -- AND FAR SOONER THAN HE EXPECTS.
FOR THE MOMENT, HOWEVER, I INTEND TO FULLY ENJOY THE FRUITS OF *MY* VICTORY.
WYNGARDE AND THE BLACK QUEEN EMBRACE LIKE LONG-LOST LOVERS. WHEN THEY FINALLY PART, JEAN'S EYES ARE LIT WITH A CRUEL, WANTON PASSION SHE'S NEVER SHOWN BEFORE.
STORM -- ALL OF YOU -- I DO NOT UNDERSTAND. IN MY HEART, I KNOW THAT IS JEAN GREY...
YET SHE ISN'T, COLOSSUS.
WHAT HAVE THEY DONE TO HER?!
IF I COULD SPEAK, NIGHTCRAWLER, I'D TELL YOU.
THANKS TO MASTERMIND, JEAN BELIEVES SHE'S PHYSICALLY SHIFTING IN TIME, RELIVING THE LIFE OF AN 18th CENTURY ANCESTOR. EVERYTHING SHE SEES -- INCLUDING US -- IS IN TERMS OF THE 1700'S.
THIS "ANCESTOR" -- LADY JEAN GREY, WIFE OF SIR JASON WYNGARDE -- KNOWS *NOTHING* OF THE X-MEN. HER ALLEGIANCE IS TO THE HELLFIRE CLUB. IF THEY ASK HER TO KILL US...
...I'VE A NASTY FEELING SHE'LL DO IT WITHOUT A SECOND THOUGHT.

I EXPECTED BETTER OF YOU. IN ALL THE YEARS YOU HAVE BEEN MY SLAVE, I HAVE NEVER MISTREATED YOU.

SLAVE?!!

I TRUSTED YOU, ONLY TO SEE THAT TRUST BETRAYED.

GODDESS, THERE'S SUCH... EVIL IN JEAN'S VOICE.

IS THIS WHAT YOU WANT, BEAUTY? THE KEYS THAT WILL FREE YOU AND YOUR COMPANIONS?

"BEAUTY" -- THE ENGLISH TRANSLATION OF MY REAL NAME, ORORO.

JEAN HAS MADE IT AN INSULT. SHE'S TAUNTING ME --

-- FLAUNTING MY HEADDRESS AND LOCKPICKS.

JEAN -- HEAR ME. WE'RE FRIENDS. I...

SILENCE! LET HER ALONE, CURSE YOU!

YOU DARE SPEAK SO TO ME, SLAVE?! I AM NOT YOUR FRIEND -- BUT YOUR MISTRESS!

I OWN YOU!

AND -- AS MY RIGHT -- MINE WILL BE THE HAND THAT ENDS YOUR WORTHLESS EXISTENCE.

KRAK!

IF ONLY I COULD SEE! LOCKED INSIDE THIS RUBY QUARTZ HELMET, I CAN ONLY GUESS AT WHAT'S GOING ON!

THE HELMET MAY NEUTRALIZE MY OPTIC BLASTS -- BUT NOT MY BRAIN! I CAN'T PHYSICALLY ACT, BUT I CAN THINK!

"I REMEMBER THE BUTTE NEAR ANGEL'S ARIZONA HOME -- A WEEK AGO.* JEAN WAS TELLING ME ABOUT HER TIMESLIPS AND RECENT, DRAMATIC UPSURGES IN HER POWER AS PHOENIX.

"THAT FRIGHTENED HER -- AND ME, TOO -- AND YET, IT FASCINATED HER AS WELL."

*SEE LAST ISSUE -- JIM.

IT'S WEIRD, HAVING YOUR PSYCHOKINETIC TALENT HOLD BACK THE POWER OF MY OPTIC BLASTS.

I WANTED TO SEE YOUR FACE, ALL OF YOUR FACE.

DISAPPOINTED?

NO. SCOTT, I'D... LIKE TO ESTABLISH A PERMANENT RAPPORT -- A PSYCHIC *BOND* -- BETWEEN US. PART OF ME IN YOUR HEAD, PART OF YOU IN MINE. I KNOW I'M ASKING A LOT -- TOTAL SHARING, TOTAL INTIMACY, TOTAL ... TRUST.

I SAY, YES.

I'LL UNDER-STAND IF YOU SAY, NO.

THAT PERSONAL, PRIVATE RAPPORT STILL EXISTS. WITH LUCK, IT COULD BECOME THE KEY TO OUR BUSTING OUT OF THIS MESS.

I TRUST YOU'VE LEARNED YOUR LESSON, BEAUTY. DEFY ME -- AND THE HELLFIRE CLUB -- AT YOUR PERIL.

JEAN -- MY DEAR FRIEND -- WHO-EVER IS RESPONSIBLE FOR TRANS-FORMING YOU INTO THE BLACK QUEEN WILL *PAY*, WHATEVER IT COSTS, HOWEVER LONG IT TAKES. THIS, NIGHTCRAWLER *SWEARS!*

HERR SHAW -- PARDON MY ASK-ING, BUT WHY ARE WE X-MEN STILL ALIVE?

THERE'S NO PROFIT IN SIMPLY KILLING YOU, *HERR* WAGNER.

YOU KNOW MY NAME?!

AMONG OTHER THINGS. SUPER-POWERED MUTANTS ARE BECOMING COMMON-PLACE IN THE WORLD. IF MY ASSOCIATES AND I CAN ISOLATE THE GENETIC QUIRK THAT CREATED US...

...AND THEN "CUSTOM BUILD"-- THROUGH GENETIC ENGINEERING -- MUTANTS AT WILL, THE POSSIBILITIES ARE... LIMITLESS. IN THAT QUEST, NIGHTCRAWLER, YOU X-MEN WILL BE OUR GUINEA PIGS.

YOU KNOW -- IN A SENSE, IT WOULD HAVE BEEN BETTER FOR YOU FOUR IF WE *HAD* KILLED YOU.

INTERLUDE: IT'S DAWN OVER MUIR ISLE, AND FOR ONCE THE SEA IS CALM AROUND THIS FORBIDDING, BARREN ROCK LOCATED JUST NORTH OF SCOTLAND'S CAPE WRATH, ALL OF 500 MILES BELOW THE ARCTIC CIRCLE.

IN MANY WAYS, THE ISLAND MIRRORS THE PERSONA OF THE WOMAN WHO OWNS IT-- REMOTE, BEAUTIFUL, ELEMENTAL, UNYIELDING.

WHEN SHE FIRST ARRIVED HERE-- AND FOR TOO MANY YEARS AFTER THAT-- MOIRA MacTAGGERT LIVED ALONE.

NOW, HER HERMITAGE IS OVER.

SHE HAS SOMEONE TO SHARE HER WORK AND HER LIFE-- SOMEONE SHE LOVES AND WHO LOVES HER. HIS NAME IS SEAN CASSIDY AND, AS THE BANSHEE, HE USED TO BE AN X-MAN.

NOW, HE IS ONLY A MAN.* AND HE IS CONTENT.

LIGHT'S ON IN MOIRA'S OFFICE. SHE'S BEEN UP ALL NIGHT AGAIN!

*BANSHEE RETIRED FROM THE X-MEN BECAUSE OF INJURIES SUFFERED IN X-MEN #119-- JOURNALIST JIM.

I'VE BEEN TRYIN' T' GET HER T' REST, BUT F'R THE LAST FEW DAYS SHE'S BEEN DRIVIN' HERSELF HARDER THAN EVER.

MOIRA DARLIN', FEEL UP TO A JOG 'ROUND THE ISLAND?

UGH-- DREADFUL THOUGHT.

WANT TO FOOL ABOUT, THEN?

THE SPIRIT IS WILLING, MY LOVE, BUT THE FLESH IS BEAT.

YE'RE TROUBLED, LASS, WANT TO TALK?

I'VE JUST FINISHED PROCESSING THE DATA SCANS PROFESSOR XAVIER MADE OF JEAN IN NEW YORK.

BAD NEWS?

SEAN, LUV-- AS PHOENIX, JEAN REALIZED HER ULTIMATE POTENTIAL AS A PSI. SHE POSSESSED THE POWER OF A GOD, BUT ONLY THE EXPERIENCE AND AWARENESS OF A YOUNG WOMAN.

SHE COULDN'T COPE WITH THAT TOTALITY OF POWER-- I DOUBT ANYONE ON EARTH COULD.

SO, TO PROTECT ITSELF FROM ITSELF, HER MIND ENGAGED A SERIES OF PSYCHIC CIRCUIT BREAKERS THAT CUT HER POWER BACK TO A LEVEL SHE COULD HANDLE.

BUT, LATELY, SOMEONE-- OR SOMETHING-- HAS BEEN RELEASING THOSE BREAKERS. THERE ARE ALMOST NONE LEFT. JEAN'S ONCE MORE TAPPING NEAR-INFINITE POWER-LEVELS.

IS THERE NOTHIN' WE CAN DO, MOIRA?

WE CAN PRAY.

89

INTERLUDE: A FULL MOON LIGHTS THE STARK, RUGGED LANDSCAPE OF THE ARIZONA DESERT ALONG THE CONTINETAL DIVIDE. IT'S THE WITCHING HOUR -- MIDNIGHT -- AND THE HIGH-FLYING ANGEL IS INDULGING IN A BIT OF EXERCISE.

BUT I DO IT, ALL THE SAME.

I LOVE IT UP HERE.

THE SKY ALWAYS CLEARS MY HEAD, RESTORES MY SENSE OF PERSPECTIVE.. IT'S MY ELEMENT, MY TRUE... HOME. AT TIMES LIKE THIS, I HATE HAVING TO RETURN TO EARTH.

AS WARREN WORTHINGTON III -- RETIRED X-MAN -- DIVES TOWARDS HIS MOUNTAIN-TOP CHALET, HIS FALCON-KEEN EYES AUTOMATICALLY SWEEP THE SURROUNDING COUNTRY-SIDE...

...SEARCHING FOR ANYTHING OUT OF THE ORDINARY, THE MEREST HINT OF TROUBLE.

HE'S A LITTLE DISAPPOINTED WHEN HE FINDS NONE.

AWAITING HIM ON THE VERANDA IS THE X-MEN'S FOUNDER -- THEIR TEACHER AND MENTOR -- PROFESSOR CHARLES XAVIER.

EVENING, PROFESSOR. I GUESS I'M NOT THE ONLY CASE OF INSOMNIA TONIGHT.

PROFESSOR, YOU'VE BEEN ON EDGE EVER SINCE CYCLOPS TOOK THE X-MEN TO NEW YORK TO CONFRONT THE HELLFIRE CLUB.

HE LEFT YOU BEHIND -- IS THAT WHAT'S BUGGING YOU?

HE HAD GOOD REASON. IF THE TEAM IS FOLLOWING A FALSE LEAD, THEN NO HARM'S DONE. IF THEY HIT PAYDIRT -- AND, HEAVEN FORBID, RUN INTO TROUBLE -- YOU'LL BE SAFE, FREE TO CARRY ON THE FIGHT.

I SHOULD BE WITH THE X-MEN, ANGEL -- MONITOR-ING THEIR PROGRESS, AIDING THEM IN BATTLE AS I DID WITH THE ORIGINAL X-MEN.

I FEEL SO... HELPLESS! I STILL CANNOT RE-ESTABLISH MY MENTAL RAPPORT WITH THE TEAM. I WON'T KNOW WHAT'S HAPPENING TO THEM UNTIL IT'S TOO LATE!

FROM THE BEGINNING, I'VE TRAINED CYCLOPS TO TAKE MY PLACE AS LEADER OF THE X-MEN. BUT WHEN THAT DAY FINALLY CAME...

... I FOUND I RESENTED IT. AND HIM. THAT RESENTMENT CAUSED ME TO MAKE SOME TERRIBLE MISTAKES, ANGEL.

I FEAR INNOCENT PEOPLE WILL SUFFER BECAUSE OF THEM.

OMINOUS WORDS -- WHOSE MEANING WILL SOON BECOME APPARENT. BUT FIRST, IT'S TIME TO RETURN TO THE *HELLFIRE CLUB*, WHERE WE FIND THAT INSTITUTION'S ANNIVERSARY PARTY -- ATTENDED BY SOME OF THE *WEALTHIEST, MOST INFLUENTIAL* PEOPLE IN AMERICA, IF NOT THE WORLD -- STILL GOING STRONG.

HOW'S THE CHAMPAGNE HOLDING OUT, MARY?

BETTER THAN MY FEET, LOU.

IT TOOK US A *WEEK* TO SET-UP, FOR THIS SHINDIG, AND IT'S GOING TO TAKE US A *MONTH* TO RECOVER.

DELIVER THIS TRAY TO *SENATOR KELLY'S* PARTY, WE'RE SUPPOSED TO GIVE HIM SPECIAL ATTENTION.

KELLY-- THE *PRESIDENTIAL CANDIDATE?* I DIDN'T KNOW HE WAS A MEMBER OF THE CLUB.

HE ISN'T. HE'S MR. SHAW'S INVITED GUEST.

SOUNDS LIKE THE COAST IS CLEAR-- 'BOUT TIME, TOO! MAIN FLOOR, EV'RYBODY OUT.

USIN' THIS DUMBWAITER TA GET OUTTA THE BASEMENT WASN'T A BAD IDEA-- THAT WAY, I BYPASS ALL THE GUARDS.

THERE'S A TIME FER SCRAPPIN' AN' A TIME FER BEIN' SNEAKY.

EITHER WAY, WOLVERINE'S THE *BEST* THERE IS.

THAT GOON I QUESTIONED WASN'T MUCH HELP-- SO I'VE BEEN FOLLOWIN' *NIGHTCRAWLER'S* SCENT. I'M STARTIN' TO PICK UP TRACES O' THE *OTHER* X-MEN, AS WELL.

TROUBLE IS, THEY'RE LEADIN' ME UP TA THE SECOND FLOOR, AN' MY DUMB-WAITER DON'T GO THAT HIGH.

NO STAIR-WAYS IN THIS HALL.

THE ONLY WAY I'M GONNA GET UPSTAIRS IS BY CUTTIN' STRAIGHT ACROSS THIS DANCE FLOOR. AN' I DON'T THINK I'M GONNA BE ABLE TA DO THAT WITHOUT MAKIN' A FUSS.

FREEZE, SUCKER!

Whoops!

MEANWHILE...

YOU'RE FAR MORE VIVACIOUS, AND EXCITING, THAN YOUR PREDECESSOR, THE WHITE QUEEN. I LIKE THAT.

I'M GLAD, SQUIRE LELAND. I LIKE YOU.

JEAN'S FLIRTING WITH THEM ALL. MASTER-MIND'S GIVEN HER THE INSTINCTS OF A MINX.

BUT I CAN'T-- I DAREN'T-- THINK ABOUT THAT. I'VE GOT TO FOCUS ON THE JOB AT HAND, NOTHING ELSE.

IF I CAN REACH JEAN THROUGH OUR PRIVATE RAPPORT, MAYBE I CAN SHATTER THE TIMESLIP ILLUSION MASTERMIND HAS CREATED.

IT'S A LONGSHOT, CYCLOPS KNOWS-- AN ALL-OR-NOTHING GAMBIT. BUT HE HAS NO ALTERNATIVE.

FOR A LONG TIME-- TO CYCLOPS, AN ETERNITY-- NOTHING HAPPENS. AND THEN ...

THE FACE MASK-- IT'S GONE! I'M WEARING MY VISOR AGAIN-- I CAN SEE!

MY GAMBLE'S PAYING OFF!

EITHER THAT, OR I'M GOING CRAZY. I'M NOT JEAN OR PROFESSOR X-- I'VE NEVER TRIED A STUNT LIKE THIS BEFORE. FOR ALL I KNOW, I COULD BE IMAGINING EVERYTHING.

I'VE GOT TO THINK POSITIVELY! NO WAY MY IMAGINATION COULD COME UP WITH A PLACE AS WEIRD AS THIS.

THE ROOM-- THE OTHERS-- HAVE DISAPPEARED. I MUST BE ON WHAT JEAN CALLS THE "ASTRAL PLANE."

I'VE MADE IT THIS FAR-- I HOPE-- BUT WHERE DO I GO FROM HERE?!

WHAT--?!! MY *CLOTHES!*

MY UNIFORM'S CHANGED INTO SOME SORT OF REVOLUTION-ARY WAR OUTFIT!

THAT DOOR-- APPEARING OUT OF NOWHERE-- IT'S THE ENTRANCE TO THE HELLFIRE CLUB!

SNAPPING JEAN OUT OF MASTERMIND'S SPELL ISN'T GOING TO BE AS EASY AS I THOUGHT.

SHE'S MAKING ME CONFORM TO THE BOGUS, 18TH-CENTURY REALITY OF HER TIMESLIPS. I DIDN'T ANTICIPATE THAT HIS CONTROL OF HER WOULD BE SO COMPLETE.

STILL-- JEAN GREY IS THE WOMAN I LOVE. I'M THE MAN SHE LOVES. THAT HAS TO COUNT FOR SOMETHING.

THERE SHE IS!

SHE'S DRESSED AS THE BLACK QUEEN--THAT'S NOT GOOD.

JEAN! IT'S ME, SCOTT!

DO I KNOW YOU, SIR? YOUR VOICE IS STRANGELY FAMILIAR, BUT YOUR GARB MARKS YOU AS AN AMERICAN REBEL, KING GEORGE'S ENEMY-- AND MINE.

TRY TO REMEMBER--! I'M *SCOTT SUMMERS.*

WE'RE LOVERS, YOU AND I -- AND WE'RE X-MEN.

YOU'RE WASTING YOUR TIME, BOY. NEITHER YOU NOR YOUR PRECIOUS X-MEN MEAN ANYTHING TO MY LADY WIFE.

BEGONE FROM THIS PLACE, SIRRAH-- OR MY HUSBAND WILL CUT YOU DOWN WHERE YOU STAND.

MASTER-MIND!

THIS IS IMPOSSIBLE! MASTERMIND HAS NO PSI-POWERS-- HE CASTS SOPHISTICATED ILLUSIONS, NOTHING MORE -- HOW COULD HE HAVE LEARNED OF JEAN'S AND MY RAPPORT?

MORE IMPORTANTLY, HOW DID HE TAKE CONTROL OF IT?!

I'VE NO CHOICE-- IF I'M TO FREE JEAN, I HAVE TO FIGHT HIM, ON HIS TURF, ON HIS TERMS.

EN GARDE, "SIR JASON"!

OHO! THE STRIPLING BARES HIS FANGS AND IMITATES THE ACTION OF THE TIGER.

POOR BOY-- YOU'VE PLAYED RIGHT INTO MY HANDS!

I'VE KNOWN OF YOUR PRECIOUS RAPPORT FROM THE MOMENT IT WAS ESTABLISHED. I KNEW YOU'D TRY TO REACH JEAN THROUGH IT. IN FACT, I WAS COUNTING ON YOU DOING PRECISELY THAT!

BUT HOW?!

YOU'VE NEVER POSSESSED THESE KINDS OF PSYCHIC POWERS!

LET THAT REMAIN MY SECRET, CYCLOPS.

WHEN I SLAY YOU IN THIS DUEL, YOUR RAPPORT--JEAN GREY'S FINAL LINK WITH THE X-MEN AND THE VIRTUOUS LIFE SHE ONCE LED--

--WILL BE SEVERED!

THEN, SHE WILL TRULY BE MINE-- BODY AND SOUL! TOGETHER, WE SHALL RULE FIRST THE HELLFIRE CLUB--

--AND THEN THE WORLD!

THE ODDS IN THIS DUEL ARE ALL IN MASTER-MIND'S FAVOR. HE KNOWS HOW TO USE A SWORD. I DON'T.

VERY NICE MOVE, CYCLOPS-- SWITCHING SWORD HANDS LIKE THAT, TRYING TO THROW ME OFF BALANCE.

YOU MAY BE A NOVICE, BUT YOU LEARN QUICKLY.

UNFORTUNATELY-- NOT QUICKLY ENOUGH TO SAVE YOU.

I WENT FOR BROKE THAT TIME, AND HE PARRIED MY ATTACK EASILY. HE'S TOYING WITH US, POSITIVE HE CAN KILL ME WHENEVER HE FEELS LIKE IT.

AND I'M AFRAID HE MAY BE RIGHT!

AT THIS POINT, LET'S RETURN TO WOLVERINE AND THE GUARD...

HANDS ON YOUR HEAD, FELLA, AND NO FAST MOVES OR-- *OWW!!*

BUB, WHERE *"FAST MOVES"* ARE CONCERNED--

THAP!

-- YOU DON'T KNOW THE MEANIN' O' THE WORDS!

GREAT-- THE CROWD'S ALREADY SPOOKED; THIS OUGHT'A PANIC 'EM FOR SURE. MAYBE I CAN TURN THAT TO MY ADVANTAGE.

WATCH OUT!

OHH!!

KEEP CALM, FOLKS!

STAY OUTTA MY WAY-- AN' YA WON'T GET HURT!

BACK-- EVERYONE *BACK!* LET SECURITY HANDLE THIS!

ANOTHER COSTUMED MANIAC-- WHAT'S HAPPENING HERE?!

WHERE'S THE *SECRET SERVICE?* AT ALL COSTS, SENATOR KELLY MUST BE PROTECTED!

HOLD IT, MISTER! THIS IS AS FAR AS YOU GO!

COME PEACEABLY, LITTLE MAN, OR IN PIECES-- YOUR CHOICE.

YA WANT ME, BUB, THEN COME AN' GET ME --

--IF YA CAN!!

I'D BETTER COOL IT WITH MY CLAWS AGAINST THESE BOZOS.

THEY MIGHT BE "INNER CIRCLE" MERCENARIES-- BUT THEY MIGHT ALSO BE LEGIT CLUB EMPLOYEES, OR RENT-A-COPS, OR EVEN SECRET SERVICE. CARVIN' 'EM UP COULD CREATE MORE HASSLES THAN IT SOLVES.

THE ODDS AGAINST WOLVERINE START OUT BAD, AND QUICKLY GET WORSE-- AND HE SOON DISAPPEARS BENEATH A VERITABLE AVALANCHE OF COSTUMED, CLUB-WIELDING BODIES.

WHILE, ON THE ASTRAL PLANE -- HIS CONSCIOUSNESS SUSPENDED BETWEEN HIS MIND AND JEAN'S -- SCOTT SUMMERS ISN'T FARING MUCH BETTER.

NO MATTER HOW HARD I TRY, MASTERMIND KEEPS PUSHING ME BACK ON THE DEFENSIVE. THE MENTAL STRAIN IS TERRIFIC -- IT'S AFFECTING MY ASTRAL FORM LIKE PHYSICAL FATIGUE.

I'M TIRING, SLOWING DOWN -- WHILE MASTERMIND IS AS FAST, AS SURE OF HIMSELF, AS EVER.

SUDDENLY...

MY SWORD!

IF I WERE A CHIVALROUS MAN, CYCLOPS, I WOULD ALLOW YOU TO SURRENDER, BUT I AM NOT CHIVALROUS.

AHRRR

AND OUR DUEL WAS-- --TO THE DEATH!!

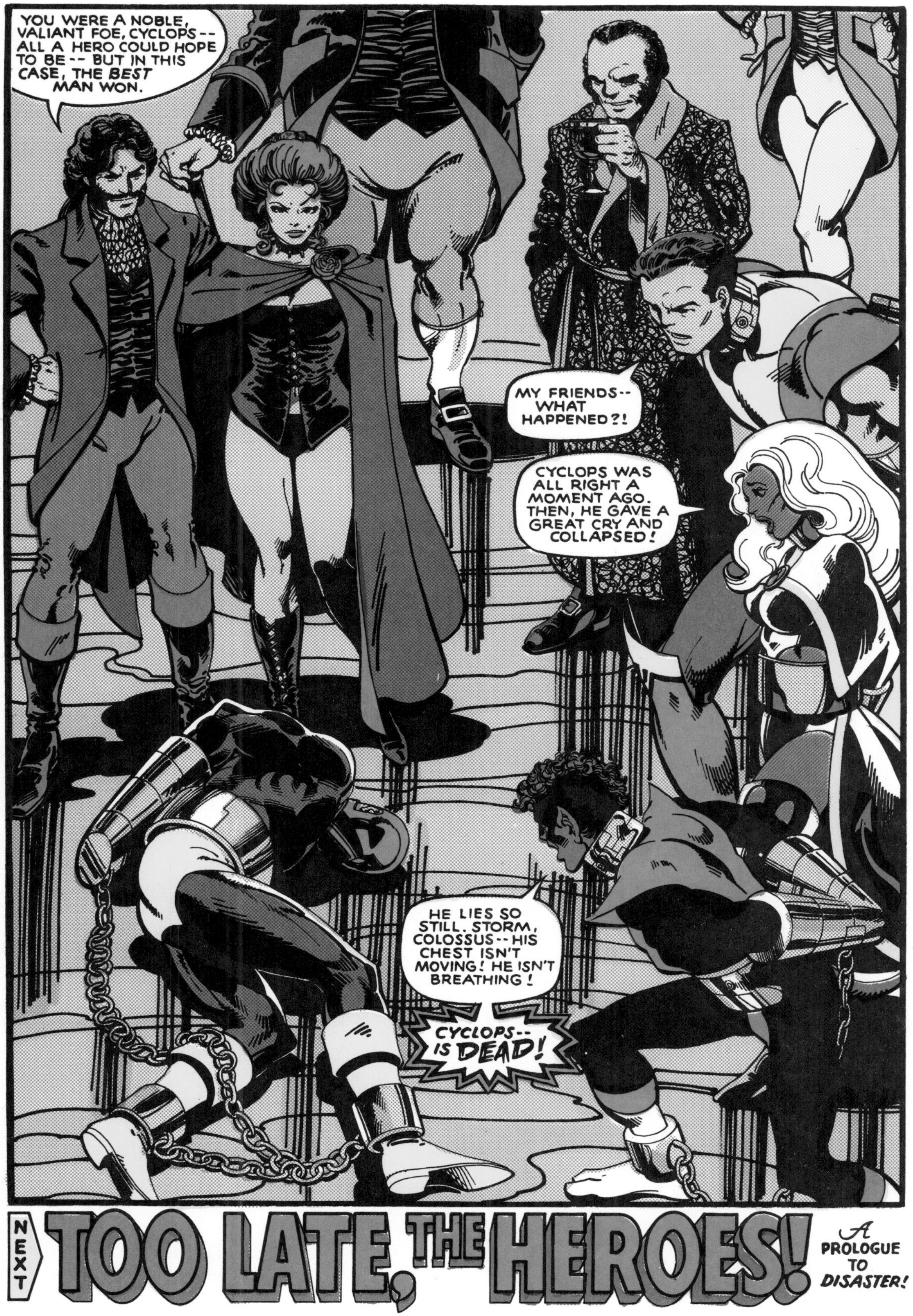
YOU WERE A NOBLE, VALIANT FOE, CYCLOPS-- ALL A HERO COULD HOPE TO BE-- BUT IN THIS CASE, THE BEST MAN WON.
MY FRIENDS-- WHAT HAPPENED?!
CYCLOPS WAS ALL RIGHT A MOMENT AGO. THEN, HE GAVE A GREAT CRY AND COLLAPSED!
HE LIES SO STILL, STORM, COLOSSUS-- HIS CHEST ISN'T MOVING! HE ISN'T BREATHING!
CYCLOPS-- IS DEAD!

NEXT TOO LATE, THE HEROES! A PROLOGUE TO DISASTER!

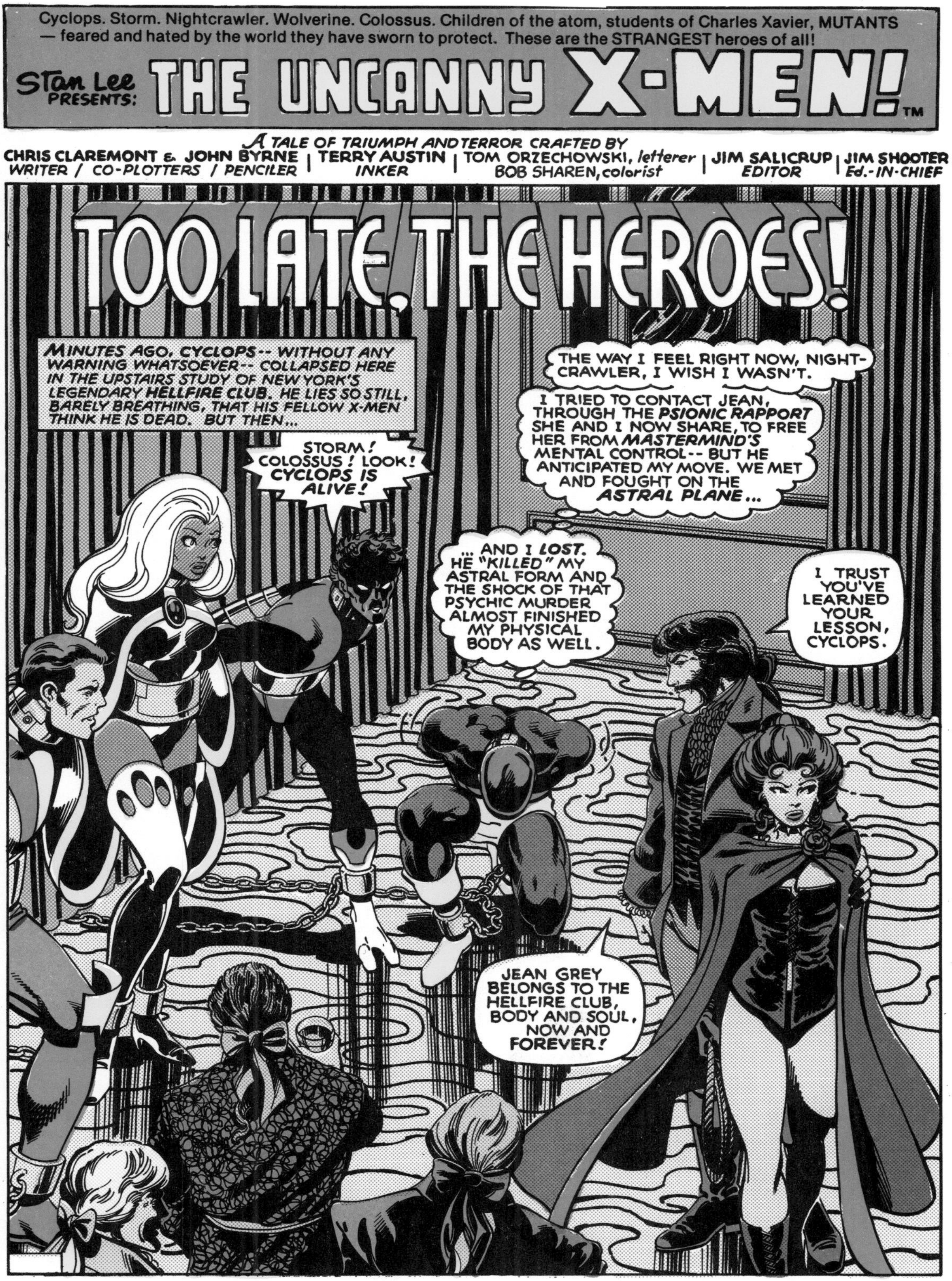
Cyclops. Storm. Nightcrawler. Wolverine. Colossus. Children of the atom, students of Charles Xavier, MUTANTS — feared and hated by the world they have sworn to protect. These are the STRANGEST heroes of all!
Stan Lee PRESENTS: THE UNCANNY X-MEN! TM
A TALE OF TRIUMPH AND TERROR CRAFTED BY
CHRIS CLAREMONT & JOHN BYRNE WRITER / CO-PLOTTERS / PENCILER | TERRY AUSTIN INKER | TOM ORZECHOWSKI, letterer BOB SHAREN, colorist | JIM SALICRUP EDITOR | JIM SHOOTER Ed.-IN-CHIEF
TOO LATE, THE HEROES!
MINUTES AGO, CYCLOPS -- WITHOUT ANY WARNING WHATSOEVER -- COLLAPSED HERE IN THE UPSTAIRS STUDY OF NEW YORK'S LEGENDARY HELLFIRE CLUB. HE LIES SO STILL, BARELY BREATHING, THAT HIS FELLOW X-MEN THINK HE IS DEAD. BUT THEN...
STORM! COLOSSUS! LOOK! CYCLOPS IS ALIVE!
THE WAY I FEEL RIGHT NOW, NIGHTCRAWLER, I WISH I WASN'T.
I TRIED TO CONTACT JEAN, THROUGH THE PSIONIC RAPPORT SHE AND I NOW SHARE, TO FREE HER FROM MASTERMIND'S MENTAL CONTROL -- BUT HE ANTICIPATED MY MOVE. WE MET AND FOUGHT ON THE ASTRAL PLANE...
... AND I LOST. HE "KILLED" MY ASTRAL FORM AND THE SHOCK OF THAT PSYCHIC MURDER ALMOST FINISHED MY PHYSICAL BODY AS WELL.
I TRUST YOU'VE LEARNED YOUR LESSON, CYCLOPS.
JEAN GREY BELONGS TO THE HELLFIRE CLUB, BODY AND SOUL, NOW AND FOREVER!

THESE HELPLESS PRISONERS OF THE HELLFIRE CLUB ARE THE UNCANNY X-MEN, THEIR MUTANT POWERS NEUTRALIZED BY INHIBITOR BONDS.

NORMALLY, OUR HEROES LOOK LIKE THIS:

NIGHTCRAWLER.

COLOSSUS.

STORM.

CYCLOPS.

BUT, THANKS TO MASTERMIND'S POWER OF ILLUSION, THEY LOOK LIKE THREE SOLDIERS IN GEORGE WASHINGTON'S CONTINENTAL ARMY AND A TURN-COAT SLAVE...

...TO THIS WOMAN, THE BLACK QUEEN OF THE HELLFIRE CLUB.

IN REALITY, SHE IS JEAN GREY, AN X-MAN--

-- BETTER KNOWN AS PHOENIX.

AT THE MOMENT, SHE BELIEVES SHE'S PHYSICALLY SHIFTING IN TIME, RE-LIVING THE LIFE OF AN 18TH-CENTURY ANCESTOR.

SHE ISN'T. HER TIME-SLIPS ARE ONLY AN ILLUSION...

...CAUSED BY A MAN JEAN KNOWS AS JASON WYNGARDE.

BUT JASON WYNGARDE IS MERELY A FAÇADE. HE IS ACTUALLY...

...MASTERMIND-- THE MUTANT MASTER OF ILLUSION!

MASTERMIND AND THESE THREE MEN ARE MEMBERS OF THE HELLFIRE CLUB'S INNER CIRCLE-- A SUPER-SECRET, SUPER-EXCLUSIVE CLUB WITHIN THE CLUB. THEIR GOAL-- TO RULE THE WORLD.

DONALD PIERCE, CYBORG-- PART HUMAN, PART SUPER-POWERED MACHINE.

HARRY LELAND-- MUTANT.

SEBASTIAN SHAW, CHAIRMAN OF THE INNER CIRCLE-- ALSO A MUTANT.

As the inner circle's cheers of victory echo through the room, a strangely somber Jean Grey slowly, deliberately looks from face to face -- her gaze lingering on Wyngarde's, lingering far longer on Cyclops'.

When, at last, she turns away, there is no mercy in her eyes.

Elsewhere in the building, the great and wealthy and powerful of America, who comprise the Hellfire Club's membership, are celebrating the club's latest anniversary, unaware of the drama being played out in the room above their heads.

While, outside on the streets, New York reels under the onslaught of a brutal mid-winter gale.

It's been raining hard since before dawn, and the water level in the sewers has been rising steadily all day -- towards a thick sheaf of power cables, whose insulation was slashed open by Wolverine when he and his fellow X-men infiltrated the club.*

*SEE X-MEN #132, PAGE 10, PANELS 6 & 7 -- SNEAKY SALICRUP.

And, speaking of the shortest, feistiest X-man...

Shaw, what's that commotion in the hall?!

I don't know. I gave strict instructions that we weren't to be disturbed.

Evenin', folks-- the name's Wolverine!

You an' me got business-- an' all the flunkies in creation ain't gonna keep me away!

Leland, you unmitigated fool! You swore to me that Wolverine drowned!

SKRASH

101

MAGNIFICENT! THIS IS MY CHANCE TO *FINISH* SHAW AS LEADER OF THE INNER CIRCLE-- AND THEN, MOVE IN TO TAKE HIS PLACE!

YOUR MAN, LELAND, MAY HAVE BOTCHED HIS JOB, SHAW-- BUT *I* WON'T!

THAT, JASON, WILL BE A PLEASURE. MORE OF ONE THAN YOU CAN POSSIBLY IMAGINE.

BLACK QUEEN-- STOP WOLVERINE!

CRIPES! JEAN'S CLOBBERIN' ME WITH A TELEKINETIC ZAP!

JEANNIE-- WHAT'RE YA DOIN'?!

JEAN-- DON'T!

AT THE SAME MOMENT, WHILE ALL EYES ARE ON WOLVERINE...

HUH?!?

BINK!

THAT VOICE -- JEAN'S VOICE, HER PRESENCE, INSIDE MY MIND. SHE'S RE-ESTABLISHED OUR *PSIONIC RAPPORT!* I CAN HEAR HER, FEEL HER, SHE'S SO... *BEAUTIFUL*-- SHINING LIKE A STAR.

SHE'S BROKEN MASTERMIND'S HOLD ON HER -- AND NOW, SHE'S TELEKINETICALLY FREEING ME AS WELL. ALL I HAVE TO DO--

--IS *OPEN* MY EYES!

GNNNGNH!

WHAK

GOT ONE, BY THE SOUND OF IT! BUT HOW MANY MORE TO GO?

I HAVE TO BE CAREFUL. JEAN'S GUIDING ME WITH A TELEPATHIC VIEW OF THE ROOM, BUT UNTIL I FIND MY *RUBY QUARTZ VISOR*, I HAVE ONLY LIMITED CONTROL OVER MY DEADLY OPTIC BLASTS.

IF I MAKE EVEN THE SLIGHTEST MISCALCU- LATION, I COULD BREAK SOMEONE'S ARMS-- OR *WORSE.*

102

WHEN THEY AMBUSHED US, SHAW AND HIS INNER CIRCLE STARTED BY THROWING US OFF-BALANCE BY HITTING US SO HARD AND SO FAST, THAT BY THE TIME WE KNEW WHAT WAS GOING ON, WE WERE BEATEN.

WHOULFFF!

SDOW

NOW, THAT SHOE'S ON THE OTHER FOOT.

TWO DOWN!

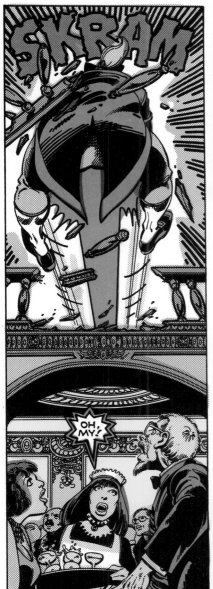

SKRAM

OH, MY!

GO, WOLVERINE!

JEANNIE! YOU'RE WORKIN' ON THE SIDE O' THE ANGELS AFTER ALL! NICE -- SNEAKY -- MOVES, LADY. YOU'RE A WOMAN AFTER MY OWN HEART.

I KNOW. I WISH I WASN'T.

HEY, LELAND! LAST TIME WE TUSSLED, YOU NEARLY TRASHED ME.*

YOU OWE ME A REMATCH, BUB, AN' I'M HERE TA COLLECT. WITH INTEREST!

*X-MEN #132--SCORE-KEEPER SALICRUP.

NEVER SAY DIE, eh, CYCLOPS? WE BEAT YOU X-MEN ONCE. WE CAN DO SO AGAIN.

YOUR VAUNTED OPTIC BLASTS MEAN NOTHING TO A MAN CAPABLE OF ABSORBING ALL FORMS OF KINETIC ENERGY. THE HARDER YOU HIT ME -- WITH ANYTHING -- THE STRONGER I GET!

WHO SAID I WAS GOING TO HIT YOU, SHAW?

WHAT--?! THE FLOOR!!

HAPPY LANDINGS!

SHAW! **SHAW!!**

DO NOT WORRY ABOUT YOUR LEADER, COMRADE PIERCE.

OOLP?!!

YOU HAVE PROBLEMS ENOUGH OF YOUR OWN.

UNHAND ME, LOUT!

YOU MADE A FATAL MISTAKE ASSAULTING ME IN YOUR *HUMAN* FORM, COLOSSUS. WITH MY CYBORG LIMBS, I CAN BEND STEEL IN MY BARE HANDS! SMASHING YOU TO A PULP SHOULD BE *CHILD'S PLAY.*

UNNNGNH!

SHOK

COLOSSUS!!

DO NOT... WORRY, NIGHTCRAWLER. MY PRIDE IS HURT WORSE THAN MY BODY.

IF THAT'S TRUE, COLOSSUS, YOU'RE LUCKIER THAN YOU DESERVE! YOU SHOULD HAVE ANTICIPATED THAT ATTACK. YOU'VE A BRAIN INSIDE THAT HEAD OF YOURS, MISTER-- START USING IT!

ARMOR UP-- PIERCE IS ALL YOURS! STORM, YOU AND NIGHTCRAWLER GO AFTER SHAW.

LEAVE MASTERMIND TO ME.

OF ALL THE CURSED LUCK! EVERY-THING WAS GOING SO WELL!

UNTIL I BROKE MY OWN FIRST LAW-- I UNDERESTIMATED THE X-MEN. I LET MY AMBITION, MY DISLIKE OF SHAW, MY DESIRE FOR HIS RANK AND POSITION IN THE INNER CIRCLE--GET THE BETTER OF ME.

LET THE OTHERS BATTER THEM-SELVES SENSELESS. FOR THE MOMENT, I THINK IT BEST NOT TO GET INVOLVED. I'LL SIMPLY CREATE AN ILLUSION THAT I'M PART OF THE WALL, AND WAIT TO SEE WHAT DEVELOPS.

WHO KNOWS? I MAY YET EMERGE VICTORIOUS.

HEADS UP, TUBBY! AN' SAY YER PRAYERS!

IT'S A MANIAC!

CALL THE POLICE-- HURRY!

DESPERATELY, INSTINCTIVELY, HARRY LELAND LASHES OUT WITH HIS MUTANT POWER, INCREASING WOLVERINE'S MASS GEOMETRICALLY AS HE FALLS.

NO!

TOO LATE, LELAND REALIZES THAT THAT'S THE LAST THING HE SHOULD HAVE DONE.

NO!!

AT THAT MOMENT, IN ONE OF THE MANY SECRET PASSAGES THAT HONEYCOMB THIS VENERABLE MANHATTAN TOWNHOUSE...

CYCLOPS IS A BORN LEADER, AS GOOD AS I EXPECTED. HE FOUND ONE OPENING, ONE FLAW IN OUR DEFENSES, AND IN A MATTER OF SECONDS HE HAD US ON THE ROPES. I LIKE THAT.

BUT HE HAD HELP-- AND I'VE AN UNCOMFORTABLE FEELING I KNOW FROM WHAT SOURCE. WYNGARDE'S PUPPET, I FEAR, HAS CUT HER STRINGS.

IF THAT'S TRUE, I PITY THE PUPPET MASTER.

WHAT-- NIGHTCRAWLER, TELEPORTING ON TOP OF ME!!

BOO! STORM SAYS I SHOULDN'T HIT YOU, HERR SHAW. THAT'S FINE WITH ME.

ANYONE CAN PUNCH. NIGHTCRAWLER IS GOING TO CLOBBER YOU IN STYLE.

WITH A SLIGHT ASSIST FROM STORM, MY FRIEND.

FOR ALL SHAW'S MUTANT STRENGTH, HE'S STILL ONLY HUMAN. HE'S VULNERABLE TO TEMPERATURE SHIFTS. SO, IF I USE MY ELEMENTAL POWERS TO SURROUND HIM WITH A FIELD OF EXTREME COLD-- A MICRO-BLIZZARD-- I SHOULD BE ABLE TO FREEZE THE FIGHT OUT OF HIM.

FOUR BLOCKS UP FIFTH AVENUE, IN AN EQUALLY IMPOSING STRUCTURE THAT HAPPENS TO BE THE HEADQUARTERS OF THE WORLD'S MIGHTIEST SUPER HERO TEAM, WE FIND...

JULIAN JAYNES
THE ORIGIN OF CONSCIOUSNESS IN THE BREAK-DOWN OF THE BICAMERAL MIND

GOOD BOOK--CAN'T WAIT TO SEE THE MOVIE.

...ONE HANK McCOY-- ALSO KNOWN AS THE BEAST-- ONCE AN X-MAN, NOW AN AVENGER, HOLDING THE FORT ALL BY HIMSELF. -

INTERESTING THEORY, TOO-- THOUGH IT'S MORE UP PROFESSOR XAVIER'S ALLEY THAN MINE. I OUGHT TO PAY HIM AND THE X-MEN A VISIT.

BRANNG!

IT'S FUNNY-- AFTER ALL THIS TIME, THERE'S STILL NO ONE AS CLOSE TO ME AS THE X-MEN. I HAVE LOTS OF PALS, BUT NO... FRIENDS. I BELONG HERE WITH THE AVENGERS, AND YET...

...AND YET...

WHOOPS!

THE ALARM! IT'S OUR HOOK-UP TO THE N.Y.P.D.

PROBABLY NOTHING-- BUT CHECKING IT OUT SURE BEATS TALKING MYSELF THROUGH A SCENE OF "AS THE WORLD TURNS". BUM-MER!

THAT'S THE SPIRIT, McCOY. HIDE YOUR FEELINGS BEHIND A FLIP, DEVIL-MAY-CARE FAÇADE.

IF YOU'VE BECOME A LONER, WHO'S TO BLAME, THE OTHERS-- OR YOU?

POLICE APB HELLFIRE CLUB REPORTS ATTACK BY GROUP BELIE[VED] TO BE X-MEN

OH, NO! THAT CAN'T BE! THE X-MEN ON A RAMPAGE?!

THERE HAS TO BE A REASON. AVENGERS PROCEDURE SAYS I SHOULD SOUND AN ALERT, SUMMON EVERY MEMBER WHO'S IN TOWN.

BUT WHAT THEN? DO WE TRASH THE X-MEN?

FOR LONG MOMENTS, HE STARES AT THE SCREEN, HIS MIND FLASHING BETWEEN HIS HIS OLD LIFE AND HIS NEW...

ERAS[E] TAPE ERAS[E]

THEN, HANK McCOY COMES TO A DECISION-- AND MAKES A FINAL, FATEFUL CHOICE. AS HE LEAVES, HE DOESN'T LOOK BACK.

MEANWHILE...

ON YOUR KNEES, YOU BOLSHEVIK BUFFOON!

I DO NOT BELIEVE THIS!

I AM STRUGGLING WITH ALL MY MIGHT, YET PIERCE IS FORCING ME BACK. HE HAS LEVERAGE ON MY HANDS. HE IS -- HURTING ME!

I HAVE FELT PAIN BEFORE. AND I HAVE FACED DEFEAT. BUT I HAVE NEVER SURRENDERED.

YOU SPEAK AS THOUGH I WAS LESS THAN HUMAN, PIERCE.

I DO NOT KNOW YOU. I HAVE NEVER THOUGHT ILL OF YOU, THREATENED YOU, HARMED YOU. YET YOU WOULD SLAY ME -- FOR NO OTHER REASON THEN THAT I AM A MUTANT?!

WHAT--?! MY-- ARM!!

ZRAKT

I AM PROUD OF WHO AND WHAT I AM, LITTLE MAN. MY HUMANITY IS NOT IN THE OUTWARD FORM I WEAR --

-- BUT IN MY SOUL!

CAN YOU SAY THE SAME?

AHHRRR!!

YES, CURSE YOU! I MAY ONLY BE HALF-A-MAN, BUT I'M MORE HUMAN THAN YOU'LL EVER BE -- FREAK!!

LIVE WIRES IN... MECHANICAL ARM-- ELECTRICAL ARC BLINDED ME!

IT TAKES A FEW SECONDS FOR COLOSSUS TO RECOVER--

--BUT WHEN HIS EYES FINALLY CLEAR...

PIERCE IS GONE!

I EXPECTED HIM TO ATTACK ME WHILE I WAS HELPLESS, BUT HE RAN AWAY INSTEAD. I MUST HAVE DAMAGED HIM MORE BADLY THAN I THOUGHT.

ELSEWHERE...

"ROUND AND ROUND AND ROUND YOU GO..."

ENJOYING YOURSELF, HERR SHAW? I AM!

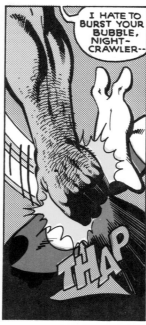

I HATE TO BURST YOUR BUBBLE, NIGHT-CRAWLER--

THAP

-- BUT YOUR SWASHBUCKLING OVERCONFIDENCE WILL BE THE DEATH OF YOU!

JUST BECAUSE I HAVE SUPER-POWERS DOESN'T MEAN I'VE FORGOTTEN HOW TO FIGHT.

GUHNFFF!

AN ACADEMIC POINT, VILLAIN. NIGHTCRAWLER HAS DONE HIS PART-- AS I WILL NOW DO MINE.

EH?! STORM!

BY HEAVEN, IT'S GOTTEN SO COLD! THE WEATHER-WITCH IS FREEZING ME TO DEATH!

I'M WEAKENING BY THE SECOND-- ALMOST NO TIME LEFT TO ACT!

OHH!

THWAK

SHE'S DOWN, BUT NOT OUT. AND THIS BLASTED COLD HAS LEFT ME TOO DRAINED -- TOO WEAK -- TO FINISH HER.

MY BODY FEELS... AS IF IT'S BEEN TURNED TO ICE!

I WANT TO STAY -- TO FIGHT -- BUT I DARE NOT.

PERHAPS THE OTHERS HAVE HAD BETTER LUCK-- BUT I DOUBT IT.

SHAW! I'VE BEEN SEARCHING ALL OVER FOR YOU!

WE'RE BEATEN, MAN-- BEATEN!

I KNOW.

HOW CAN YOU BE SO CALM?!

I'VE LOST BATTLES BEFORE, PIERCE. THE WAR GOES ON. WE'LL LEARN FROM TONIGHT'S MISTAKES...

... AND NEXT TIME THE OUTCOME WILL BE DIFFERENT. COME ALONG. THERE IS MUCH TO DO.

UPSTAIRS...

CYCLOPS IS DOING HIS BEST TO CALM THE PARTY-GUESTS, WONDERING WHY HIS WORDS ONLY SEEM TO MAKE THINGS WORSE--

--UNAWARE THAT MASTERMIND'S ILLUSION POWER IS GIVING THE CROWD A COMPLETELY DIFFERENT VIEW OF HIS ACTIONS.

AT THAT MOMENT, THE WATER LEVEL IN A CERTAIN NEARBY STORM SEWER...

...REACHES A CERTAIN BANK OF EXPOSED CABLES...

... AND...

HEY! WHO TURNED OUT THE LIGHTS?!

THAT'S ALL WE NEED! NOW, WE'LL HAVE A REAL PANIC ON OUR HANDS.

AND IF SHAW'S GOONS ARE RESPONSIBLE, WE COULD BE SITTING DUCKS FOR A COUNTER-ATTACK!

109

Y'KNOW, CYKE, WE GOTTA STOP MEETIN' LIKE THIS.

WOLVERINE!

CRIPES, HE STARTLED ME! I WAS ON GUARD-- EXPECTING TROUBLE-- YET HE CREPT RIGHT UP BEHIND ME WITHOUT MY NOTICING!

YOU LOOK OKAY. WHAT HAPPENED TO LELAND?

DON'T ASK.

IF THAT MEANS WHAT I THINK IT DOES, PROFESSOR X IS GOING TO HAVE A FIT. FIND NIGHTCRAWLER AND STORM. WE'RE GETTING OUT OF HERE.

TOO BAD I HATE LEAVIN' A FIGHT HALF-FINISHED.

BUT YOU'RE THE BOSS.

SHE STANDS MOTIONLESS, A SHADOW AMONG SHADOWS, FEELING DARK FIRE CONSUME HER SOUL. HER FACE IS SUPERNALLY CALM. HER FACE LIES.

JEAN GREY IS TERRIFIED-- MORE AFRAID NOW THAN SHE'S EVER BEEN--

--BECAUSE SHE KNOWS WHAT IS HAPPENING TO HER. AND SHE CANNOT STOP IT.

THE HELLFIRE CLUB DID ITS BEST-- AND IT WASN'T GOOD ENOUGH.

I'VE LOST MY TELEPATHIC TAP ON JEAN'S MIND. THAT MEANS SHE MUST HAVE BROKEN MY CONTROL-- BUT HOW? I ANTICIPATED EVERY CONTINGENCY.

SHE LAUGHS TO HERSELF. THE MAN IS SUCH A FOOL. SHE WILL ENJOY WHAT HAPPENS NEXT.

AND, REALIZING THAT, SHE WEEPS.

YOU MADE A MISTAKE, JASON. YOU "SLEW" THE MAN I LOVED BEFORE MY EYES. INSTEAD OF SEVERING MY LAST CONNECTION WITH THE X-MEN, THAT ACTED LIKE A BUCKET OF ICE WATER IN MY FACE.

INSTEAD OF ENSLAVING ME FOREVER, YOU SHOCKED ME AWAKE. YOU SET ME FREE.

TOO LATE.

NO! I COMPENSATED FOR THAT REACTION -- MY POWER SHOULD HAVE ...

YOUR POWER IS NOTHING!

YOU--!! DO YOU HAVE ANY IDEA WHAT YOU'VE *DONE*-- WHAT FORCES YOU'VE SET IN MOTION?!!

JEAN-- NO! PLEASE!

AAGKGH!

YOU CAME TO ME WHEN I WAS VULNERABLE. YOU FILLED THE EMOTIONAL VOID WITHIN ME. YOU MADE ME TRUST YOU-- PERHAPS EVEN LOVE YOU--

-- AND ALL THE WHILE, YOU WERE *USING* ME!

JEAN-- NO MORE-- I BEG YOU!

YOU'RE ... *KILLING* ME!

I INTEND TO DO A LOT WORSE THAN THAT, MASTER-MIND.

BUT, FIRST, I WANT TO KNOW HOW YOU REACHED INTO MY MIND. YOU'RE AN ILLUSIONIST, NOT A TELEPATH.

M- MINDTAP MECHANISM-- WHITE QUEEN'S DESIGN. ALLOWED ME TO PROJECT ILLUSIONS DIRECTLY INTO YOUR MIND...

... AS WELL AS MONITOR YOUR THOUGHTS...

USE A TELEPATH TO ENSNARE A TELEPATH-- INGENIOUS. THIS DEVICE ENABLED YOU TO TAILOR YOUR ILLUSIONS TO FIT MY MOST PRIVATE FANTASIES --THE REPRESSED, DARK SIDE OF MY SOUL.

YOU GAVE ME WHAT I SECRETLY WANTED --

-- AND USED THAT TO DESTROY ME!

IT'S ONLY FAIR THAT I RETURN THE COMPLIMENT.

THROUGH ME, YOU SOUGHT *POWER*.

VERY WELL, THEN, I'LL GRANT YOUR WISH.

NO.

I'LL GIVE YOU POWER, JASON WYNGARDE--

P-PLEASE --NO!

--SUCH AS NO LIVING BEING HAS EVEN *DREAMED* OF.

AT JEAN'S TOUCH, HIS MIND EXPANDS AT THE SPEED OF THOUGHT, RACING INSTANTLY FROM ONE SIDE OF REALITY TO THE OTHER, THROUGH ALL THE INFINITE REACHES OF SPACE AND TIME.

IN THE BLINK OF AN EYE, MASTERMIND FINDS HIMSELF IN TOUCH WITH THE UNIVERSE-- HIS BRAIN FLOODED WITH ALL THE MYRIAD, ABSOLUTE, CONTRA-DICTORY TRUTHS OF EXISTENCE.

HE SCREAMS. UNABLE TO COPE, HE RUNS. UN-ABLE TO ESCAPE, HE DROWNS. HE IS, AFTER ALL, ONLY HUMAN-- A MAN OF LIMITED AWARE-NESS, LIMITED POWER, LIMITED ABILITY, TRANS-FORMED IN A TWINKLING INTO A GOD.

SOME PEOPLE CAN HANDLE THE EXPERIENCE.

SOME PEOPLE CAN'T.

ENJOY YOUR "TRIP", JASON. YOU WON'T BE COMING BACK.

IN A WAY, I ENVY YOU. YOU'RE AT PEACE.

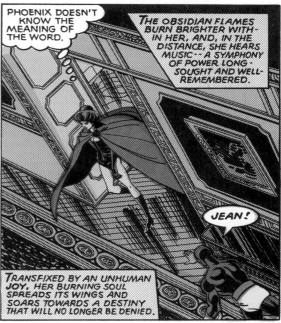

PHOENIX DOESN'T KNOW THE MEANING OF THE WORD.

THE OBSIDIAN FLAMES BURN BRIGHTER WITH-IN HER, AND, IN THE DISTANCE, SHE HEARS MUSIC-- A SYMPHONY OF POWER LONG-SOUGHT AND WELL-REMEMBERED.

JEAN!

TRANSFIXED BY AN UNHUMAN JOY, HER BURNING SOUL SPREADS ITS WINGS AND SOARS TOWARDS A DESTINY THAT WILL NO LONGER BE DENIED.

I'VE BEEN SEARCHING ALL OVER FOR YOU. ARE YOU ALL RIGHT?

SCOTT-- I... I...

SOMETHING'S WRONG! SHE'S DAMPING DOWN THE PSYCHIC RAPPORT WE SHARE--HIDING FROM ME!

MASTERMIND WAS UP HERE -- IS HE --?!!

STILL CONTROLLING ME? NO. I... TOOK CARE OF HIM.

WHAT'S THE MATTER? JEAN, TALK TO ME-- LET ME HELP!

YOU CAN'T HELP, MY LOVE. NO ONE CAN.

JEAN-- WAIT!

ALL PRESENT, CYKE-- WHAT NOW?

WE RUN FOR IT, SHORT-STUFF!

I'M RECEIVING MULTIPLE MENTAL IMPRESSIONS -- THE POLICE ARE CLOSING IN ON THIS BUILDING, AND THEY MEAN TO ARREST THE X-MEN.

IF THEY CAPTURE US, YOU CAN BET SHAW AND THE HELLFIRE CLUB WILL MAKE ANY CRIMINAL CHARGES STICK. SO, LET'S SCOOT!

THIS MOMENT IS YOURS, X-MEN. ENJOY IT WHILE YOU CAN.

BECAUSE, BEFORE I'M FINISHED, YOU'LL BE KNOWN THROUGHOUT THE LAND -- THROUGH-OUT THE WORLD --

--AS PUBLIC ENEMY NUMBER ONE!

WHY WON'T JEAN LET ME REACH HER-- ON ANY LEVEL? WHAT IS SHE SO AFRAID OF?!

NOTHING MUCH I CAN DO ABOUT IT NOW -- AT LEAST, UNTIL WE'RE SAFELY ON OUR WAY. ONCE WE'RE AIRBORNE, THOUGH, AND THE PRESSURE'S OFF, THEN MAYBE SHE'LL TALK TO ME.

CYCLOPS TOUCHES A CONTROL STUD ON HIS WRISTWATCH...

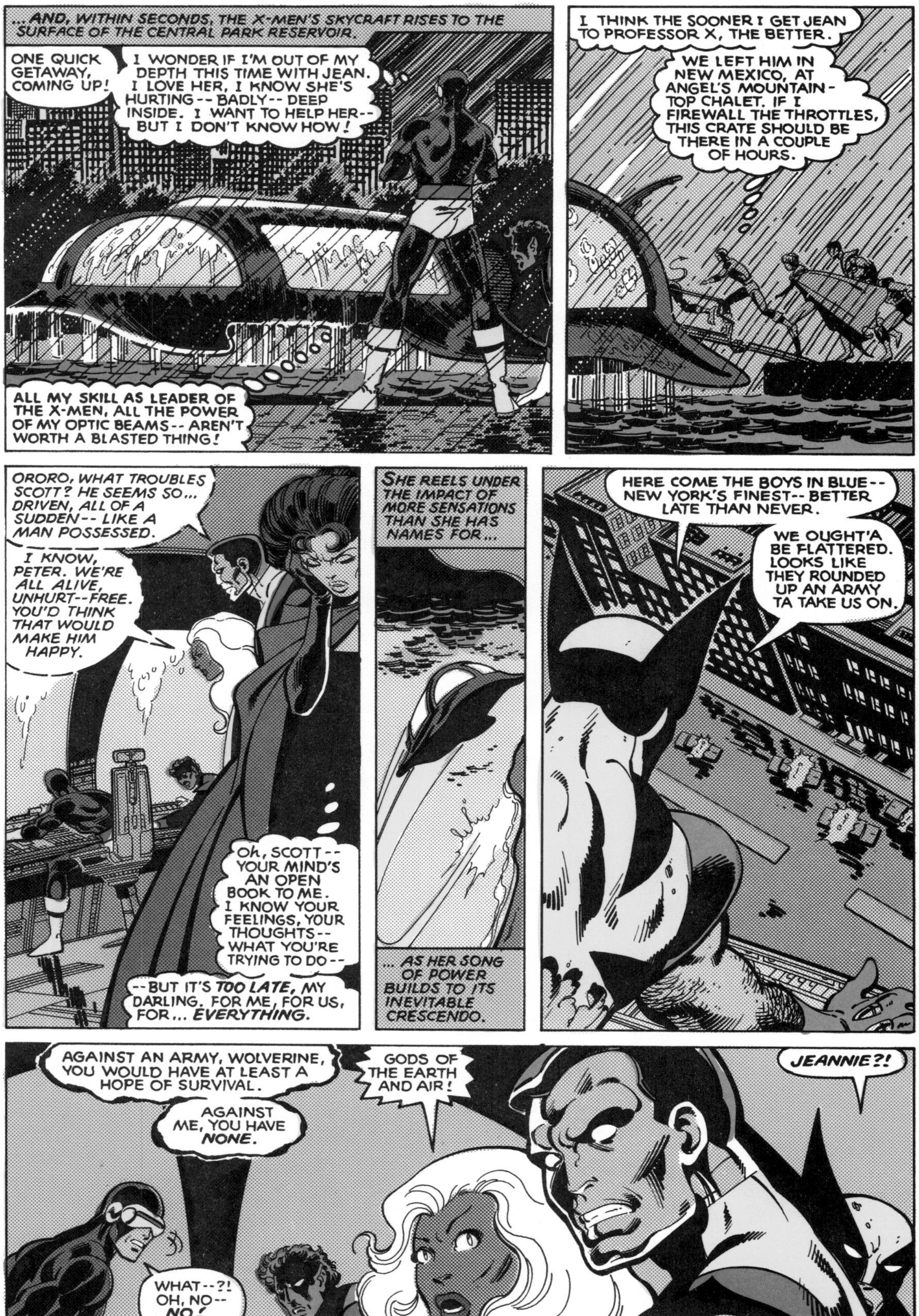
...AND, WITHIN SECONDS, THE X-MEN'S SKYCRAFT RISES TO THE SURFACE OF THE CENTRAL PARK RESERVOIR.
ONE QUICK GETAWAY, COMING UP!
I WONDER IF I'M OUT OF MY DEPTH THIS TIME WITH JEAN. I LOVE HER, I KNOW SHE'S HURTING-- BADLY-- DEEP INSIDE. I WANT TO HELP HER-- BUT I DON'T KNOW HOW!
ALL MY SKILL AS LEADER OF THE X-MEN, ALL THE POWER OF MY OPTIC BEAMS-- AREN'T WORTH A BLASTED THING!
I THINK THE SOONER I GET JEAN TO PROFESSOR X, THE BETTER.
WE LEFT HIM IN NEW MEXICO, AT ANGEL'S MOUNTAIN-TOP CHALET. IF I FIREWALL THE THROTTLES, THIS CRATE SHOULD BE THERE IN A COUPLE OF HOURS.
ORORO, WHAT TROUBLES SCOTT? HE SEEMS SO... DRIVEN, ALL OF A SUDDEN-- LIKE A MAN POSSESSED.
I KNOW, PETER. WE'RE ALL ALIVE, UNHURT--FREE. YOU'D THINK THAT WOULD MAKE HIM HAPPY.
Oh, SCOTT-- YOUR MIND'S AN OPEN BOOK TO ME. I KNOW YOUR FEELINGS, YOUR THOUGHTS-- WHAT YOU'RE TRYING TO DO--
--BUT IT'S TOO LATE, MY DARLING. FOR ME, FOR US, FOR... EVERYTHING.
SHE REELS UNDER THE IMPACT OF MORE SENSATIONS THAN SHE HAS NAMES FOR...
...AS HER SONG OF POWER BUILDS TO ITS INEVITABLE CRESCENDO.
HERE COME THE BOYS IN BLUE-- NEW YORK'S FINEST-- BETTER LATE THAN NEVER.
WE OUGHT'A BE FLATTERED. LOOKS LIKE THEY ROUNDED UP AN ARMY TA TAKE US ON.
AGAINST AN ARMY, WOLVERINE, YOU WOULD HAVE AT LEAST A HOPE OF SURVIVAL.
AGAINST ME, YOU HAVE NONE.
GODS OF THE EARTH AND AIR!
JEANNIE?!
WHAT--?! OH, NO-- NO!

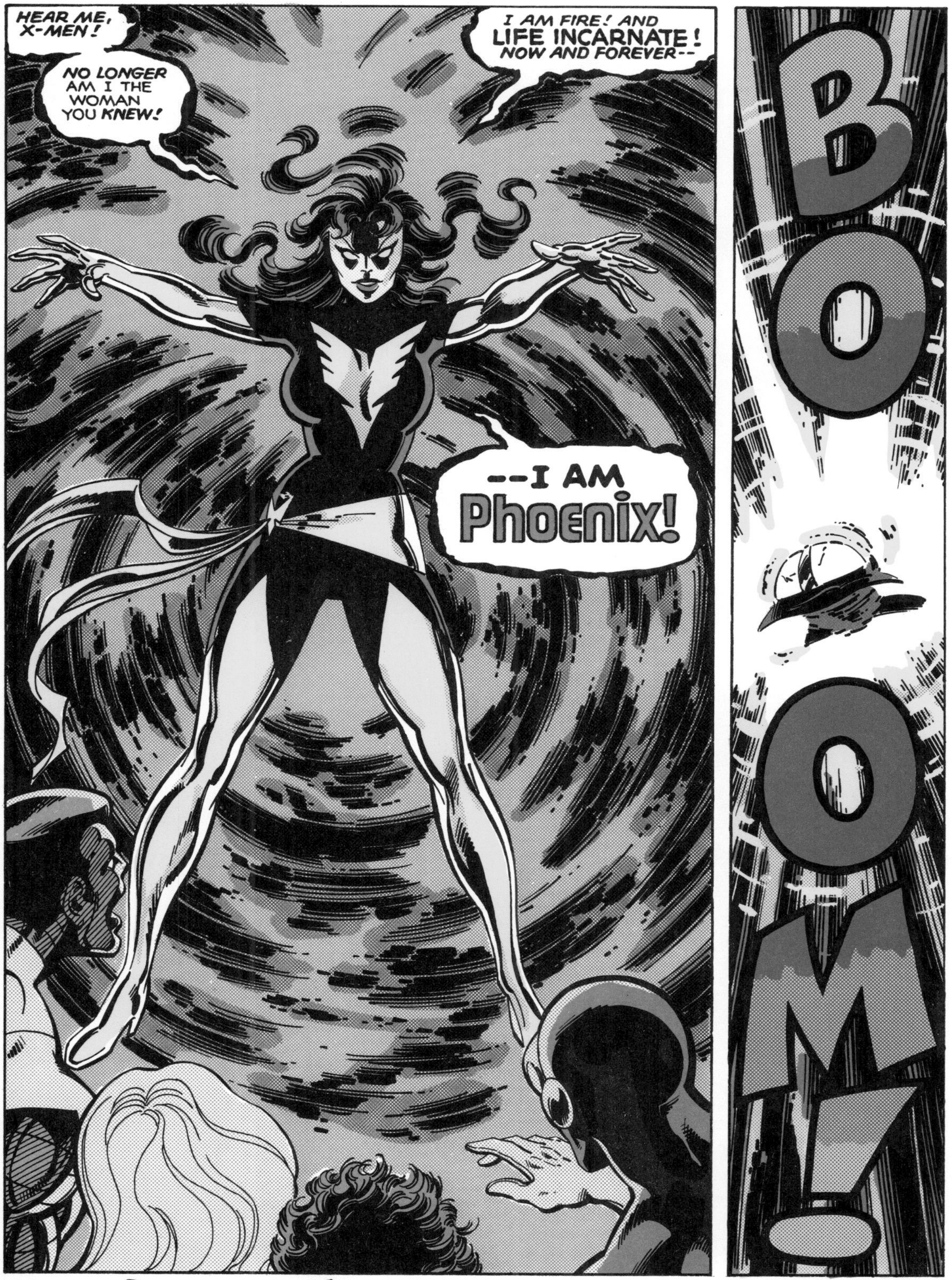
HEAR ME, X-MEN!
NO LONGER AM I THE WOMAN YOU KNEW!
I AM FIRE! AND LIFE INCARNATE! NOW AND FOREVER--
--I AM Phoenix!
BOOM!

NEXT Dark Phoenix!

Cyclops. Storm. Nightcrawler. Wolverine. Colossus. Children of the atom, students of Charles Xavier, MUTANTS — feared and hated by the world they have sworn to protect. These are the STRANGEST heroes of all!!

STAN LEE PRESENTS: THE UNCANNY X-MEN!™

CHRIS CLAREMONT & **JOHN BYRNE**
WRITER / CO-PLOTTERS / PENCILER | **TERRY AUSTIN**
INKER | TOM ORZECHOWSKI, *letterer*
BOB SHAREN, *colorist* | **JIM SALICRUP**
EDITOR | **JIM SHOOTER**
Ed.-IN-CHIEF

WITNESS THE BIRTH OF A GOD!

HER NAME IS *JEAN GREY.* A YOUNG WOMAN OF EXTRAORDINARY BEAUTY, STRENGTH, COURAGE, PASSION. A SUPER-POWERED MUTANT TELEPATH/ TELEKINETIC. A CHARTER MEMBER OF THE UNCANNY X-MEN.

NONE OF THAT HAS CHANGED. AND YET -- *EVERYTHING* HAS CHANGED.

HER FIRST ACT -- A THOUSAND FEET ABOVE MANHATTAN'S CENTRAL PARK -- IS THE SEEMING DESTRUCTION OF THOSE SHE LOVES BEST IN THE WORLD: THE X-MEN!

JEAN -- NO!

BY THE WHITE WOLF!

ACH, NEIN -- NOT ANOTHER AIRCRAFT DESTROYED!

COLOSSUS: A FALL FROM THIS HEIGHT WILL NOT HARM MY ARMORED FORM. I WILL LAND FIRST-- SO THAT I CAN EITHER HELP CATCH THE OTHERS...

...OR TRY TO STOP PHOENIX IF SHE ATTACKS US AGAIN.

WHAT HAS HAPPENED TO JEAN, THOUGH?! WHAT COULD HAVE CAUSED THIS TERRIBLE TRANSFORMATION?!

KTHOOM

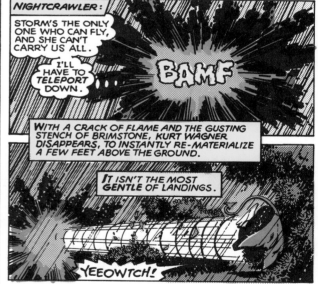

NIGHTCRAWLER: STORM'S THE ONLY ONE WHO CAN FLY, AND SHE CAN'T CARRY US ALL. I'LL HAVE TO TELEPORT DOWN.

BAMF

WITH A CRACK OF FLAME AND THE GUSTING STENCH OF BRIMSTONE, KURT WAGNER DISAPPEARS, TO INSTANTLY RE-MATERIALIZE A FEW FEET ABOVE THE GROUND.

IT ISN'T THE MOST GENTLE OF LANDINGS.

YEEOWTCH!

STORM AND WOLVERINE:

I HAVE YOU!

OBLIGED, 'RORO.

I WOULD HAVE DONE AS MUCH FOR ANY X-MAN, WOLVERINE. EVERYONE IS ACCOUNTED FOR -- SAVE CYCLOPS.

THERE HE IS! PHOENIX IS GOING AFTER HIM! BUT TO SAVE HIM, OR--?!

I CAN'T AFFORD TO TAKE THE RISK!

THE TEAM IS OFF-BALANCE. I MUST BUY US TIME TO REGAIN OUR BEARINGS-- TO FIGURE OUT WHAT IS HAPPENING AND HOW TO DEAL WITH IT.

BUT-- I DO NOT WANT TO HURT JEAN...

AT STORM'S MENTAL COMMAND, THE GALE CLOSES IN AROUND THE FOUR MUTANTS, ITS WINDS SHOVING HER-- AND HER BURDEN-- ONE WAY...

...SHOVING PHOENIX THE OTHER.

I'VE DONE MY BEST, CYCLOPS-- BUT I FEAR IT WILL ONLY BE A BRIEF RESPITE.

THANKS -- BOTH OF YOU.

COLOSSUS? NIGHT-CRAWLER?!

WE ARE WELL, CYCLOPS.

WE'RE ALIVE, ANYWAY.

FIGURES-- WE GET AWAY FROM THE HELLFIRE CLUB WITH OUR SKINS INTACT, ONLY TO GET TRASHED BY ONE OF OUR OWN! OI-FLIPPING-VEY!

SUDDENLY...

YOURS WAS AN ADMIRABLE PLOY, STORM. BUT ESCAPING ME WON'T BE THAT EASY.

WHY ARE YOU ATTACKING US? FOR PITY'S SAKE, JEAN-- WHY?!

ASK NOT FOR PITY FROM DARK PHOENIX, MY LOVE. THERE IS NONE IN HER.

SHE STRIKES LIKE THE ANGEL OF DEATH-- TERRIBLE IN HER UNHUMAN BEAUTY-- AS ELEMENTAL, AS MAJESTIC, AS THE STARS IN THE HEAVENS.

119

AND AS IRRESISTABLE.

JEAN'S ENJOYING THIS! USING HER POWER IS TURNING HER ON -- ACTING LIKE THE ULTIMATE PHYSICAL/EMOTIONAL STIMULANT!

WE HAVE TO STOP HER -- BUT *HOW?!*

I MUST REMEMBER -- DESPITE HER ACTIONS, PHOENIX IS NO VILLAIN, BUT OUR DEAR FRIEND. WE WISH TO *HELP* HER.

IF I CAN TANGLE HER IN THE BRANCHES OF THIS TREE...

YOU'LL ENSNARE *NO ONE*, COLOSSUS.

SAVE, PERHAPS, YOUR-SELF.

LENIN'S GHOST!

SHE -- SHE TELEKINETICALLY TRANSFORMED ME BACK INTO MY *HUMAN* SELF. I'M NO LONGER STRONG ENOUGH TO HOLD THIS TREE -- !

HANG ON, PETEY! I'LL GET YOU OUTTA THERE!

NO, YOU WON'T, WOLVERINE.

CRIPES! JEANNIE CHANGED THE TREE INTA *SOLID GOLD!*

IT MUST WEIGH TONS -- *WHOUMPH!*

JEAN -- NO MORE, I BEG YOU!

WE ARE YOUR *FRIENDS!* LET US HELP YOU -- PLEASE!

IT IS TOO LATE FOR "*HELP*", ORORO. FOR ME, FOR YOU -- FOR THE *UNIVERSE.*

AND DARK PHOENIX HAS NO FRIENDS.

SHE WAS LIKE THIS WHEN SHE SAVED THE UNIVERSE. *

BUT THEN, HER POWER WAS TEMPERED BY JOY, AND *LOVE.*

*SEE X-MEN #108 -- JIM

THERE IS NO JOY -- NO LOVE -- IN DARK PHOENIX. I SENSE PAIN, GREAT SADNESS -- AND AN AWFUL, ALL-CONSUMING *LUST.*

AYE, ORORO -- TAKE YOUR BEST SHOT.

I'D RATHER END THIS QUICKLY.

AARRGH!

FOR ALL YOUR SKILL--AND POWER-- ORORO, YOU HAVEN'T A PRAYER AGAINST ME. I CAN PICK YOUR MIND CLEAN IN THE BLINK OF AN EYE-- KNOW YOUR PLANS THE MOMENT YOU THINK OF THEM.

"AND MY POWER... DEFIES COMPREHENSION."

STORM! IMAGES -- HITTING ME THROUGH THE PSYCHIC RAPPORT I SHARE WITH JEAN-- BLACK FLAMES CONSUMING HER SOUL! MYSTICAL ALLUSIONS -- I DON'T UNDERSTAND--LOST... DROWNING... ALONE ...

CYCLOPS, WE'RE THE ONLY ONES LEFT! WHAT CAN WE DO?!

NOT A THING, NIGHTCRAWLER.

SHE HITS THEM A HUNDRED DIFFERENT WAYS AT ONCE--

-- AND THE LAST TWO X-MEN DROP IN THEIR TRACKS.

I DIDN'T WANT THIS, MY DEAR ONES -- AND YET, IT WAS SOMETHING I HAD TO DO.

BY STRIKING YOU DOWN, I CUT MYSELF FREE OF THE LAST TIES BINDING ME TO THE PERSON I WAS, THE LIFE I LED.

FOR A MOMENT, THE GODDESS-MASQUE SLIPS -- AND JEAN GREY'S FACE SHATTERS WITH A GRIEF THAT TRANSCENDS THOUGHT.

BUT THE MOMENT PASSES, THE HUMANITY FADES -- PERHAPS FOREVER -- AND ONLY DARK PHOENIX REMAINS.

YOU AND I ARE QUITS NOW, X-MEN. OUR PATHS WILL CROSS NO MORE.

MY DESTINY LIES IN THE STARS!

SHE REACHES FOR THE SKY-- SUMMONING THE LIGHTNING -- LAUGHING AS THE AWESOME BOLTS OF ENERGY CARESS HER BODY LIKE A LOVER.

TIME: FIVE MINUTES EARLIER. PLACE: THE HELLFIRE CLUB, ON NEW YORK'S FASHIONABLE FIFTH AVENUE.

THE X-MEN HAVE JUST *FLED* INTO THE GALE-SWEPT NIGHT, A STEP AHEAD OF THE POLICE UNITS ASSEMBLED TO *ARREST* THEM.

ON THE SURFACE, THE CASE LOOKS CUT AND DRIED. THE X-MEN BROKE INTO THE CLUB DURING A PARTY CELEBRATING ITS ANNIVERSARY.

THEY RAMPAGED THROUGH THE BUILDING, TERRORIZING THE GUESTS AND LEAVING TWO CLUB MEMBERS-- HARRY LELAND AND JASON WYNGARDE-- IN NEED OF IMMEDIATE HOSPITALIZATION.

TO ALL CONCERNED, THE X-MEN ARE OBVIOUSLY CRIMINALS.

BUT, IN REALITY, THEY ARE NOT.

IF ANYTHING, THEY ARE *VICTIMS*-- OF A PLOT HATCHED BY SEBASTIAN SHAW, HEAD OF THE CLUB'S SECRET INNER CIRCLE, A GROUP OUT, SIMPLY, TO RULE THE WORLD.

SEBASTIAN, I... I AM SORRY ABOUT LELAND.

THANK YOU, ROBERT. THAT'S VERY KIND.

THE X-MEN WERE OUR HELPLESS PRISONERS YET STILL THEY ESCAPED AND DEFEATED US. WE UNDERESTIMATED THEM-- AND LELAND AND WYNGARDE PAID THE PRICE. *

*FOR FULL DETAILS, SEE THE LAST THREE ISSUES--JIM.

THE MAN WITH SHAW IS U.S. SENATOR ROBERT KELLY-- PRESIDENTIAL CANDIDATE-- INTELLIGENT, ARTICULATE, DECENT, POPULAR, GIVEN A GOOD CHANCE OF WINNING IN NOVEMBER. HE AND SHAW ARE OLD FRIENDS.

MR. SHAW, SENATOR KELLY ...

... MY MEN HAVE SEARCHED THE CLUB. THERE'S NO SIGN OF THE MUTIES.

OBVIOUSLY, CAPTAIN-- BECAUSE THE X-MEN ARE NO LONGER *INSIDE* THE BUILDING!

MR. SHAW SAW THEM RUNNING TOWARDS CENTRAL PARK.

I SUGGEST YOU SHOW SOME INIATIVE AND GET YOUR PEOPLE IN THERE AFTER THEM-- BEFORE THEY GET AWAY!

WITH ALL DUE RESPECT, SENATOR, WE'RE OUT OF OUR LEAGUE HERE. MY OFFICERS AREN'T EQUIPPED TO FIGHT SUPER-POWERED MUTANTS. TACKLING THE X-MEN WOULD BE SUICIDE.

YOU WANT RESULTS-- CALL THE AVENGERS, OR THE FANTASTIC FOUR, OR SHIELD.

BY ALL MEANS, DO SO, CAPTAIN.

THERE IS, HOWEVER, ANOTHER ALTERNATIVE-- ALBEIT A LONG TERM ONE-- THAT WOULD DEAL MOST EFFECTIVELY WITH THIS MUTANT MENACE, AND AT THE SAME TIME BE COMPLETELY, UNQUESTION- ABLY UNDER FEDERAL GOVERNMENT CONTROL.

OH? WHAT'S THAT?

SENTINELS.

CAP'N-- SOMETHING'S HAPPENING IN THE PARK!

LOOK!

EH?! GOOD HEAVENS!

LIGHTNING-- BOLTS AS BRIGHT AS THE SUN ITSELF, STRIKING THE PARK. IT'S INCREDIBLE-- IMPOSSIBLE!

WHAT COULD BE CAUSING IT?!

STORM'S THE WEATHER- WITCH-- THIS IS HER KIND OF STUNT. BUT WHAT'S THE POINT?

THE BOLTS ARE BUILDING IN INTENSITY.

AND THEN...

PHOENIX!!

SAINTS PRESERVE US!

AT THAT MOMENT-- IN THE BAXTER BUILDING, HOME OF THE *FANTASTIC FOUR*--

SHEESH, STRETCHO-- I WUZ JUST GETTIN' ALL NICE AN' LATHERED UP WHEN YA HADDA GO AN' HIT THE *RED ALERT*.

WHAT HAPPENED, REED--GALACTUS STEP ON YANCY STREET OR SOMETHIN'?

THIS IS SERIOUS, BEN! I'M REGISTERING AN ENERGY READING OF UNBELIEVABLE PROPORTIONS-- FROM SOMEONE WHOSE POWER COULD *RIVAL* THAT OF GALACTUS.

... ON MANHATTAN'S WEST SIDE...

THAT FIREBIRD IMAGE -- THE MOMENT IT APPEARED--

... MY *SPIDER-SENSE* WENT CRAZY!

... IN GREENWICH VILLAGE...

BY HOGGOTH!

I SENSE IMAGES OF GREAT MYSTIC POWER, GREAT PASSION --GREAT... *EVIL*. BUT WHAT MEANING DO THEY HAVE FOR *DR. STRANGE*?

... AND ON THE EDGE OF SPACE...

CAN IT BE? I SENSE A *KINDRED SOUL!*

A CHILD OF THE STARS-- SO LIKE THE *SILVER SURFER**, AND YET, NOT LIKE ME AT ALL.

SHE IS HUMAN, FLAWED-- AND THAT FLAW BIDS FAIR TO *DESTROY* HER. I MUST AID HER IF I CAN...

*FOR MORE OF THE SILVER SURFER, SEE *EPIC ILLUSTRATED* #1 -- JIM.

"... FOR MORE THAN A SINGLE TERRAN LIFE HANGS IN THE BALANCE. LEFT UNCHECKED, THIS FORCE COULD THREATEN THE ENTIRE *COSMOS!* "

BUT EVEN AS THE SKY-RIDER OF THE SPACE-WAYS SPEEDS 'ROUND THE GLOBE -- EVEN AS OTHERS BECOME AWARE OF HER EXISTENCE --

--THE *DARK PHOENIX* BIDS FAREWELL TO HER HOMEWORLD...

...AND SOARS SPACEWARD TO FULFILL HER *MALEFIC DESTINY*.

AS SHE LIFTS OFF, SHE JUST MISSES AN AVENGERS QUINJET GOING THE OTHER WAY.

HEY!! THAT FIREBIRD IMAGE I SAW-- THAT WAS JEAN'S *PHOENIX EFFECT.* AND BENEATH IT-- THE PARK'S ON *FIRE!*

I'D BETTER GET DOWN THERE-- *FAST!*

WITHOUT A FALSE MOVE OR PAUSE, THE QUINJET DROPS TO A LANDING NEAR THE RESEVOIR ...

... AND *HANK McCOY--* ALSO KNOWN AS THE *BEAST,* X-MAN TURNED AVENGER--STEPS OUT UNDER A SUPERNALLY CLEAR, STAR-FLECKED SKY.

FASCINATING.

BEFORE THE PHOENIX-EFFECT APPEARED, A FULL-FLEDGED GALE WAS RAGING OVER THE CITY.

NOW, IT'S DISAPPEARED.

THE GROUND-- CHARRED, SMOKING, STILL BURNING IN PATCHES. THE FIRE MUST HAVE EXPLODED UP AND OUT-- IGNITING THE TREE-TOPS WHILE LEAVING THIS CENTRAL AREA RELATIVELY UNTOUCHED.

BUT THE X-MEN-- ARE THEY *ALL* RIGHT?!

SCOTT?! SCOTTY-- IT'S HANK!

I... HEAR YOU... OL' BUDDY.

≥KOFF≤ ≥KOFF≤

THROAT... RAW-- CAN HARDLY TALK.

I'M... OKAY-- SEE TO OTHERS.

AND, SHORTLY...

MEIN GOTT-- THAT SOLID GOLD OAK TREE SHOULD SOLVE NEW YORK'S FISCAL CRISIS FOR SURE.

STORM? ORORO?!

MY LUNGS... CLOGGED-- DIFFICULT TO BREATHE. ALSO... FEEL BROILED. OTHERWISE, CYCLOPS, I AM-- AS EVER-- READY FOR ACTION.

DON'T LOOK NOW, SCOTTY, BUT I THINK THE LADY JUST CRACKED A JOKE.

OOOMPH!

MOVE IT, YOU TWO! I'M NOT HOLDING THIS ALL NIGHT!

MINUTES LATER...

...ANYWAY, CYKE-- INSTEAD OF SOUNDING AN AVENGERS ALERT WHEN I HEARD THE POLICE CALL ABOUT THE X-MEN, I *ERASED* THE TAPE AND CAME TO SEE IF I COULD HELP.*

I GUESS-- ONCE AN X-MAN, *ALWAYS* AN X-MAN.

*IT HAPPENED LAST ISH-- JIM.

HANK'S HIDING IT WELL, BUT THAT CHOICE IS TEARING HIM APART. HE LOVES BEING AN AVENGER. I HOPE WE CAN MAKE IT UP TO HIM.

...LET'S TURN OUR ATTENTION WEST-WARD ACROSS THE CONTINENT...

AS THE QUINJET ARROWS ACROSS THE BRONX, TOWARDS THE X-MEN'S WESTCHESTER COUNTY HEADQUARTERS...

...TO THE NEW MEXICO MOUNTAIN-TOP HOME OF ANOTHER FORMER X-MAN: *WARREN WORTHINGTON III*, BETTER KNOWN AS THE HIGH-FLYING ANGEL!

HIS HOUSE-GUEST IS THE X-MEN'S FOUNDER AND MENTOR, PROFESSOR CHARLES XAVIER.

I FELT A TREMENDOUS BURST OF PSIONIC ENERGY, MOIRA -- AS IF SOMEONE HAD TRIGGERED A GIANT-SIZED PSYCHIC *H-BOMB*.

THE EFFECT PASSED QUICKLY.

I CAN CONFIRM WHAT YOU ALREADY SUSPECT, CHARLES. THE SOURCE WAS *JEAN*.

I THINK PHOENIX IS OUT OF CONTROL.

ON THE OTHER END OF THE PHONE IS *MOIRA MacTAGGERT* -- XAVIER'S ASSOCIATE IN MUTANT RESEARCH -- AND THE MAN SHE LOVES, *SEAN CASSIDY* -- BANSHEE, A RETIRED X-MAN.

OVER THE PAST FEW HOURS, MY REMOTE SCANS SHOW PHOENIX' POWER INCREASING ALONG A GEOMETRIC CURVE, WITH NO END IN SIGHT. SHE ALREADY DWARFS ANY MUTANT WE'VE ALREADY CHARTED.

IF YOU WANT A CONVENIENT BUZZ-WORD DESCRIPTION FOR HER, "COSMIC" FITS THE BILL NICELY.

"MOIRA SOUNDED TERRIFIED -- AND I'VE NEVER SEEN THE PROFESSOR LIKE THIS. NOT SO MUCH SCARED AS... *HAUNTED*.

PROFESSOR, WHAT'S HAPPENED?

THE SIMPLE EXPLANATION, WARREN, IS THAT POWER CORRUPTS, AND ABSOLUTE POWER CORRUPTS *ABSOLUTELY*. PHOENIX IS THE ULTIMATE EXPRESSION OF JEAN'S POTENTIAL AS A PSI.

TOO MUCH POWER, I FEAR, TOO SOON. JEAN IS TOO YOUNG -- SHE LACKS THE... *AWARENESS* NECESSARY TO CONTROL HER NOW LIMITLESS ABILITIES.

WE MUST RETURN TO NEW YORK, ANGEL -- *AT ONCE*. I AM PARTLY TO BLAME FOR THIS TRAGEDY. I MUST DO WHAT I CAN TO RESOLVE IT, WHATEVER THE COST.

MONTHS AGO -- A LIFETIME AGO -- WHEN HER POWER SAVED THE UNIVERSE, JEAN GREY HAD A VISION OF HERSELF AS TIPHERETH...

...HEART AND SOUL OF THE MYSTIC TREE OF LIFE. SHE WAS A DREAM, REPRESENTING THE ORDER AND HARMONY OF THINGS. SHE WAS ALL THAT WAS GREAT IN US.

BUT NOW, THE DREAM IS TWISTED. SHE KNOWS THIS -- KNOWS WHAT SHE WAS, WHAT SHE HAS BECOME -- AND SHE DOES NOT CARE.

WHAT MATTERS IS THAT DARK PHOENIX LIVES! AND ALL CREATION IS HER DOMAIN -- TO DO WITH AS SHE PLEASES.

MEANWHILE, ABOARD STARCORE ONE -- A UNITED NATIONS SUN-WATCH STATION -- PHOENIX' ARRIVAL IN THE VICINITY HAS NOT GONE UNNOTICED.

DR. CORBEAU TO THE COMMAND DECK -- ON THE DOUBLE!

DOCTOR CORBEAU -- WHAT'S HAPPENING?!

I'M NOT SURE. SOME KIND OF ENERGY BEAM -- VERY SMALL, INCREDIBLY POWERFUL, VECTORING SUNWARD FROM THE EARTH!

LOCK ALL SENSORS ON IT! I WANT A FULL-RANGE SCAN!

EVEN AS THE NOBEL-PRIZE WINNING CREATOR OF STARCORE YELLS HIS ORDERS, PHOENIX LOOPS THE SUN, SKIMMING ITS SURFACE AND USING THE "SLINGSHOT-EFFECT" TO BOOST HER SPEED A THOUSAND-FOLD.

BY THE TIME CORBEAU FINISHES HIS SENTENCE, SHE IS SHOOTING PAST JUPITER.

SECONDS AFTER THAT, SHE IS WELL INTO THE VAST EMPTINESS OF INTER-STELLAR SPACE--

WITH RIDICULOUS, TERRIFYING EASE, SHE CREATES A STAR-GATE -- AND THIS PERSONAL SPACE/TIME HURLS HER INSTANTLY OUT OF THE MILKY WAY...

--AND HER JOURNEY HAS ONLY JUST BEGUN.

...AND INTO A GALAXY FAR, FAR AWAY.

TRANSITION TOOK MORE OUT OF ME THAN I ANTICIPATED. MY POWER IS CONSIDERABLE--AND GROWING --BUT, FOR THE MOMENT, IT'S STILL FINITE.

LIKE IT OR NOT-- I STILL HAVE LIMITS.

I'M RAVENOUS. BEFORE I GO ON, I NEED SUSTENANCE.

THIS STAR SHOULD DO NICELY.

WITHOUT A THOUGHT OF THE CONSEQUENCES, SHE DIVES INTO THE HEART OF A MAIN SEQUENCE, G-TYPE STAR MUCH LIKE OUR OWN SUN.

ITS DIAMETER IS A MILLION MILES; SURFACE TEMPERA-TURE, 6,000° CENTI-GRADE; CORE TEMPERATURE, WELL OVER 2,000 TIMES THAT-- 14 MILLION DEGREES!

NORMALLY, THIS STAR COULD EXPECT TO 'LIVE' FOR ANOTHER SIX BILLION YEARS.

IN REALITY, ITS FUTURE CAN BE MEASURED IN A MATTER OF MINUTES...

...AS IT IS SUDDENLY, COMPLETELY, CONSUMED BY DARK PHOENIX.

ORBITING THE STAR IS A SYSTEM OF ELEVEN PLANETS. THE FOURTH IS INHABITED-- BY AN ANCIENT, PEACE- LOVING CIVILIZATION.

ON THE PLANETARY DAYSIDE, THEY SEE THE LIGHT FIRST-- THE AWFUL LIGHT OF ARMAGEDDON-- FILLING THE SKY FROM HORIZON TO HORIZON TEN MINUTES AFTER LEAVING THE MURDERED STAR.

MANY WHO SEE THIS LIGHT-- THE LAST THING THEY WILL EVER SEE-- ARE CONFUSED, FRIGHTENED. A VERY FEW-- WHO REALIZE AT ONCE WHAT HAS HAPPENED-- HAVE TIME TO CURSE CRUEL FATE OR MAKE THEIR PEACE WITH THEIR GOD. THEN, THEY ALL DIE.

FOLLOWING THE LIGHT-- AT A COMPARATIVE SNAIL'S PACE-- COMES THE *HEAT FLARE.* THE INSTANT IT HITS, THE ATMOSPHERE AND OCEANS ON THE DAYSIDE BOIL AWAY, THE STEAM AND SUPERHEATED AIR WHIRLING AROUND THE GLOBE IN A FLAMING SHOCK-WAVE THAT OBLITERATES ALL IN ITS PATH.

THOSE FEW AWAKE ON THE NIGHTSIDE ARE TREATED TO A SPECTACULAR, ONCE IN A LIFETIME *AURORA BOREALIS,* BEFORE DEATH CLAIMS THEM.

BUT HALF THE WORLD DIES IN ITS SLEEP. THEY ARE THE *LUCKY* ONES.

AND IN THE CENTER OF THE *SUPER-NOVA* SHE CREATED, DARK PHOENIX THRILLS TO THE ABSOLUTE POWER THAT IS HERS. SHE IS IN *ECSTACY.*

YET SHE KNOWS THAT THIS IS ONLY THE BEGINNING-- THAT WHAT SHE FEELS NOW IS *NOTHING* COMPARED TO WHAT SHE EXPERIENCED WITHIN THE GREAT M'KRANN CRYSTAL. *

SHE CRAVES THAT ULTIMATE SENSATION...

*X-MEN #108, AGAIN -- JIM.

... AND SHE WILL PAY *ANY* PRICE TO ACHIEVE IT ONCE MORE.

HOWEVER, ON THE FRINGES OF THIS *DOOMED* SYSTEM, APPEARS A POSSIBLE *OBSTACLE* TO HER *DAEMONIC* QUEST--

GIVE ME *TACTICAL!*

-- A SHI'AR IMPERIAL BATTLE CRUISER, FIRST OF ITS CLASS, AND ONE OF THE DEADLIEST WARCRAFT THE EMPIRE HAS EVER SEEN, TOURING THE CO-DOMINIONS ON ITS MAIDEN VOYAGE.

D'BARI HAS JUST GONE SUPER-NOVA, SCIENCE OFFICER. EXPLANATION?

I HAVE NONE, MILORD CAPTAIN.

D'BARI WAS AN AVERAGE, G-NORMAL STAR, ÉLUKE. IT MIGHT FLARE, BUT NOT EXPLODE.

STELLAR EXPANSION CEASING -- VISIBLE CONTRACTION NOW EVIDENT IN PHOTOSPHERE. IT'S ACTING LIKE A PROPER SUPER-NOVA, MILORD, BUT AT A FANTASTICALLY ACCELERATED RATE.

MILORD, BASED ON THIS MORNING'S STARSCAN, D'BARI WAS A PERFECTLY HEALTHY STAR. WE CHARTED NO ABNORMAL MATRICES, ON ATOMIC OR SUB-ATOMIC LEVELS.

THIS SHOULD NOT-- COULD NOT-- HAVE OCCURRED.

UNLESS... SOMETHING *MADE* IT.

MILORD, SENSORS NOW REGISTER A FIELD ANAMOLY, MOVING OUT FROM THE CORE OF THE STAR. THIS IS INCREDIBLE--!

THE ANAMOLY IS REGISTERING ALL ACROSS THE SPECTRUM -- AS ENERGY... AND AS A *LIFEFORM* -- AND AT LEVELS SO EXTREME THAT OUR INSTRUMENTS CAN-NOT CALIBRATE IT!

MAIN SCREEN -- FULL MAGNIFICATION.

THERE, JUBER. THAT MUST BE IT.

SHARRA AND K'YTHRI PRESERVE US!

IT APPEARS TO BE HUMANOID, BUT WHAT KIND OF CREATURE *IS* IT?!

SOUND BATTLE STATIONS, ÉLUKE. WE WILL ENGAGE.

IS THAT WISE, MILORD?

IT IS *NECESSARY*. B'DARI WAS AN ALLY OF THE EMPIRE, SCIENCE OFFICER. FIVE BILLION PEOPLE -- *EXTERMINATED* BY THAT... THING. THEY MUST BE AVENGED!

"MORE IMPORTANTLY, THIS ENTITY SEEMS TO ABSORB ITS LIFE ENERGY FROM THE STARS IT CONSUMES. IT MUST BE STOPPED *NOW*-- BEFORE IT SLAUGHTERS ANY OTHER WORLDS. AND BEFORE ITS POWER BECOMES SO GREAT THAT NO FORCE IN CREATION CAN STAND AGAINST IT.

"MAIN BATTERIES-- *FIRE!*"

WHAT--?!!

A PLASMA BOLT! SOMEONE'S *SHOOTING* AT ME!

WHOEVER YOU ARE, YOU'VE JUST MADE A BIG MISTAKE.

SCRATCH ONE PROPULSION NACELLE!

I'VE CRIPPLED THEM--

--NOW TO *MIND-SCAN* THE VESSEL, FIND OUT WHAT I'M FACING.

WELL! IT'S ONE OF *LILANDRA'S* GRAND FLEET!

THE FOOLS -- HURT AS THEY ARE, THEY STILL MEAN TO FIGHT ME. IF THAT'S WHAT CAPTAIN LORD JUBER WANTS, HOWEVER, DARK PHOENIX WILL BE MORE THAN HAPPY TO OBLIGE HIM.

WARP POWER DOWN TO 40%; WEAPONRY DOWN BY HALF-- THE SAME GOES FOR SHIELD STRENGTH.

WE'RE LUCKY TO BE ALIVE, JUBER! LET'S GET OUT OF HERE WHILE WE CAN!

DO YOU HONESTLY THINK WE CAN *OUTRUN* OUR FOE, ELUKE -- OR THAT IT WILL LET US GO? WHATEVER OUR FATE, MY FRIEND, WE WILL MEET IT WITH HONOR.

COMMUNICATIONS -- ESTABLISH *INSTA-LINK* WITH IMPERIAL CENTER! THIS HAS ABSOLUTE PRIORITY! I MUST SPEAK WITH THE *EMPRESS!*

AND, ON THE ANCIENT WORLD THAT IS THE RULING SEAT OF MUCH OF THIS ALIEN GALAXY, IN THE BEDCHAMBER OF THE WOMAN WHO, ONLY RECENTLY-- AND WITH CONSIDERABLE RELUCTANCE -- CLAIMED THE SHI'AR THRONE AS HER OWN...

LILANDRA! MAJESTY!!

EH...??

MY LORD CHAMBERLAIN? WHAT'S THE MATTER?!

MINUTES LATER, AFTER A HURRIED EXPLANATION...

JUBÉR IS ONE OF MY BEST CAPTAINS -- I TRAINED HIM MYSELF. IF HE'S USING THE INSTA-LINK HIS SITUATION MUST BE SERIOUS.

ARAKI, CAN'T YOU TELL ME *ANYTHING*?!

NO MORE THAN I ALREADY HAVE -- I, TOO, WAS AWAKENED FROM A SOUND SLEEP.

ALL OUR ANSWERS AWAIT US IN THE *WAR ROOM.*

SOON...

LILANDRA -- CAN YOU *SEE* IT?!

WE'RE BEATEN -- NO WEAPONS, NO POWER! MY CREW... MOSTLY DEAD. SHIP A RUINED, GUTTED HULK.

ENTITY CLOSING. TAKE MY HAND, JUBER, MY CAPTAIN, MY FRIEND -- I THINK THIS IS THE END.

ARAKI -- BEHIND THEM, THAT IMAGE --!

WARSHIP?

I SEE IT, MAJESTY. WOULD I WERE BLIND.

FAREWELL, LILANDRA --!

JUBÈR!!

TECHNICIAN -- REGAIN CONTACT!

IMPOSSIBLE, MAJESTY. THERE'S NOTHING OUT THERE FOR US TO CONTACT.

JUBÈR'S SHIP -- IS *GONE.*

LILANDRA -- THAT BIRD IMAGE...

I RECOGNIZED IT, OLD FRIEND -- THE *PHOENIX.*

WHAT WE'VE FEARED FROM THE BEGINNING -- AND PRAYED WE'D NEVER HAVE TO FACE -- HAS COME TO PASS.

SUMMON MY MINISTERS, CHAMBERLAIN. THE THREAT MUST BE DEALT WITH, ONCE AND FOR ALL -- NO MATTER WHAT THE COST.

EARTH -- SPECIFICALLY, A VENERABLE MANSION LOCATED ON GRAYMALKIN LANE, A FEW MILES OUTSIDE THE WESTCHESTER COUNTY TOWN OF *SALEM CENTER*.

ITS OFFICIAL TITLE IS "PROFESSOR XAVIER'S SCHOOL FOR GIFTED YOUNGSTERS." IN ADDITION, HOWEVER -- QUITE UNKNOWN TO THE NEIGHBORS -- IT SERVES AS HOME AND HEADQUARTERS OF THE X-MEN.

THESE YOUNG MUTANTS HAVE SEEN GOOD TIMES AND BAD, BUT IN ALL THE YEARS SINCE THE TEAM'S FOUNDING, THEY'VE NEVER FACED A MOMENT QUITE LIKE THIS.

EVER SINCE WE RETURNED FROM NEW YORK, SCOTT HAS JUST SAT THERE -- NOT EATING, NOT SPEAKING.

HE'S TAKING THIS VERY HARD, ORORO.

IF THERE WAS ONLY SOME WAY TO HELP...

DON'T GET YER HOPES UP, PETEY.

GIVING UP, WOLVERINE? I FIND THAT HARD TO BELIEVE.

I MAY BE STUBBORN, 'RORO, BUT I AIN'T STUPID. I'M A REALIST AN', REALISTICALLY, JEANNIE *TRASHED* US WITHOUT EVEN RAISIN' A SWEAT.

YOU THINK A REMATCH'LL END ANY DIFF'RENTLY?

IT MIGHT, SHORT-STUFF.

TEAMWORK WILL HELP. AND I THINK I CAN WHIP UP SOME GADGETS THAT COULD MAKE THE ODDS A BIT MORE EQUAL.

A... "BIT"?

THAT'S BETTER THAN NOTHING, FUZZY-- EH?!

OH, NO! NO!!

SCOTT, WHAT'S WRONG?!

IT'S *PHOENIX* -- I CAN SENSE HER IN MY MIND, THROUGH THE *PSIONIC RAPPORT* WE SHARE. SHE'S... RETURNING TO EARTH--

--AND SHE'S *HUNGRY!*

NEXT Child of Light and Darkness!

133

Cyclops. Storm. Nightcrawler. Wolverine. Colossus. Children of the atom, students of Charles Xavier, MUTANTS — feared and hated by the world they have sworn to protect. These are the STRANGEST heroes of all!

Stan Lee PRESENTS: THE UNCANNY X-MEN! ™

child of light and darkness!

CHRIS CLAREMONT · JOHN BYRNE | TERRY AUSTIN | TOM ORZECHOWSKI, *letterer* | JIM SALICRUP | JIM SHOOTER
WRITER · CO-PLOTTERS · PENCILER | INKER | GLYNIS WEIN, *colorist* | EDITOR | EDITOR-IN-CHIEF

IMPERIAL CENTER -- RULING SEAT OF A GALACTIC EMPIRE LOCATED HALFWAY ACROSS THE KNOWN UNIVERSE FROM EARTH...

SEE, MY FRIENDS! THE *PHOENIX-ENTITY* APPROACHES HER HOMEWORLD, SOL 3-- *EARTH!*

FELLOW MINISTERS-- RISE AND HAIL *LILANDRA,* MAJESTRIX SHI'AR!

THIS EMERGENCY MEETING OF HER GRAND COUNCIL IS NOW IN SESSION.

THANK YOU, ARAKI.

HONORABLE BEINGS, WE NOW FACE A THREAT THE LIKE OF WHICH THE SHI'AR EMPIRE-- INDEED, THE ENTIRE UNIVERSE-- HAS NEVER KNOWN.

BESIDE IT, EVEN *GALACTUS* MAY PALE TO INSIGNIFICANCE. TO FEED HIS INFERNAL HUNGER, HE CONSUMES WORLDS.

TO FEED HERS, PHOENIX MAY CONSUME *ALL THAT EXISTS.*

TUOKS'ENHAAMIN, BEGIN THE BRIEFING.

UPON ARRIVING IN IMPERIAL SPACE, AS ALL CAN SEE IN THIS HOLOGRAM FIELD, THE PHOENIX-ENTITY PLUNGED INTO THE HEART OF *D'BARI,* A MAIN SEQUENCE, G-TYPE STAR.

IN A MATTER OF SECONDS, SHE ADVANCED IT TO *SUPER-NOVA* STAGE.

"THE RESULTANT STELLAR EXPLOSION DESTROYED NOT ONLY D'BARI, BUT ITS INHABITED PLANETS AS WELL."

AFTER LEAVING D'BARI, PHOENIX WAS INTERCEPTED BY OUR NEWEST, MOST POWERFUL BATTLE CRUISER. THE SHIP ATTACKED...

...AND WAS DESTROYED AS QUICKLY, AS EASILY, AS COMPLETELY, AS THE STAR. *

*SEE LAST ISH-- JIM.

136

WHEN I FIRST MET PHOENIX, SHE WAS A TERRAN FEMALE NAMED JEAN GREY, A BENEFICENT ENTITY. SHE AND HER FELLOW X-MEN HELPED STOP MY MAD BROTHER FROM UNLEASHING *ARMAGEDDON.* ∗

NOW, IT SEEMS, THE CHILD IS BENEFICENT NO LONGER. I FEAR AS WELL THAT SHE MEANS TO PICK UP WHERE MY BROTHER LEFT OFF.

∗X-MEN #'S 107 & 108 --JIM.

MINISTERS, IF THE EMPIRE-- IF THE *UNIVERSE* -- IS TO SURVIVE...

...PHOENIX MUST BE *DESTROYED.*

AT THAT MOMENT, ON EARTH, IN A MANSION KNOWN THROUGHOUT THE WORLD...

...MR. PRESIDENT, IT'S THE SAME ENERGY MATRIX THAT STARCORE MONITORED EARLIER THIS EVENING. ONLY NOW IT'S FAR MORE POWERFUL, AND HEADING STRAIGHT FOR THE EARTH!

THANK YOU, DR. COAHBEAU. JOEL, GET ME THE AVENGERS!

AND, IN NEW YORK...

GOODNESS GRACIOUS! THAT'S A SPECIAL ALERT!

ONLY THE PRESIDENT CAN ACTIVATE IT-- AND ONLY THEN IN TIMES OF THE GRAVEST DANGER. I'VE NEVER HEARD IT SOUNDED IN EARNEST.

I PRAY THIS IS ONLY ANOTHER TEST.

MR. JAHVIS, AH UNDERSTOOD THAT AN AVENJUH WAS ALWAYS SUPPOSED TO BE ON MONITUH DUTY. AH'VE BEEN CALLING FOAH SOME TIME, WITHOUT RESPONSE!

AN ENERGY FORCE OF UNKNOWN ORIGINS, BUT CONSIDERABLE POWER, IS APPROACHING EARTH.

IF THIS IS SOME EXTRATERRESTRIAL ATTACK, I WANT THE AVENJUHS READY TO DEAL WITH IT.

YES, SIR. I'LL ASSEMBLE THEM AT ONCE.

AFTER THE TRANSMISSION ENDS...

MASTER *BEAST* WAS ON MONITOR DUTY. THERE'S NO SIGN OF A STRUGGLE-- SO I DOUBT HE WAS KIDNAPPED. BUT NO MESSAGE FROM HIM, EITHER.

WHAT HAPPENED TO HIM?! WHERE COULD HE HAVE GONE?!

ANSWER: THE BEAST, ANSWERING CYCLOPS' SECRET CALL FOR HELP, HAS RETURNED TO HIS OLD ALMA MATER, PROFESSOR CHARLES XAVIER'S **SCHOOL FOR GIFTED YOUNGSTERS**— SECRET HOME AND HEADQUARTERS OF THE UNCANNY **X-MEN.**

GENTLY DOES IT... *GENTLY*...

BEFORE HE JOINED THE AVENGERS, *HANK McCOY* WAS A CHARTER MEMBER OF THIS MUTANT TEAM. TONIGHT HE DISCOVERED THAT OLD LOYALTIES DIE VERY HARD.

BY GEORGE, I'VE GOT IT!

GOT WHAT, HANK?

YOUR BASIC MNEMONIC SCRAMBLER. SLAP THIS ON JEANNIE'S HEAD AND SHE SHOULDN'T BE ABLE TO THINK A COHERENT THOUGHT, MUCH LESS READ MINDS OR THROW TELEKINETIC FORCE BOLTS.

GOOD WORK, BEAST.

I'VE NEVER HEARD SUCH PAIN IN CYCLOPS' VOICE SOON NOW WE WILL HAVE TO FIGHT THE WOMAN HE LOVES — PERHAPS TO THE DEATH. THAT KNOWLEDGE IS EATING HIM UP INSIDE.

SCOTT, I...

JUST A SEC, STORM.

I CAN'T OPEN MY EYES, EVEN THE TINIEST FRACTION, UNTIL I'VE PUT ON MY SPECIAL RUBY QUARTZ GLASSES, OR MY OPTIC BLASTS COULD PUNCH A TRUCK-SIZED HOLE IN THE WALL.

I'VE HAD TO BE THIS CAREFUL SINCE BEFORE I JOINED THE X-MEN. I'LL HAVE TO STAY THIS CAREFUL TILL THE DAY I DIE.

ORORO WANTS TO HELP ME, TO COMFORT ME. BUT I CAN'T GIVE IN. NOT YET. IF I GIVE FULL REIN TO MY FEELINGS, I'LL... *SHATTER.*

FOR JEAN'S SAKE, AS MUCH AS EVERYONE ELSE'S, I HAVE TO STAY STRONG... IN CONTROL.

MEANWHILE, IN THE MANSION'S *DANGER ROOM,* THE REST OF THE X-MEN WORK OUT WITH A MACHINE WHOSE BLADES WHIRL ABOUT THE ROOM AT VARYING HEIGHTS AND DEADLY SPEED.

I AVOIDED BEING CRUSHED BY TELEPORTING ONTO ONE OF THE BLADES AND RIDING IT...

...BUT *YOU* MUST STOP THE "SUPER SPANNER," COLOSSUS, BEFORE ITS SPINNING BLADES CRUSH BOTH YOU AND WOLVERINE!

I AM *TRYING* TO, NIGHTCRAWLER!

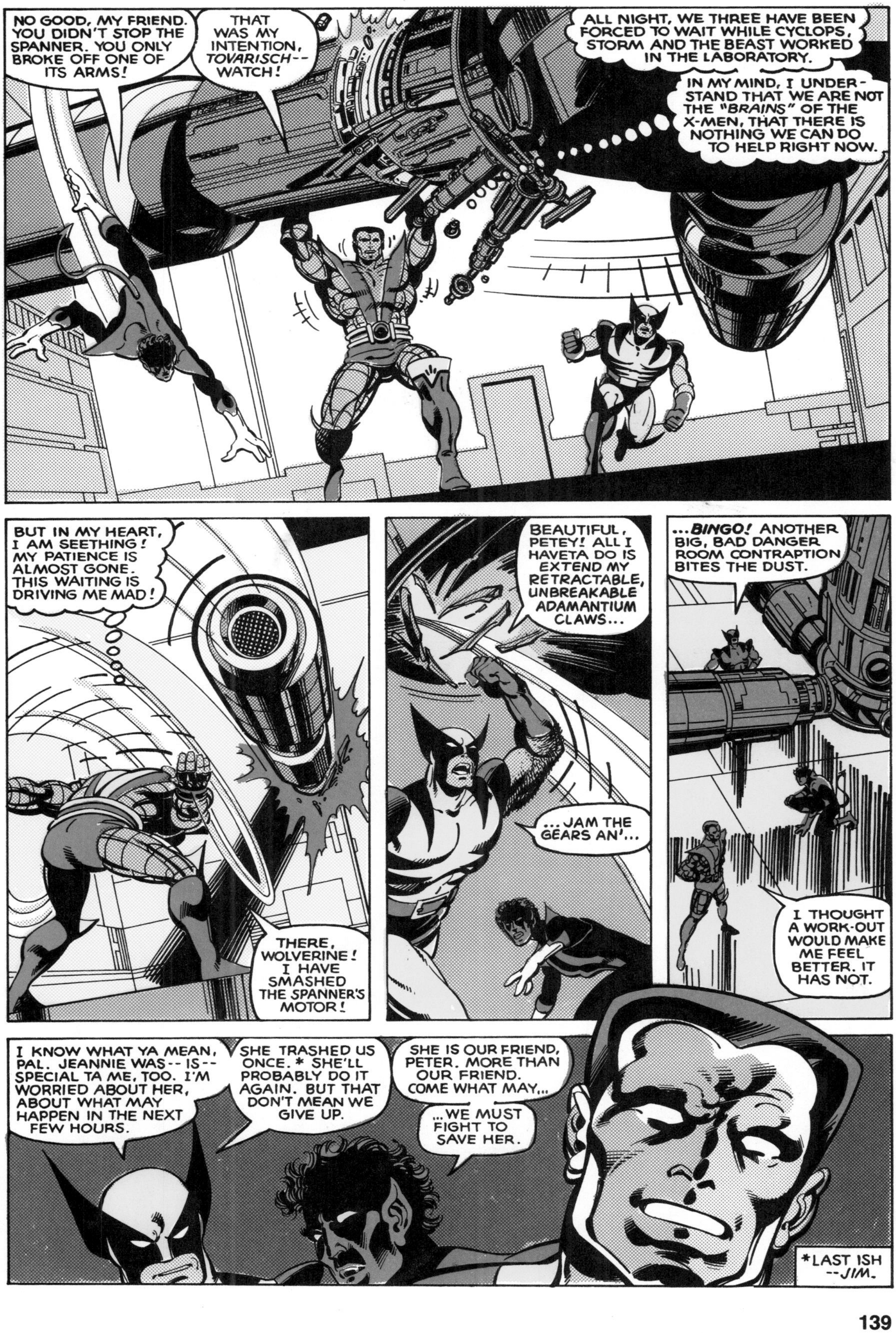
NO GOOD, MY FRIEND. YOU DIDN'T STOP THE SPANNER. YOU ONLY BROKE OFF ONE OF ITS ARMS!
THAT WAS MY INTENTION, TOVARISCH-- WATCH!
ALL NIGHT, WE THREE HAVE BEEN FORCED TO WAIT WHILE CYCLOPS, STORM AND THE BEAST WORKED IN THE LABORATORY.
IN MY MIND, I UNDERSTAND THAT WE ARE NOT THE "BRAINS" OF THE X-MEN, THAT THERE IS NOTHING WE CAN DO TO HELP RIGHT NOW.
BUT IN MY HEART, I AM SEETHING! MY PATIENCE IS ALMOST GONE. THIS WAITING IS DRIVING ME MAD!
THERE, WOLVERINE! I HAVE SMASHED THE SPANNER'S MOTOR!
BEAUTIFUL, PETEY! ALL I HAVETA DO IS EXTEND MY RETRACTABLE, UNBREAKABLE ADAMANTIUM CLAWS...
...JAM THE GEARS AN'...
...BINGO! ANOTHER BIG, BAD DANGER ROOM CONTRAPTION BITES THE DUST.
I THOUGHT A WORK-OUT WOULD MAKE ME FEEL BETTER. IT HAS NOT.
I KNOW WHAT YA MEAN, PAL. JEANNIE WAS-- IS-- SPECIAL TA ME, TOO. I'M WORRIED ABOUT HER, ABOUT WHAT MAY HAPPEN IN THE NEXT FEW HOURS.
SHE TRASHED US ONCE.* SHE'LL PROBABLY DO IT AGAIN. BUT THAT DON'T MEAN WE GIVE UP.
SHE IS OUR FRIEND, PETER. MORE THAN OUR FRIEND. COME WHAT MAY,...
...WE MUST FIGHT TO SAVE HER.
*LAST ISH --JIM.

ANNANDALE-ON-HUDSON, NEW YORK-- A SLEEPY LITTLE COLLEGE HAMLET SOME 50 MILES (AS THE PROVERBIAL CROW FLIES) NORTHWEST OF THE X-MEN'S MANSION/HEADQUARTERS.

THIS HOUSE ON ANNANDALE ROAD IS WHERE JEAN GREY WAS BORN, WHERE SHE GREW UP.

SHE RETURNS AS-- Dark Phoenix.

SHE LEFT HERE YEARS AGO TO BECOME THE X-MAN, MARVEL GIRL.

FOR A TIME, THE YOUNG GODDESS STANDS, UNMOVING, IN THE FRONT YARD, WONDERING WHY SHE CAME BACK HERE.

THEN...

CREEEAK

THE LOOK, THE SMELL, THE FEEL OF EVERYTHING IS FAMILIAR, UNCHANGED. AND YET, THESE MEMORIES AND EXPERIENCES NOW SEEM TO BELONG TO SOMEONE ELSE.

THIS IS JEAN GREY'S HOME, NOT DARK PHOENIX'S.

JEAN GREY IS A GENTLE, LOVING WOMAN WHO CARED SO MUCH FOR THOSE SHE LOVED THAT SHE DEFIED DEATH ITSELF TO SAVE THEM. PHOENIX IS A DESTROYER OF WORLDS WHO CARES ONLY FOR HERSELF.

YET JEAN GREY IS DARK PHOENIX.

SHE WAS ONCE ALL THAT IS GREAT IN HUMANITY. SHE HAS BECOME ALL THAT IS TERRIBLE.

WHO'S THERE?!

WOULD YOU BELIEVE, THE WICKED WITCH OF THE WEST?

EH?! THAT VOICE! IT CAN'T BE--!

JEAN!!

THIS IS FANTASTIC! MY GOODNESS, GIRL, WE HAVEN'T HEARD FROM YOU IN WEEKS! WHY DIDN'T YOU WRITE OR CALL?!

Oh, NO! PLEASE, NO! MY TELEPATHIC POWER IS SO SENSITIVE, I CAN'T BLOCK OUT DAD'S THOUGHTS. HE'S AN OPEN BOOK TO ME! NOTHING'S SECRET, NOTHING'S SACRED, ANYMORE!

ELAINE! SARAH! COME DOWNSTAIRS! LOOK WHO'S HERE!

HIYA, LITTLE SISTER. LONG TIME, NO SEE!

WOW! MOM WASN'T KIDDING, JEAN. YOU *HAVE* CHANGED!

IT'S WONDERFUL TO SEE YOU, DEAR.

IT'S THE SAME WITH MOM AND SARAH, TOO! I CAN'T HELP READING THEIR MINDS!

I WAS... IN THE NEIGHBORHOOD. I THOUGHT I'D DROP IN.

THAT COSTUME...! IT'S TRUE, THEN, WHAT MOM TOLD ME? YOU *ARE* SOME KIND OF SUPER HERO.

YOU LOOK THIN, JEAN. ARE YOU EATING ENOUGH?

I'M FINE, MOM.

I'M *NOT* FINE! GET OUT OF MY MIND, ALL OF YOU! GET OUT! *GET OUT!!*

I NEVER SHOULD HAVE COME HERE. I CAN *"READ"* MOM'S LOVE FOR ME, HER CONCERN. BUT BENEATH THAT, ON A PRIMAL LEVEL-- BURIED SO DEEPLY SHE PROBABLY ISN'T EVEN AWARE THE FEELING EXISTS-- SHE'S SCARED OF ME.

IT'S AWFULLY LATE FOR AN IMPROMPTU VISIT, JEAN. IS ANYTHING WRONG?

DAD'S WORRIED ABOUT ME, BUT HE'S AS EDGY AS MOM.

AND SARAH'S *TERRIFIED.* SHE HAS TWO KIDS. SHE KNOWS NOW THAT I'M A MUTANT. SHE'S WONDERING IF THEY'RE MUTANTS TOO-- IF THEY'LL TURN OUT LIKE ME.

WELL, WHAT'S SO WRONG WITH THAT?! I AM DARK PHOENIX. I AM *POWER INCARNATE!*

I HOLD THE FATE OF THE *UNIVERSE* IN MY HANDS!

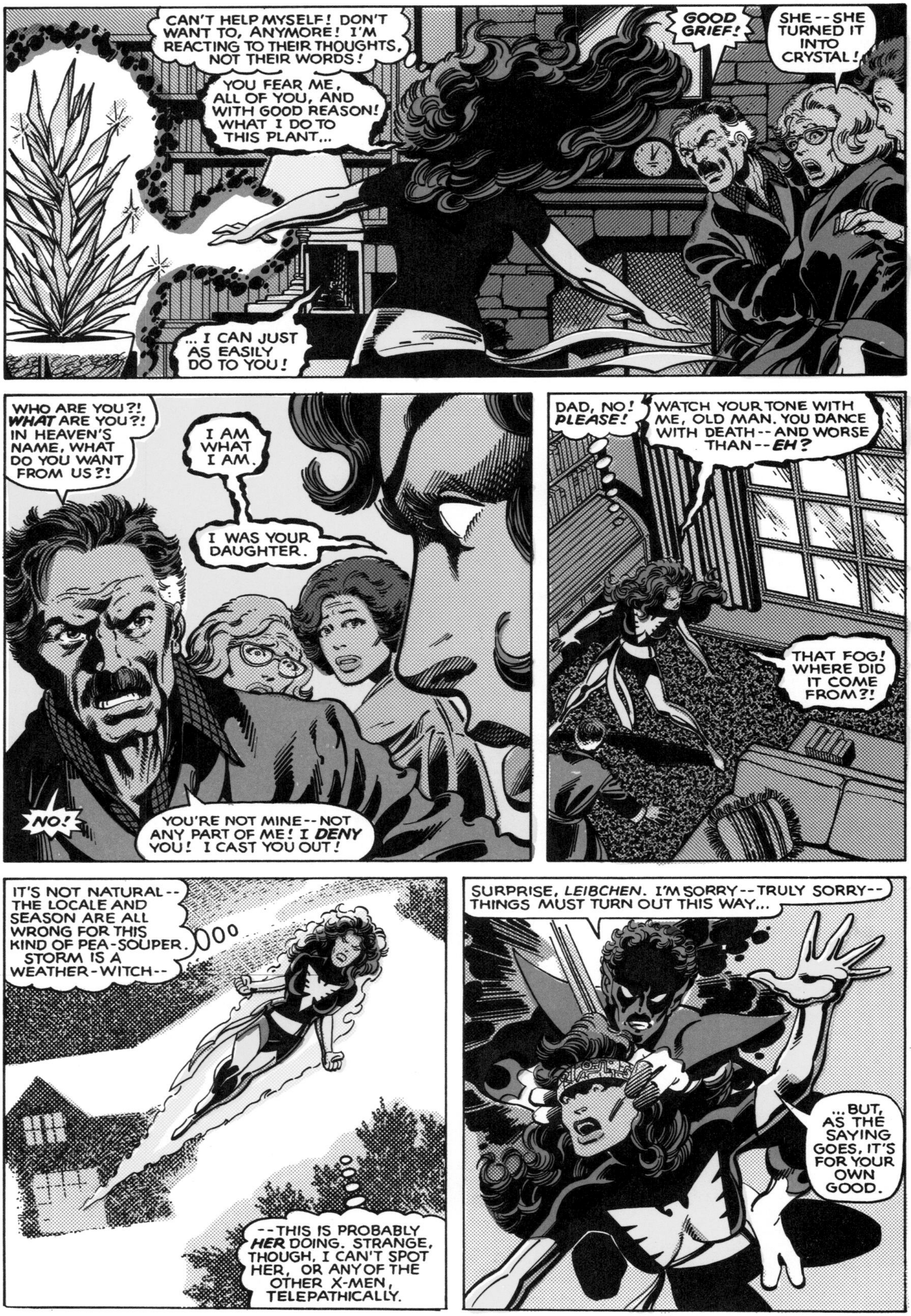

CAN'T HELP MYSELF! DON'T WANT TO, ANYMORE! I'M REACTING TO THEIR THOUGHTS, NOT THEIR WORDS!
YOU FEAR ME, ALL OF YOU, AND WITH GOOD REASON! WHAT I DO TO THIS PLANT...
...I CAN JUST AS EASILY DO TO YOU!
GOOD GRIEF!
SHE--SHE TURNED IT INTO CRYSTAL!
WHO ARE YOU?! WHAT ARE YOU?! IN HEAVEN'S NAME, WHAT DO YOU WANT FROM US?!
I AM WHAT I AM.
I WAS YOUR DAUGHTER.
NO!
YOU'RE NOT MINE--NOT ANY PART OF ME! I DENY YOU! I CAST YOU OUT!
DAD, NO! PLEASE!
WATCH YOUR TONE WITH ME, OLD MAN. YOU DANCE WITH DEATH--AND WORSE THAN--EH?
THAT FOG! WHERE DID IT COME FROM?!
IT'S NOT NATURAL--THE LOCALE AND SEASON ARE ALL WRONG FOR THIS KIND OF PEA-SOUPER. STORM IS A WEATHER-WITCH--
--THIS IS PROBABLY HER DOING. STRANGE, THOUGH, I CAN'T SPOT HER, OR ANY OF THE OTHER X-MEN, TELEPATHICALLY.
SURPRISE, LEIBCHEN. I'M SORRY--TRULY SORRY--THINGS MUST TURN OUT THIS WAY...
...BUT, AS THE SAYING GOES, IT'S FOR YOUR OWN GOOD.

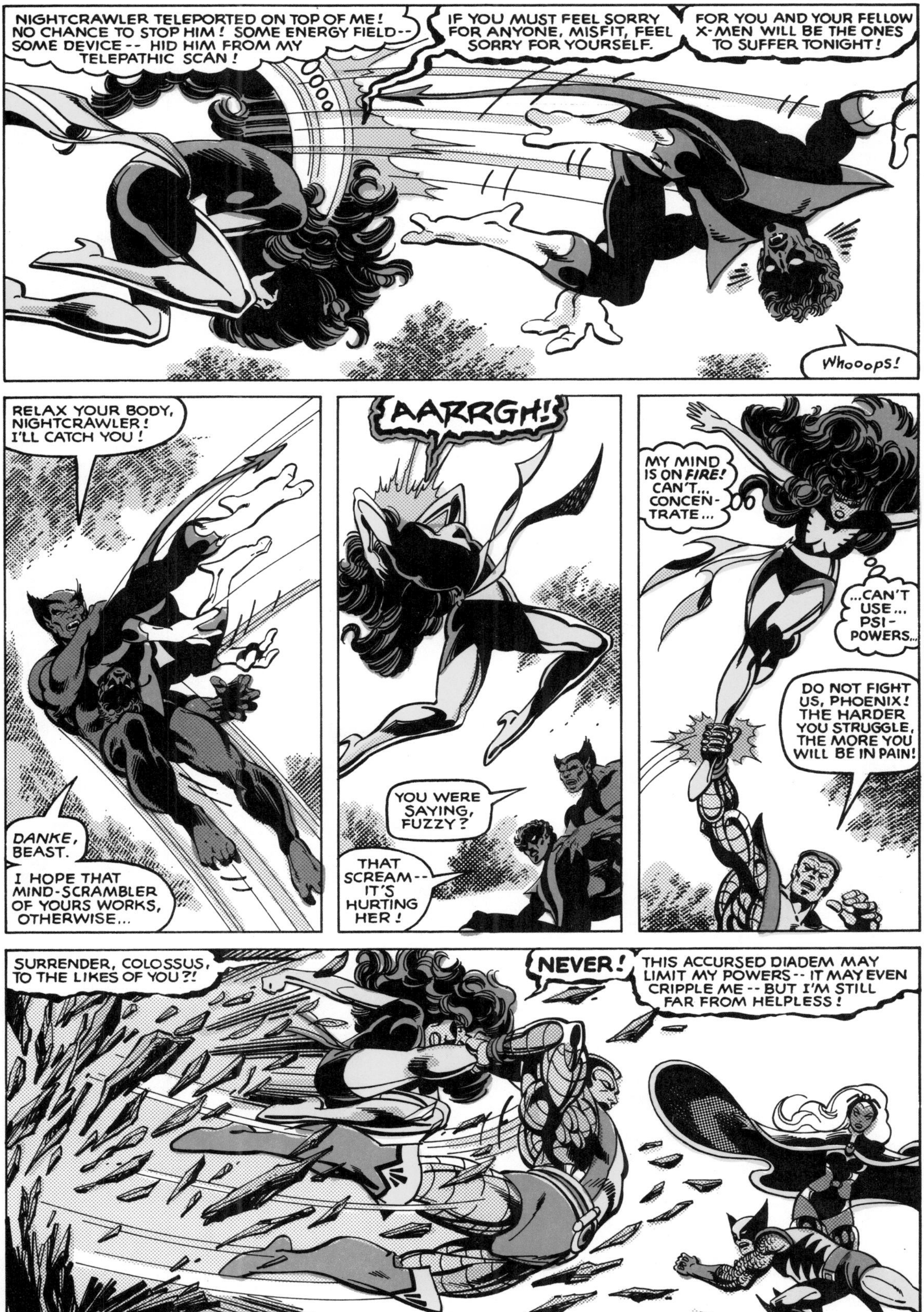

NIGHTCRAWLER TELEPORTED ON TOP OF ME! NO CHANCE TO STOP HIM! SOME ENERGY FIELD-- SOME DEVICE -- HID HIM FROM MY TELEPATHIC SCAN!
IF YOU MUST FEEL SORRY FOR ANYONE, MISFIT, FEEL SORRY FOR YOURSELF.
FOR YOU AND YOUR FELLOW X-MEN WILL BE THE ONES TO SUFFER TONIGHT!
Whooops!
RELAX YOUR BODY, NIGHTCRAWLER! I'LL CATCH YOU!
DANKE, BEAST.
I HOPE THAT MIND-SCRAMBLER OF YOURS WORKS, OTHERWISE...
AARRGH!
YOU WERE SAYING, FUZZY?
THAT SCREAM -- IT'S HURTING HER!
MY MIND IS ON FIRE! CAN'T... CONCEN-TRATE...
...CAN'T USE... PSI-POWERS...
DO NOT FIGHT US, PHOENIX! THE HARDER YOU STRUGGLE, THE MORE YOU WILL BE IN PAIN!
SURRENDER, COLOSSUS, TO THE LIKES OF YOU?!
NEVER!
THIS ACCURSED DIADEM MAY LIMIT MY POWERS -- IT MAY EVEN CRIPPLE ME -- BUT I'M STILL FAR FROM HELPLESS!

SHE WON'T YIELD! NO MORE THAN ANY OF US WOULD, WERE OUR POSITIONS REVERSED. EVIL THOUGH DARK PHOENIX IS...

...SHE IS STILL JEAN GREY, WITH ALL OF JEAN'S STRENGTH AND COURAGE.

YOU ARE CLOSER TO ME THAN MY OWN SISTER, STORM, YET I WON'T HESITATE TO STRIKE YOU DOWN.

I DON'T WANT THIS, JEAN! NONE OF US DO!

IN THE NAME OF THE LOVE WE SHARE--

--LET US *HELP* YOU!

IN THE NAME OF THE LOVE WE SHARED, ORORO --

-- I WILL WEEP OVER YOUR GRAVE.

UNNNGNH!!

TEMPER, TEMPER, CARROT-TOP!

BEAST!

WE'RE RUNNING OUT OF TIME! MY SCRAMBLER-DIADEM'S GLOWING -- JEAN'S FIGHTING ITS EFFECTS, DRAWING ON MORE AND MORE RAW POWER. SHE'S BURNING IT OUT!

HOLD HER OFF-BALANCE FOR A MOMENT LONGER, BUB, AN' I'LL SETTLE THIS FRACAS...

...THE ONLY WAY IT *CAN* BE SETTLED.

WOLVERINE -- WHAT'RE YOU *DOING?!?*

EV'RYONE ELSE IS HOLDIN' BACK.

THEY KEEP THINKIN' OF DARK PHOENIX AS JEANNIE. THEY'RE TRYIN' TA CAPTURE HER WITHOUT HURTIN' HER ANY MORE THAN THEY HAVE TO. BUT THAT WON'T WORK. EVEN WITH THE BEAST'S FRAMMISTAT CHOPPIN' HER POWER...

... SHE'S STILL TOO STRONG FER US -- AN' GETTIN' STRONGER ALL THE TIME. I GOT NO CHOICE. I GOTTA END THIS -- NOW! *PERMANENTLY!*

FORGIVE ME, DARLIN'.

SNIKT

D-DO IT, WOLVERINE!

STRIKE! WHILE THE HUMAN PART OF ME IS STILL IN CONTROL. FINISH ME WITH YOUR CLAWS, I BEG YOU... I DON'T WANT TO--

--HURT YOU!!

FOR AN INSTANT *JEAN* WAS BACK... I COULDN'T...

WHOULLMPGH!

WHAT A PITY, HANK. I'VE *OVERLOADED* YOUR PRECIOUS SCRAMBLER.

THIS WAS AN ADMIRABLE PLOY, X-MEN...

...BUT A PLOY THAT *FAILED.*

WITH A THOUGHT, SHE FREEZES THE FIVE OF THEM WHERE THEY STAND, INSTANTLY TRANSFORMING THEM INTO LIVING STATUES.

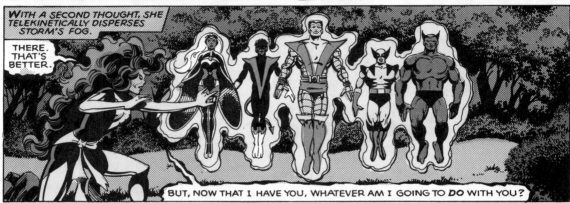

WITH A SECOND THOUGHT, SHE TELEKINETICALLY DISPERSES STORM'S FOG.

THERE. THAT'S BETTER.

BUT, NOW THAT I HAVE YOU, WHATEVER AM I GOING TO *DO* WITH YOU?

JEAN, IF THERE IS ANYTHING *HUMAN* REMAINING WITHIN YOU,...

THERE ISN'T.

...*HEAR ME!* REMEMBER WHAT YOU WERE, WHAT YOU MEANT TO US AND WE, TO YOU. I...

HUSH, COLOSSUS. YOUR APPEAL IS HEARD -- AND *DENIED.*

ANY LAST THOUGHTS, "*LITTLE BROTHER,*" BEFORE FINAL SENTENCE IS PASSED?

AIIIEARRGH!

STOP IT, JEAN.

CYCLOPS!

I WAS WONDERING WHEN YOU'D TURN UP.

"HAVE YOU COME TO FIGHT?"

"I HOPE SO."

"I CAME TO *TALK*. I WON'T *LISTEN!*"

"THEN, KILL ME. I CAN'T STOP YOU. I WON'T EVEN *TRY*. BE TRUE TO YOUR MALEFIC DESTINY, PHOENIX-- *KILL ME...*"

"...IF YOU *CAN*."

"BUT IF YOU CAN'T, THEN ASK YOURSELF WHY. YOU'RE DARK PHOENIX-- POWER INCARNATE. NO FORCE IN EXISTENCE CAN STAND AGAINST YOU. THE X-MEN HAVE DEFIED YOU, FOUGHT YOU-- YET WE LIVE."

"WHY?!"

"YOU'RE ...NOT WORTH KILLING."

"THAT'S ONE ANSWER. BUT THERE'S ANOTHER. TRUE, YOU'RE DARK PHOENIX, BUT YOU'RE ALSO STILL *JEAN GREY*. NO MATTER HOW HARD YOU TRY, YOU CAN'T EXORCISE THAT PART OF YOURSELF. IT'S TOO FUNDAMENTAL.

YOU CAN'T KILL US BECAUSE YOU *LOVE* US. AND WE LOVE *YOU*."

"DARK PHOENIX KNOWS *NOTHING* OF LOVE!"

"Oh? FOR LOVE OF THE X-MEN, YOU SACRIFICED YOUR LIFE. FOR LOVE OF ME, YOU RESURRECTED YOURSELF. FOR LOVE OF THE WHOLE UNIVERSE, YOU ALMOST DIED A SECOND TIME TO SAVE IT.

KNOW NOTHING OF LOVE?! JEAN, YOU *ARE* LOVE!"

"YOUR EXISTENCE, YOUR VERY *CREATION*, SPRINGS FROM LOVE, FROM THE *NOBLEST* EMOTIONS A HUMAN CAN ATTAIN.

AND NOW, YOU WANT TO *DENY* THAT? TO DENY *YOURSELF?*"

"YES!"

"NO."

"I... *HUNGER*, SCOTT--FOR A JOY, A RAPTURE, BEYOND ALL COMPREHENSION. THAT NEED IS A PART OF ME, TOO.

IT... *CONSUMES* ME."

IT DOESN'T HAVE TO. TRUST ME. LET ME HELP-- JEAN!!

≥OHH!!≤

PROFESSOR XAVIER?!? WHAT HAVE YOU DONE!?!

WHILE YOU DISTRACTED HER, I WAS ABLE TO APPROACH AND MIND-BLAST PHONIX. I-I HAD NO ALTERNATIVE.

NOW STAND ASIDE--AT ONCE! I DO NOT WISH YOU TO BE HURT.

YOU HEARD OUR "MENTOR," MY LOVE, AWAY WITH YOU!

≥URRRGH!≤

MEDDLING OLD FOOL--

--YOU HAVE JUST SIGNED YOUR DEATH WARRANT!

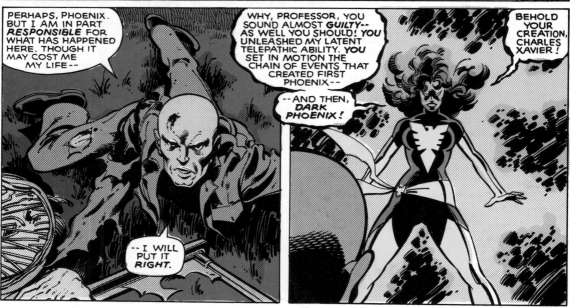

PERHAPS, PHOENIX. BUT I AM IN PART RESPONSIBLE FOR WHAT HAS HAPPENED HERE. THOUGH IT MAY COST ME MY LIFE--

-- I WILL PUT IT RIGHT.

WHY, PROFESSOR, YOU SOUND ALMOST GUILTY-- AS WELL YOU SHOULD! YOU UNLEASHED MY LATENT TELEPATHIC ABILITY. YOU SET IN MOTION THE CHAIN OF EVENTS THAT CREATED FIRST PHOENIX--

--AND THEN, DARK PHOENIX!

BEHOLD YOUR CREATION, CHARLES XAVIER!

I AM WHAT WAS, WHAT IS, WHAT WILL BE-- THE BLACK ANGEL, *CHAOS-BRINGER!* I-- AM-- POWER!

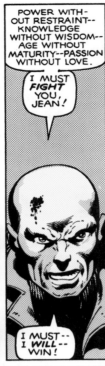

POWER WITHOUT RESTRAINT-- KNOWLEDGE WITHOUT WISDOM-- AGE WITHOUT MATURITY--PASSION WITHOUT LOVE.

I MUST *FIGHT* YOU, JEAN!

I MUST-- I *WILL*-- WIN!

WILL YOU?

THE PHOENIX RISES, THE *PSI-WAR* BEGINS! THE INSANE YOUNG TELEPATH...

... VERSUS HER TEACHER...

... IN A DEATH-DUEL BETWEEN THE STRONGEST MUTANT MINDS ON EARTH.

THE STRUGGLE IS *EPIC*--

--WAGED SIMULTANEOUSLY ON ALL THE INFINITE PLANES OF EXISTENCE.

NOT LONG AGO, YET FOR JEAN, A *LIFETIME* AGO, PHOENIX BOUND A ROGUE NEUTRON GALAXY WITHIN A STASIS-FIELD OF LIVING ANTI-ENERGY, THEREBY PREVENTING THAT ULTIMATE *BLACK HOLE* FROM DESTROYING THE ENTIRE UNIVERSE.

NOW, IN MUCH THE SAME WAY, CHARLES XAVIER SEEKS TO BIND DARK PHOENIX ONCE MORE...

...WITHIN AN UNBREACHABLE NETWORK OF PSIONIC CIRCUIT BREAKERS.

THE END COMES SUDDENLY. ONE MOMENT, THE PHOENIX-EFFECT IS LIGHTING UP THE COUNTRYSIDE LIKE A SMALL SUN.

JEAN!!

THE NEXT, JEAN GREY COLLAPSES TO THE GROUND LIKE A PUPPET WITH ITS STRINGS CUT.

WOULD... HAVE LOST-- BUT I ... SENSED JEAN... FIGHTING HER PHOENIX-SELF... *HELPING* ME...

BLESS YOU, CHILD. I AM ...SO *PROUD* OF YOU...

JEAN? SHE'S SO STILL. I'M NOT EVEN SURE SHE'S ALIVE. I WANT HER TO LIVE--

--BUT WHAT IF SHE HASN'T CHANGED? WHAT IF SHE'S STILL DARK PHOENIX?!

I'LL *LOVE* HER JUST THE SAME.

FOR BETTER, WORSE, RICHER, POORER, SICKNESS, HEALTH-- TILL DEATH DO US PART.

HI.

H-HI, YOUR-SELF.

IF I DIDN'T KNOW BETTER, I'D SAY THOSE THOUGHTS I JUST PICKED UP SOUNDED LIKE A *PROPOSAL.*

THEY DID, DIDN'T THEY?

WHAT DO YOU SAY, RED?

I SAY, YES!

NEXT ISSUE: THE END OF AN EPIC -- A 35 -PAGE MASTERWORK!

The FATE of THE PHOENIX!

Seventeen years ago, this month, *Stan Lee* and *Jack Kirby* chronicled the first adventure of one of the strangest super hero teams ever created — and a *legend* was born! Today, *Chris Claremont*, *John Byrne* and *Terry Austin* proudly celebrate that anniversary and *reaffirm* that legend!

Stan Lee PRESENTS: THE UNCANNY X-MEN!™

I AM -- THE WATCHER!

SINCE *TIME IMMEMORIAL*, I AND OTHERS OF MY RACE HAVE BEHELD THE MYRIAD WONDERS OF THE UNIVERSE. OUR CHARGE -- OUR MOST SACRED TRUST -- IS THAT WE EVER OBSERVE, BUT *NEVER* INTERFERE.

YEARS AGO, I BEHELD THE BIRTH OF *JEAN GREY*. I WATCHED HER GROW FROM CHILD TO WOMAN, WATCHED HER TAKE HER DESTINED PLACE AS ONE OF THE *X-MEN*. I SAW HER *DIE*...

... AND I SAW HER *REBORN* AS PHOENIX! THOUGH SHE DID NOT KNOW IT THEN, JEAN HAD BECOME *ONE* WITH A PRIMAL FORCE SECOND ONLY TO THAT OF THE *CREATOR*. IT WAS MORE POWER THAN SHE -- OR ANY HUMAN -- COULD EVER HOPE TO CONTROL. IN TIME, IT TWISTED AND WARPED HER SOUL -- UNTIL PHOENIX WAS TRANSFIGURED INTO *DARK PHOENIX!*

THE X-MEN FOUGHT TO SAVE THEIR FRIEND, TO RETURN JEAN GREY TO HER HUMANITY, AND AFTER AN EPIC STRUGGLE, THEY *SUCCEEDED*. BUT THEN, AT THE VERY MOMENT OF THEIR TRIUMPH, THE X-MEN *VANISHED* FROM THE FACE OF THE EARTH.

THIS DRAMA'S FINAL ACT IS ABOUT TO BEGIN. BEFORE IT IS ENDED, THESE YOUNG MUTANTS WILL BE PUT TO THE *ULTIMATE* TEST. IF THEY ARE FOUND WANTING, THE ENTIRE *UNIVERSE* MAY WELL PAY THE PRICE.

153

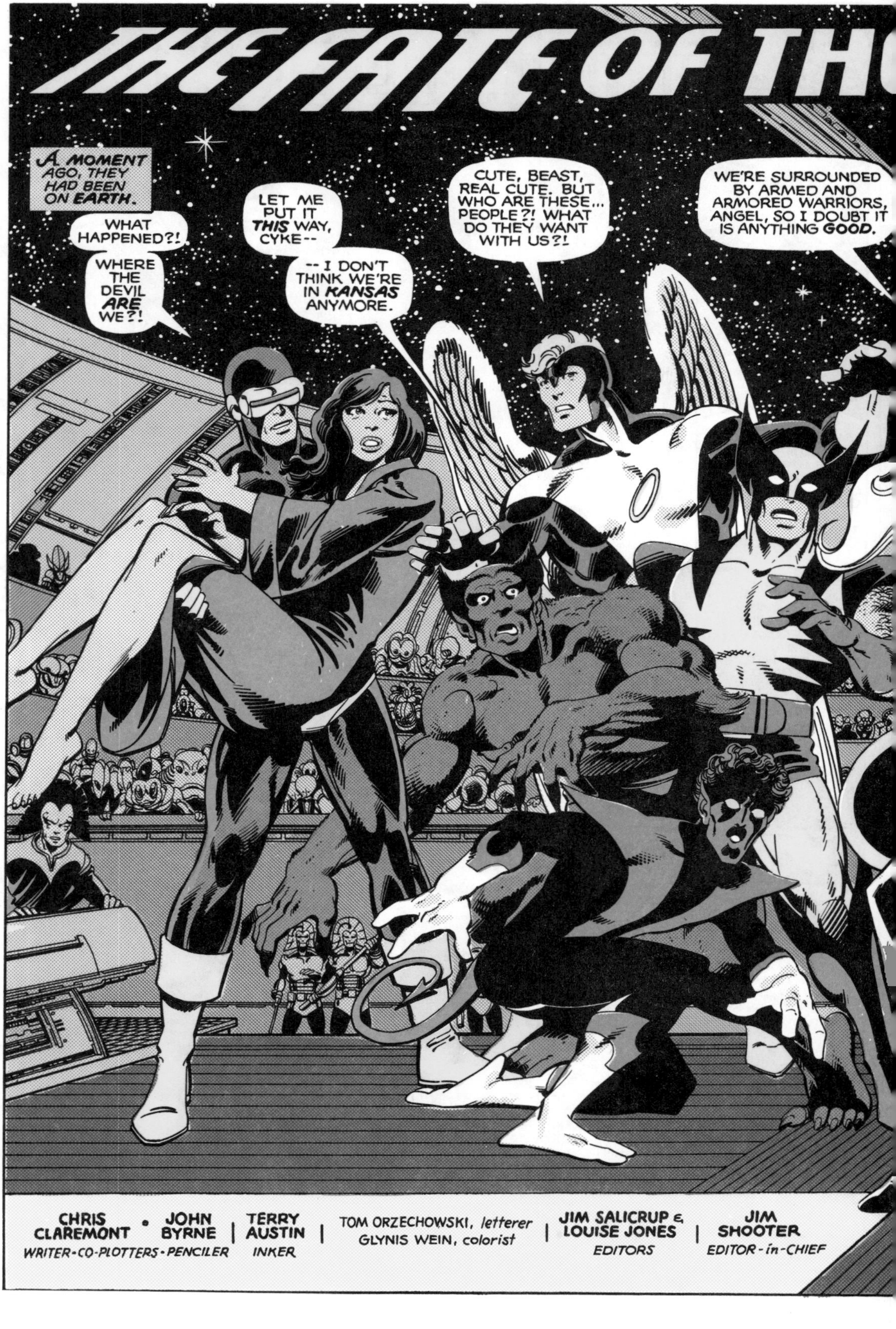
THE FATE OF TH
A MOMENT AGO, THEY HAD BEEN ON EARTH.
WHAT HAPPENED?!
WHERE THE DEVIL ARE WE?!
LET ME PUT IT THIS WAY, CYKE--
-- I DON'T THINK WE'RE IN KANSAS ANYMORE.
CUTE, BEAST, REAL CUTE. BUT WHO ARE THESE... PEOPLE?! WHAT DO THEY WANT WITH US?!
WE'RE SURROUNDED BY ARMED AND ARMORED WARRIORS, ANGEL, SO I DOUBT IT IS ANYTHING GOOD.
CHRIS CLAREMONT • JOHN BYRNE
WRITER-CO-PLOTTERS-PENCILER
TERRY AUSTIN
INKER
TOM ORZECHOWSKI, letterer
GLYNIS WEIN, colorist
JIM SALICRUP & LOUISE JONES
EDITORS
JIM SHOOTER
EDITOR-in-CHIEF

PHOENIX!

PROFESSOR XAVIER, I DO NOT UNDERSTAND. WE WERE IN THE GARDEN OF JEAN'S PARENT'S HOUSE...

AND, NOW, WE ARE ON THE CARGO DECK OF A SHI'AR IMPERIAL DREADNOUGHT. I RECOGNIZE IT. THIS IS THE FLAGSHIP OF LILANDRA'S GRAND FLEET!

AND IF IT IS HERE, THEN LILANDRA-- THE WOMAN I LOVE-- CANNOT BE FAR...!

X-MEN! HEED THE WORDS OF GLADIATOR, PRAETOR OF THE IMPERIAL GUARD!

YOU STAND IN THE PRESENCE OF LILANDRA-- MAJESTRIX SHI'AR, EMPRESS!

YOUR FATE IS IN HER HANDS!

LILANDRA?! WHAT'S THIS ALL ABOUT?!

THE X-MEN WERE YOUR FRIENDS! WHY HAVE YOU KIDNAPPED US?!

TRUE, CYCLOPS. THE X-MEN *ARE* MY FRIENDS. I OWE YOU MY LIFE, MY FREEDOM, MY THRONE-- MORE THAN I CAN EVER REPAY. BUT, AS EMPRESS, MY FIRST RESPONSIBILITY IS TO MY PEOPLE.

TO ENSURE THEIR SAFETY-- TO ENSURE THE SAFETY OF THE ENTIRE UNIVERSE--

-- PHOENIX MUST BE *DESTROYED!*

PHOENIX?! *ME?!*

WHY?!?

AS I RECALL, LILANDRA, PHOENIX STOPPED YOUR *BROTHER* FROM SINGLE-HANDEDLY DESTROYING THE UNIVERSE. *

IS THIS HOW YOU REPAY HER?!

*X-MEN #108--JIM.

WE HAD NO QUARREL WITH PHOENIX THEN, CYCLOPS. SHE SEEMED A *BENEFICENT* ENTITY. THOUGH WE SUSPECTED THE FULL EXTENT OF HER POWER-- AND *FEARED* IT-- WE DID NOTHING.

WE BELIEVED-- *I* BELIEVED-- THAT JEAN COULD COPE WITH HER NEAR-INFINITE ABILITIES. I WAS WRONG.

GLADIATOR-- CONTINUE.

WHEN PHOENIX RETURNED TO SHI'AR SPACE, SHE WAS NO LONGER BENEFICENT. SHE HAD BEEN TRANS-FORMED INTO THE BLACK ANGEL OF LEGEND-- *CHAOS-BRINGER*--

--RAVAGER OF WORLDS.

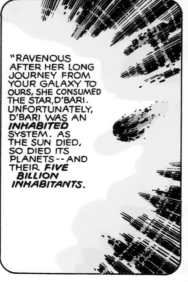

"RAVENOUS AFTER HER LONG JOURNEY FROM YOUR GALAXY TO OURS, SHE CONSUMED THE STAR, D'BARI. UNFORTUNATELY, D'BARI WAS AN *INHABITED* SYSTEM. AS THE SUN DIED, SO DIED ITS PLANETS-- AND THEIR *FIVE BILLION INHABITANTS.*

"A SHI'AR WARSHIP INTERCEPTED PHOENIX, AND FOUGHT HER.

"SHE DESTROYED IT, AS WELL, BEFORE RETURNING TO EARTH." *

* SEE X-MEN #135 -- JIM.

156

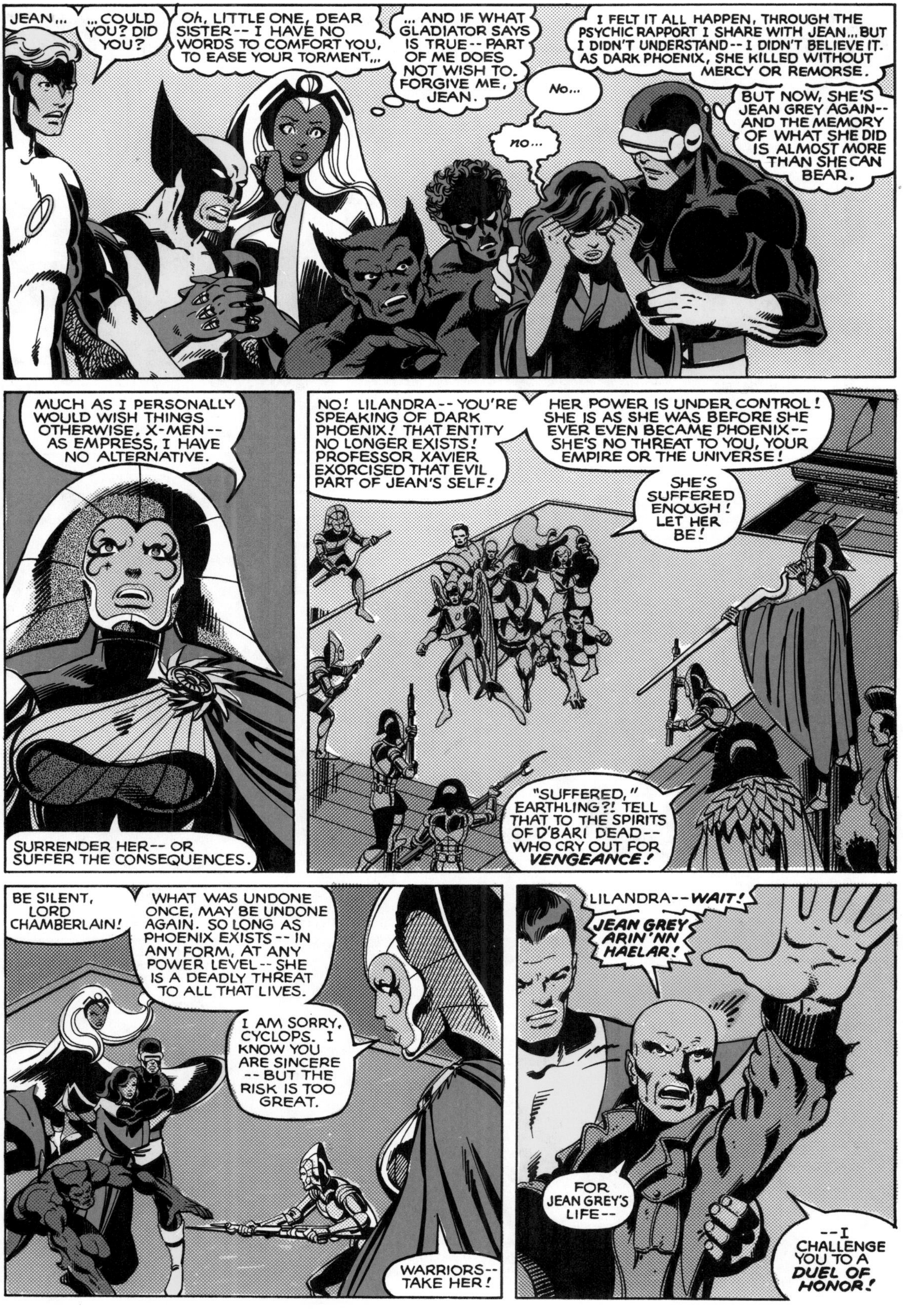
JEAN...
...COULD YOU? DID YOU?
Oh, LITTLE ONE, DEAR SISTER-- I HAVE NO WORDS TO COMFORT YOU, TO EASE YOUR TORMENT...
...AND IF WHAT GLADIATOR SAYS IS TRUE-- PART OF ME DOES NOT WISH TO. FORGIVE ME, JEAN.
No...
no...
I FELT IT ALL HAPPEN, THROUGH THE PSYCHIC RAPPORT I SHARE WITH JEAN... BUT I DIDN'T UNDERSTAND -- I DIDN'T BELIEVE IT. AS DARK PHOENIX, SHE KILLED WITHOUT MERCY OR REMORSE.
BUT NOW, SHE'S JEAN GREY AGAIN-- AND THE MEMORY OF WHAT SHE DID IS ALMOST MORE THAN SHE CAN BEAR.
MUCH AS I PERSONALLY WOULD WISH THINGS OTHERWISE, X-MEN-- AS EMPRESS, I HAVE NO ALTERNATIVE.
SURRENDER HER-- OR SUFFER THE CONSEQUENCES.
NO! LILANDRA-- YOU'RE SPEAKING OF DARK PHOENIX! THAT ENTITY NO LONGER EXISTS! PROFESSOR XAVIER EXORCISED THAT EVIL PART OF JEAN'S SELF!
HER POWER IS UNDER CONTROL! SHE IS AS SHE WAS BEFORE SHE EVER EVEN BECAME PHOENIX-- SHE'S NO THREAT TO YOU, YOUR EMPIRE OR THE UNIVERSE!
SHE'S SUFFERED ENOUGH! LET HER BE!
"SUFFERED," EARTHLING?! TELL THAT TO THE SPIRITS OF D'BARI DEAD-- WHO CRY OUT FOR VENGEANCE!
BE SILENT, LORD CHAMBERLAIN!
WHAT WAS UNDONE ONCE, MAY BE UNDONE AGAIN. SO LONG AS PHOENIX EXISTS -- IN ANY FORM, AT ANY POWER LEVEL-- SHE IS A DEADLY THREAT TO ALL THAT LIVES.
I AM SORRY, CYCLOPS. I KNOW YOU ARE SINCERE -- BUT THE RISK IS TOO GREAT.
WARRIORS-- TAKE HER!
LILANDRA--WAIT!
JEAN GREY ARIN'NN HAELAR!
FOR JEAN GREY'S LIFE--
--I CHALLENGE YOU TO A DUEL OF HONOR!

MAGNIFICENT, CHARLES. YOU LEARNED *MUCH* ABOUT THE SHI'AR DURING YOUR TOO-BRIEF STAY ON MY HOMEWORLD. THE *"ARIN'NN HAELAR"* IS THE ONE CHALLENGE THAT *CANNOT* BE REFUSED.

CHARLES, MY BELOVED, HAD THE FATES WEAVED A DIFFERENT TAPESTRY, WE MIGHT HAVE HAD THE STARS. INSTEAD, WE FACE NOTHING BUT THE ASHES OF DYING DREAMS.

WELL, EMPRESS? DO YOU ACCEPT?

MAJESTRIX, THE *KREE* AGREED THAT THIS PHOENIX-ENTITY BE EXPUNGED. NOTHING WAS SAID OF ANY *"DUEL OF HONOR."*

EXCUSE ME, CHARLES. IT SEEMS I MUST CONSULT WITH MY... ALLIES.

AND SO, AFTER A COMMUNICATIONS INSTA-LINK HAS BEEN ESTABLISHED BETWEEN LILANDRA'S FLAGSHIP AND THE THRONEWORLDS OF THE KREE AND SKRULL EMPIRES-- FEUDING GALACTIC STATES AS ANCIENT AND MIGHTY AS THE SHI'AR...

THE X-MEN WILL FIGHT, REGARDLESS. THESE TERRANS ARE A STUBBORN BREED-- BUT *HONORABLE.* THEIR WORD CAN BE TRUSTED.

THE SUPREME INTELLIGENCE OF THE KREE HAS NO OBJECTION TO THIS DUEL.

NOR DO I, RK'LLL, EMPRESS OF THE SKRULLS...

PROVIDED THAT THE X-MEN ARE NOT PERMITTED TO WIN.

AND, TO INSURE THIS, OUR REPRESENTATIVES ARE REQUIRED TO MONITOR THE BATTLE.

MY LEIGE, *NO!* I MUST STAND BESIDE THIS MIS-BEGOTTEN MATE OF A MUDWORM?! YOU ASK *TOO MUCH* OF ME!

THEN STAY BEHIND, SKRULL! THE PETTY BICKERING BETWEEN YOUR TWO ... ES DOES NOT CONCERN ME.

I AM HERE FOR ONE REASON: TO END FOREVER THE THREAT OF PHOENIX. HINDER ME IN ANY WAY, ALIEN--

--AND YOUR LIFE IS *FORFEIT!*

158

YOUR GAMBIT WAS SUCCESSFUL, CHARLES. I *ACCEPT* YOUR CHALLENGE.

I PRAY YOU WILL NOT LIVE TO *REGRET* WHAT YOU'VE DONE THIS DAY.

PROFESSOR XAVIER HAD NO RIGHT TO ISSUE THAT CHALLENGE IN *ALL* OUR NAMES WITH-OUT CONSULTING US...

...BUT IT DID BUY US TIME TO CONSIDER OUR ALTERNA-TIVES... WHETHER WE *WANT* TO FIGHT FOR HER.

HOW CAN WE LET ONE OF OUR OWN BE CONDEMNED WITHOUT A FAIR TRIAL -- OR ANY TRIAL AT ALL?

I THOUGHT YOU KNEW THE X-MEN BETTER THAN THAT, LILANDRA.

EASY, BEAST.

YOUR COURAGE AND LOYALTY DO YOU CREDIT, BEAST.

YOU WILL HAVE A DAY TO REST, TO RECOVER YOUR STRENGTH, TO PREPARE.

THE DUEL BEGINS AT *DAWN.*

JEAN GREY.

ONLY HOURS AGO -- IS THAT ALL? -- AS DARK PHOENIX, I HELD THE WHOLE UNIVERSE IN THE PALM OF MY HAND.

FOR A WHILE, I WAS ALMOST *GOD.*

I WAS TERRIBLE -- YET BEAUTIFUL. AN *ANGEL.* I DIDN'T WANT THAT AWESOME POWER. I DIDN'T MEAN TO DO WHAT I DID.

BUT I DID IT JUST THE SAME.

NOW, THE TIME HAS COME TO PAY THE PRICE.

GOD... MERCIFUL GOD, HELP ME. GIVE ME STRENGTH.

MILADY?

Eh?!

IS THIS THE GARMENT YOU REQUESTED?

IT IS. IT LOOKS FINE. LEAVE IT THERE, PLEASE. I'LL LET YOU KNOW IF THERE ARE ANY PROBLEMS.

I'D LIKE TO BE ALONE.

NIGHTCRAWLER.

FOR ALL BEAST'S BRAVADO, I'VE A NASTY FEELING THIS MAY BE THE BATTLE WHERE OUR LUCK RUNS OUT.

I AND THE OTHER NEW X-MEN HAVE FOUGHT THE IMPERIAL GUARD BEFORE. HE HAS NOT. THEY'RE ALIEN SUPER-BEINGS, WITH ABILITIES AS VARIED AND POWERFUL AS OUR OWN. THE LAST TIME WE MET, IT TOOK A MINOR *MIRACLE* FOR US TO DEFEAT THEM.

BUT THEN AGAIN, MIRACLES SEEM TO BE THE X-MEN'S STOCK IN TRADE. WHO KNOWS, WE MIGHT PULL OFF AN *UPSET* AT THAT.

I WISH I FELT AS CONFIDENT ABOUT THE *REASON* FOR THIS DUEL. I ONCE THOUGHT I WOULD DEFY THE *DEVIL* HIMSELF FOR JEAN. NOW... I'M NOT SO SURE.

AS A CHILD, IN THE CIRCUS, I KNEW PEOPLE WHO HAD SURVIVED THE *HOLOCAUST* -- THE NAZI DEATH CAMPS. I STILL CANNOT FORGIVE THE BUTCHERS RESPONSIBLE FOR THOSE ATROCITIES. HOW THEN CAN I FORGIVE JEAN ?!

I WISH I KNEW WHAT TO DO, WHICH WAY TO CHOOSE. PERHAPS A SHOWER WILL HELP ME DECIDE. THE WORKOUT CERTAINLY ISN'T DOING MUCH GOOD.

I COULD *TELEPORT* TO THE FLOOR -- BUT I THINK I'LL RUN DOWN THE WALL INSTEAD. IT'S MORE FUN.

EAT YOUR HEART OUT, SPIDER-MAN! ANYTHING YOU CAN CLIMB, I CAN CLIMB BETTER...

FUN? OH, WHAT'S THE USE... TRY THOUGH I MIGHT, I CAN'T GET JEAN FROM MY MIND!

‹WHOOPS!›

THE WALL IS A FRICTIONLESS SURFACE!

MY TOES AND FINGERS CAN'T GET A GRIP!

RELAX, CRAWLER, I'VE GOT YOU!

ANGEL!

THANKS! IT REALLY WASN'T NECESSARY. I COULD HAVE JUST AS EASILY TELEPORTED TO SAFETY.

NO PROBLEM. I NEEDED THE EXERCISE. I'VE BEEN *WARREN WORTHINGTON THE THIRD* -- BOY BILLIONAIRE -- TOO MUCH LATELY.

THE HIGH-FLYING ANGEL, ON THE OTHER HAND...

... IS A WEE BIT OUT OF SHAPE.

YOU SOUND SAD.

DO I? PERHAPS IT'S BECAUSE I'VE DISCOVERED *DOUBTS* WHERE I DIDN'T EXPECT TO FIND ANY. IN A FEW HOURS, WE'RE SUPPOSED TO FIGHT FOR JEAN -- AND I DON'T KNOW YET IF I CAN. AND THAT, KURT... THAT *HURTS.*

WOLVERINE:

NICE DIGS. AN OKAY PLACE TO SPEND THE NIGHT-- BUT I'D GO BATTY IF I WAS FORCED TO LIVE HERE.

'COURSE, THIS TIME TOMORROW, I MAY NOT HAVE'TA WORRY ABOUT LIVIN' *ANYWHERE*.

I AIN'T SCARED OF DYIN'-- NEVER HAVE BEEN. IT'LL HAPPEN TO ME ONE DAY, WHETHER I WANT IT TO OR NOT, SO WHY WASTE TIME WORRYIN' ABOUT IT.

AS FOR ANYTHING ELSE-- SHOOT, THERE AIN'T MUCH FOR A MAN WITH UNBREAK-ABLE ADAMANTIUM BONES AN' RAZOR-SHARP ADAMANTIUM CLAWS TO BE SCARED *OF*.

STILL... I'VE GOT A *BAD* FEELING ABOUT THIS FIGHT.

SNIKT!

NOBODY UNDERSTANDS JEANNIE LIKE I DO-- THAT SHE'S BECOME TWO *SEPARATE* ENTITIES: JEAN GREY, AN' PHOENIX.

JEAN AIN'T A KILLER. SHE CAN'T BE HELD RESPONSIBLE FOR PHOENIX'S ACTIONS.

BUT CAN THE PROFESSOR'VE REALLY SPLIT THE TWO ENTITIES APART...

... SUPRESSING PHOENIX AND LEAVING JEAN ? I HOPE SO. BUT IF PUSH COMES TA SHOVE -- IF I HAVETA MAKE A CHOICE --

-- I STAND BY JEANNIE ALL THE WAY!

BEAST:

IT'S BEEN A LONG TIME SINCE I LOST MY TEMPER LIKE THAT. BUT I'M NOT ABOUT TO BACK DOWN, EVEN IF I HAVE TO STAND ALONE.

THE *LAW* SEPARATES HUMANITY FROM ITS ANIMAL ANCESTORS.

AND, LIKE IT OR NOT, THE LAW PROTECTS *EVERYONE*-- GOOD, EVIL, VICTIM, CRIMINAL. IT *HAS* TO, OR IT-- AND CIVILIZATION-- AREN'T WORTH BEANS.

IF JEAN WERE SATAN INCARNATE, I'D STILL GRANT HER THE FULL BENEFIT OF THE LAW !

AFTER ALL, WE ONLY HAVE *LILANDRA'S* WORD FOR WHAT HAPPENED AND THAT PHOENIX STILL EXISTS INSIDE OF JEAN. IF SHE WANTS JEAN'S LIFE, SHE SHOULD PROVE HER CASE IN A PROPER COURT-- BEYOND A REASONABLE DOUBT--

--AND GIVE JEAN A CHANCE TO DEFEND HERSELF. LILANDRA'S EXERCISE IN RAW, NAKED POWER-- MIGHT MAKING RIGHT-- IS AS REPRE-HENSIBLE IN ITS OWN WAY AS DARK PHOENIX'S...

AND I, FOR ONE, AM NOT GOING TO STAND FOR IT !

WELL, HELLLL-*LO!*

I AM YOUR MASSEUSE, SIR. I HAVE BEEN SENT TO LOOK AFTER YOUR EVERY NEED.

Oh, MY STARS AND GARTERS !

161

COLOSSUS.

≥Yawwww*WWWWNN!*≤

IS IT DAWN, ALREADY? HAVE I SLEPT THE WHOLE NIGHT THROUGH?

THE MOMENT OF TRUTH FAST APPROACHES. I KNOW DARK PHOENIX IS EVIL; I HAVE FELT HER POWER. YET, I ALSO KNOW JEAN GREY; I HAVE FELT HER LOVE. I OWE HER MY LIFE! WHEN WE X-MEN FOUGHT DARK PHOENIX, WE WERE NOT TRYING TO DESTROY HER...

...BUT *CURE* HER WE FOUGHT OUT OF LOVE. THAT HAS NOT CHANGED.

TO LEAVE JEAN TO PHOENIX'S FATE NOW -- AFTER HAVING STRUGGLED SO HARD TO SAVE HER -- WOULD BE A DENIAL OF THAT LOVE. SUCH A BETRAYAL, I CANNOT -- I WILL NOT -- COMMIT.

HE CONCENTRATES -- AND IN THE BLINK OF AN EYE A BODY OF FLESH AND BLOOD AND BONE AND SINEW BECOMES ONE OF NIGH-INVINCIBLE ORGANIC STEEL!

STORM.

DAWN, ON EARTH, THAT IS MARKED BY THE ETERNAL BEAUTY OF A *SUNRISE.*

HERE, BY THE CHIME OF AN ALARM. I PREFER THE SUNRISE.

OH, FOR THOSE HAPPY DAYS WHEN I WAS SIMPLY ORORO, WIND-RIDER.

I WAS *FREE.*

I WAS ALONE, THEN.

NOW, I AM NEITHER ALONE NOR FREE. AND RARELY HAPPY.

YET, I CHOSE TO JOIN THE X-MEN, TO LEAVE MY AFRICAN HOME OF MY OWN FREE WILL. THE X-MEN HAVE BECOME MY FAMILY, AND JEAN GREY THE BELOVED *SISTER* I NEVER HAD.

HOW IRONIC. DARK PHOENIX SYMBOLIZES ALL I ABHOR. BUT-- KNOWING THAT SHE IS JEAN, I FIND... THAT I CAN NO MORE DENY HER THAN I CAN MYSELF. I... *LOVE* JEAN. AS PART AND PARCEL OF THAT LOVE, I SHALL USE MY ELEMENTAL POWERS TO DEFEND HER TO THE DEATH.

CYCLOPS.

TODAY'S CONTEST IS NOT A DUEL TO THE DEATH... BUT IN TRYING TO SAVE JEAN, ONE OF US... OR ALL OF US... MIGHT DIE...

AND I CAN'T HELP THINKING, WHAT IF LILANDRA'S *RIGHT*? SUPPOSE WE WIN TODAY, AND THEN THE PSYCHIC CIRCUIT BREAKERS THAT PROFESSOR XAVIER PLACED IN JEAN'S MIND *FAIL*?!

DARK PHOENIX WILL BE FREE ONCE MORE, WITH THE WHOLE UNIVERSE AT HER MERCY, AND IT WILL HAVE BEEN *OUR* FAULT. I'VE BEEN WRESTLING WITH THIS PROBLEM-- THIS *FEAR*-- ALL NIGHT; I STILL DON'T HAVE AN ANSWER. MAYBE THERE ISN'T ONE.

DAMN IT, IT ISN'T FAIR! AFTER ALL WE'VE BEEN THROUGH--AFTER ALL THE *GOOD* THAT JEAN'S DONE-- TO HAVE IT END LIKE THIS!

I GUESS THAT'S WHAT THE PEOPLE ON D'BARI THOUGHT, WHEN THEIR SUN EXPLODED.

I'VE BEEN A LEADER TOO LONG. I CAN SEE LILANDRA'S POSITION AS CLEARLY AS MY OWN.

AND IF OUR POSITIONS WERE *REVERSED*, WOULD I BE ACTING ANY DIFFERENTLY THAN SHE?

I'D LIKE TO THINK, YES. IF VENGEANCE IS DEMANDED, LET *GOD* METE IT OUT. ME-- I'D RATHER ERR ON THE SIDE OF *MERCY*.

NO MATTER WHAT THE COST?

WHAT?! JEAN! YOU READ MY MIND!

I NO LONGER HAVE THE POWER OF PHOENIX, SCOTT--

--BUT I'M STILL A *TELEPATH*. AND WE STILL SHARE OUR *PSYCHIC RAPPORT*.

YOU'RE DRESSED AS *MARVEL GIRL*! WHY?!

I'M NOT SURE --NOSTALGIA? PRIDE? I STARTED AS MARVEL GIRL, AND THAT'S HOW I'LL *FINISH*.

SCOTT, AM I WORTH IT? I DESTROYED A WORLD--IN MY MIND, I CAN STILL HEAR THE SCREAMS OF THE DYING--AND IT FELT... *GOOD!* I DON'T WANT WANT THAT FEELING EVER AGAIN. AND YET-- I *DO*!

I KNOW. BUT TO GIVE UP--

--THAT'LL BE LIKE SAYING THAT DARK PHOENIX HAS *WON*. THAT YOU ARE EVIL. YOU'RE *NOT*!

JEAN, WHATEVER HAPPENS, KNOW THAT *I* LOVE YOU. AND I'LL STAND BY YOU.

AND I, YOU, SCOTT-- WITH ALL MY HEART!

163

LATER...

IT'S BEEN NEARLY *EIGHT* YEARS SINCE APOLLO 17, THE LAST LUNAR MISSION. MANY BELIEVE MAN WILL NOT WALK ON THE MOON AGAIN BEFORE THE TURN OF THE CENTURY. EVEN THEN, THAT WOULD BE A SHAME AND A TERRIBLE WASTE.

IT TOOK AMERICA'S ASTRONAUTS THREE DAYS TO MAKE THE JOURNEY FROM EARTH TO MOON. LILANDRA'S FLAGSHIP DOES IT IN *MINUTES*.

MEANWHILE, ON THE FLAGSHIP'S TRANSPORTER DECK...

I JUST WANT TO TELL YOU THAT I'M FIGHTING FOR JEAN. I WON'T ASK ANY OF YOU TO JOIN ME-- I HAVEN'T THE RIGHT-- AND I WON'T THINK ANY THE LESS OF YOU IF YOU DECIDE NOT TO.

SCOTT, WE, *uh*, TALKED THIS OUT AMONGST OURSELVES BEFORE YOU GOT HERE. WE'RE ALL AGREED. WE'RE WITH YOU AND JEAN, TO THE END!

THANKS, WARREN. TH-THANKS, ALL OF YOU.

THE X-MEN AND THE IMPERIAL GUARD WILL FIGHT UNTIL ONE TEAM OR THE OTHER IS DEFEATED. IF THE X-MEN WIN, THOSE WHO SURVIVE WILL BE SET FREE. IF MY IMPERIALS WIN ...

... PHOENIX-- JEAN GREY-- IS *OURS*, TO DO WITH AS WE WILL. WILL YOU ABIDE BY THESE TERMS, CYCLOPS?

WE WILL. YOU HAVE OUR *WORD* ON THAT.

I WISH YOU WELL, X-MEN. TODAY, I MUST PLAY THE ROLE OF *EXECUTIONER*-- YET I WOULD GIVE ANYTHING TO BE FIGHTING BY YOUR SIDE.

BEAM THEM DOWN, TECHNICIAN.

THE X-MEN FACE *HOPELESS* ODDS, MAJESTRIX...

...BUT THEY ARE EXCEPTIONAL BEINGS. SUPPOSE... THEY *WIN*?

THEY WILL *NOT* WIN, ARAKI.

YOU HAVE *MY* WORD ON THAT.

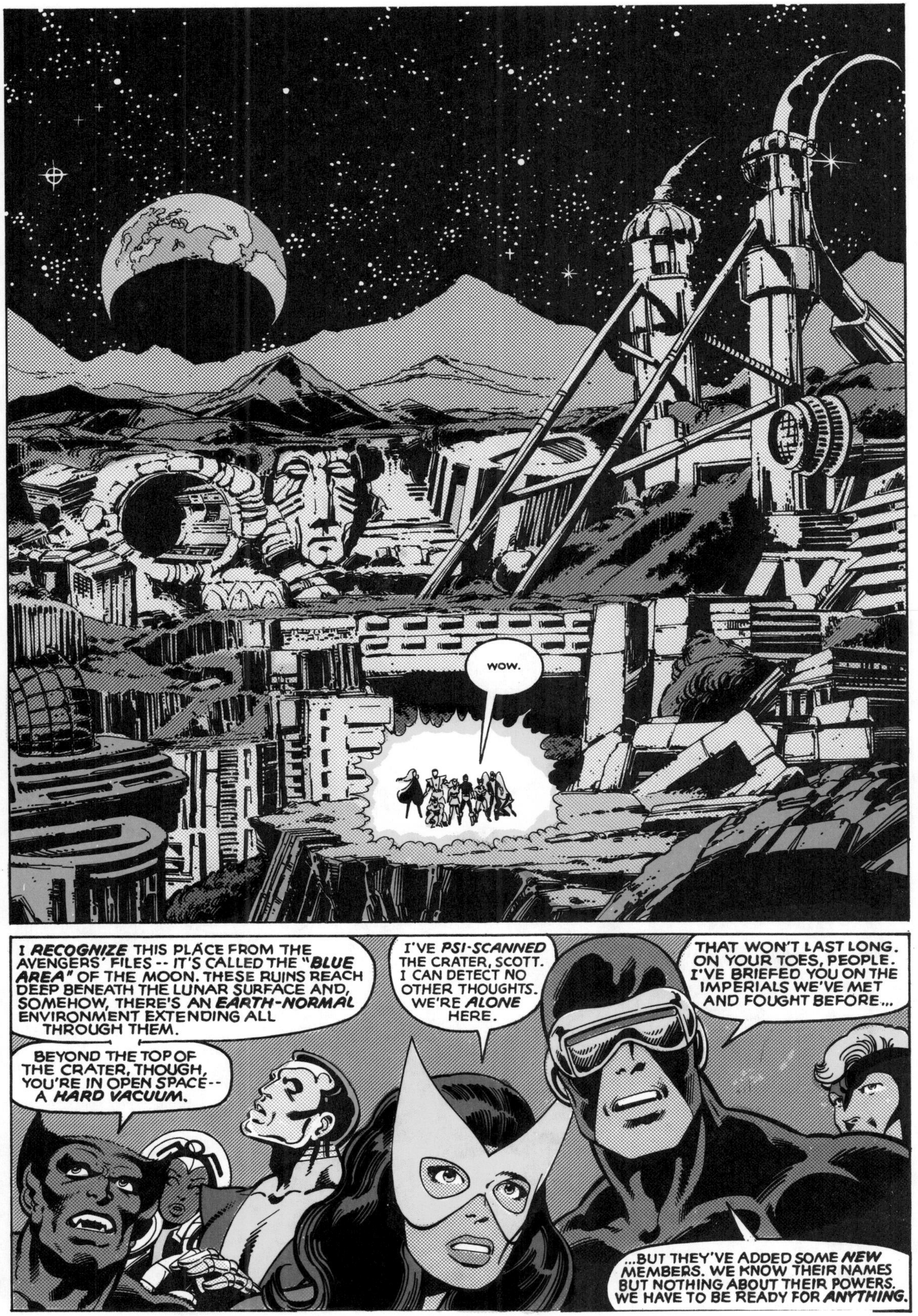
WOW.
I RECOGNIZE THIS PLACE FROM THE AVENGERS' FILES -- IT'S CALLED THE "BLUE AREA" OF THE MOON. THESE RUINS REACH DEEP BENEATH THE LUNAR SURFACE AND, SOMEHOW, THERE'S AN EARTH-NORMAL ENVIRONMENT EXTENDING ALL THROUGH THEM.
BEYOND THE TOP OF THE CRATER, THOUGH, YOU'RE IN OPEN SPACE -- A HARD VACUUM.
I'VE PSI-SCANNED THE CRATER, SCOTT. I CAN DETECT NO OTHER THOUGHTS. WE'RE ALONE HERE.
THAT WON'T LAST LONG. ON YOUR TOES, PEOPLE. I'VE BRIEFED YOU ON THE IMPERIALS WE'VE MET AND FOUGHT BEFORE...
...BUT THEY'VE ADDED SOME NEW MEMBERS. WE KNOW THEIR NAMES BUT NOTHING ABOUT THEIR POWERS. WE HAVE TO BE READY FOR ANYTHING.

HOLD IT! NOW I'M PICKING UP MULTIPLE TELEPATHIC IMPRESSIONS! THEY JUST POPPED INTO "VIEW"!

THERE, JEANNIE!

THAT FLASH O' LIGHT ON THE FAR SIDE O' THE CRATER MUST BE THE GUARD TELEPORTIN' DOWN!

I'LL TAKE A LOOK-SEE, CYKE.

HAVE YOU FORGOTTEN -- WE'RE ON THE MOON! COMPENSATE FOR THE LIGHTER GRAVITY, BEFORE--!

ANGEL -- NO!

AND WHILE I'M AT IT -- MAYBE I'LL GET IN SOME FAST FIRST-LICKS BEFORE THE OPPOSITION GETS THEIR BEARINGS.

WHAT?! ≥AARRRGKGH!≤

MY WINGS -- ONE SWEEP TOOK ME OUT OF THE CRATER! THEY SHOULDN'T HAVE DONE THAT!

NO AIR! I CAN'T BREATHE! AND THE COLD -- FREEZING ME SOLID! GOT TO... STAY... CONSCIOUS...

HE'S MOVING, CYCLOPS-- TRYING TO BREAK HIS FALL! HE'S STILL ALIVE!

I'LL CATCH HIM!

BE CAREFUL, STORM! I DON'T WANT YOU FLYING OFF INTO SPACE, AS WELL!

THE LIMITED ENVIRONMENT WITHIN THIS CRATER WILL MAKE IT HARD FOR ME TO EFFECTIVELY USE MY ELEMENTAL POWERS. I WON'T HAVE SUFFICIENT ATMOSPHERIC "TOOLS" TO WORK WITH.

GO LIMP, ANGEL! I HAVE YOU!

MUCHAS GRACIAS, STORM. I... I ACTED WITHOUT THINKING, AS USUAL. UP HERE, MY WINGS WILL TAKE ME FARTHER, FASTER.

I'VE PULLED SOME DODO STUNTS IN MY DAY. THIS ONE'S RIGHT IN CHARACTER.

YOU MADE A *MISTAKE*, ANGEL. THAT IS ALL.

I HAVE A *KNACK* FOR DOING THAT.

WARREN! HOW DO YOU--?!

FEEL, SCOTT? *D-U-M-B.* I SCREWED UP.

NEXT TIME, BUDDY, *THINK*-- WHERE YOU ARE, WHAT YOU'RE DOING. THERE ARE ONLY EIGHT OF US, WARREN.

WITH JEAN'S LIFE AT STAKE, WE CAN'T AFFORD *ANY* MISTAKES. YOU GOT AWAY WITH IT ONCE. DON'T PUSH YOUR LUCK.

CYCLOPS, WOLVERINE HAS SPOTTED THE IMPERIAL GUARD. THEY ARE NEAR-BY, HEADING THIS WAY!

DO WE MAKE A STAND, BOSS?

WHEN WE'RE READY, WOLVERINE, AND ON *OUR* TERMS.

WE'LL START WITH *HIT-AND-RUN* TACTICS, TO THROW THE IMPERIALS OFF-BALANCE AND WHITTLE DOWN THEIR FORCES.

FOR NOW, WE SPLIT UP. WE'VE GOT THESE RUINS, BEAST; LET'S USE 'EM TO OUR BEST ADVANTAGE.

Oh, GOODY! I JUST LOVE PLAYING HIDE-'N'-SEEK!

ANY TELEPATHIC SIGN OF THE IMPIES, JEAN?

I'M AFRAID NOT, WARREN. *ORACLE* MUST BE BLOCKING MY PROBES. I DON'T WANT TO PUSH TOO HARD. SHE MIGHT BE ABLE TO *BACK-TRACK* THE SCAN TO US.

GOOD MOVE, JEAN--uh-oh!

THIS PLAZA'S WIDE OPEN-- ALMOST NO COVER. A PERFECT PLACE FOR AN AMBUSH.

TAKE THE POINT, NIGHTCRAWLER.

AS YOU COMMAND, FEARLESS LEADER.

BUT, BEFORE THE GERMAN-BORN MUTANT CAN EVEN TAKE A STEP...

WATCH OUT!

FGOOM

SCOTT!!

YOU CANNOT HIDE FROM US, X-MEN; YOU CANNOT ESCAPE. AND NO MATTER HOW HARD YOU TRY, YOU WILL NOT WIN!

WE'LL SEE ABOUT THAT, STARBOLT. ANGEL-- TAKE OFF!

THIS ALBINO LADY IS CALLED ORACLE. ACCORDING TO CYKE'S BRIEFING BEFORE WE BEAMED DOWN, SHE HAS PSI-POWERS LIKE MARVEL GIRL'S.

THE OTHER GUY IS SMASHER. I'LL HANDLE HIM.

NIGHT-CRAWLER AND JEANNIE CAN HANDLE THE LADIES.

ZARK!

YOU GUYS HEAR THAT? CYKE'S FIRIN' HIS OPTIC BLASTS-- AT PRETTY NEAR FULL POWER, TOO.

SOUNDS LIKE THE FIGHT'S STARTED WITHOUT US.

ZARK!

MY FRIENDS, SHOULD WE NOT GO TO THEIR AID?

WE SHOULD NOT, COLOSSUS--MUCH AS WE'D LIKE TO. FOR THE MOMENT, CYKE'S TEAM IS ON ITS OWN, JUST AS WE ARE.

DON'T WORRY, THOUGH, THERE ARE PROBABLY MORE THAN ENOUGH VILLAINS TO GO 'ROUND.

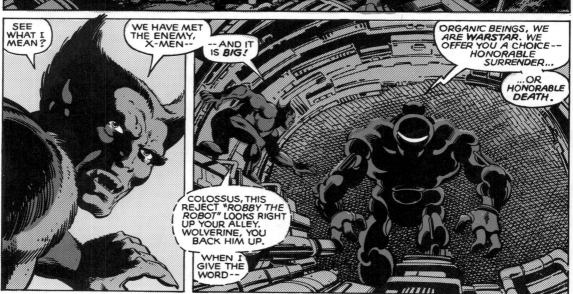

SEE WHAT I MEAN?

WE HAVE MET THE ENEMY, X-MEN--

--AND IT IS BIG!

ORGANIC BEINGS, WE ARE WARSTAR. WE OFFER YOU A CHOICE-- HONORABLE SURRENDER...

...OR HONORABLE DEATH.

COLOSSUS, THIS REJECT "ROBBY THE ROBOT" LOOKS RIGHT UP YOUR ALLEY. WOLVERINE, YOU BACK HIM UP.

WHEN I GIVE THE WORD--

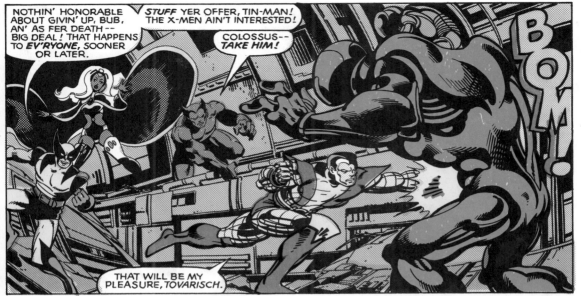

NOTHIN' HONORABLE ABOUT GIVIN' UP, BUB, AN' AS FER DEATH -- BIG DEAL! THAT HAPPENS TO EV'RYONE, SOONER OR LATER.

STUFF YER OFFER, TIN-MAN! THE X-MEN AIN'T INTERESTED!

COLOSSUS-- TAKE HIM!

BOM!

THAT WILL BE MY PLEASURE, TOVARISCH.

IF THAT'S THE WAY YOU WANT IT, TERRANS.

YOU TAKE CARE OF COLOSSUS, C'CLL-- THIS FUZZY ONE IS ALL MINE!

HEY! THERE'S TWO OF THEM!

THAT, STORM, IS MY CUE TA GET INVOLVED. GIMME ABOUT FIVE SECONDS, AN' WE'LL KNOW IF THESE SUCKERS ARE WORTH THE METAL THEY'RE MADE OUT OF.

MY APOLOGIES, WOLVERINE--

--BUT THAT, I CANNOT ALLOW!

GLADIATOR! HE RIPPED UP THE FLOOR-- KNOCKED US INTO SOME SORT OF PIT!

RRRIP!

CAUGHT YOU! THIS IS GETTING TO BE A HABIT, YOU KNOW-- SNATCHING X-MEN FROM THE BRINK OF DOOM.

YUP--AN', AS EVER, 'RORO, I'M OBLIGED.

WE'VE FALLEN A PRETTY FAIR PIECE.

THAT WE HAVE. AND FLYING BACK TO THE OTHERS WON'T BE EASY, EITHER. IT TAKES ME FAR MORE CONCENTRA-TION THAN USUAL TO GENERATE WINDS HERE, AND MANIPU-LATE THEM.

WOLVERINE, LOOK!

THAT BUILDING-- IT'S PURE CRYSTAL!

IT'S TOTALLY UNLIKE THE RUINS AROUND IT, AND IT SEEMS BRAND NEW.

GUESS WHAT, STORM, IT'S GOT A WATCH-DOG TOO!

I AM CALLED EARTHQUAKE, MAMMALS--

--BEHOLD THE REASON WHY!

THE GROUND--!!

CAN'T KEEP MY BALANCE!

HOLY--?! ORORO...

WOLVERINE!

HE--FELL RIGHT THROUGH THAT WALL! BUT I CAN'T GO AFTER HIM UNTIL I'VE DEALT WITH EARTHQUAKE.

I MUST NOT LET THE IMPERIAL SEE HOW MUCH EFFORT IT TAKES ME TO USE MY ELEMENTAL POWERS. STRAIN IS INCREDIBLE, BUT I MUST NOT-- I WILL NOT-- FAIL!

YOU-- EARTHQUAKE! YOU CLAIM TO CONTROL THE EARTH BENEATH OUR FEET!

LEARN NOW, VILLAIN, THAT STORM CONTROLS THE WIND AND RAIN-- ELEMENTS THAT GRIND THE EARTH DOWN TO POWDER!

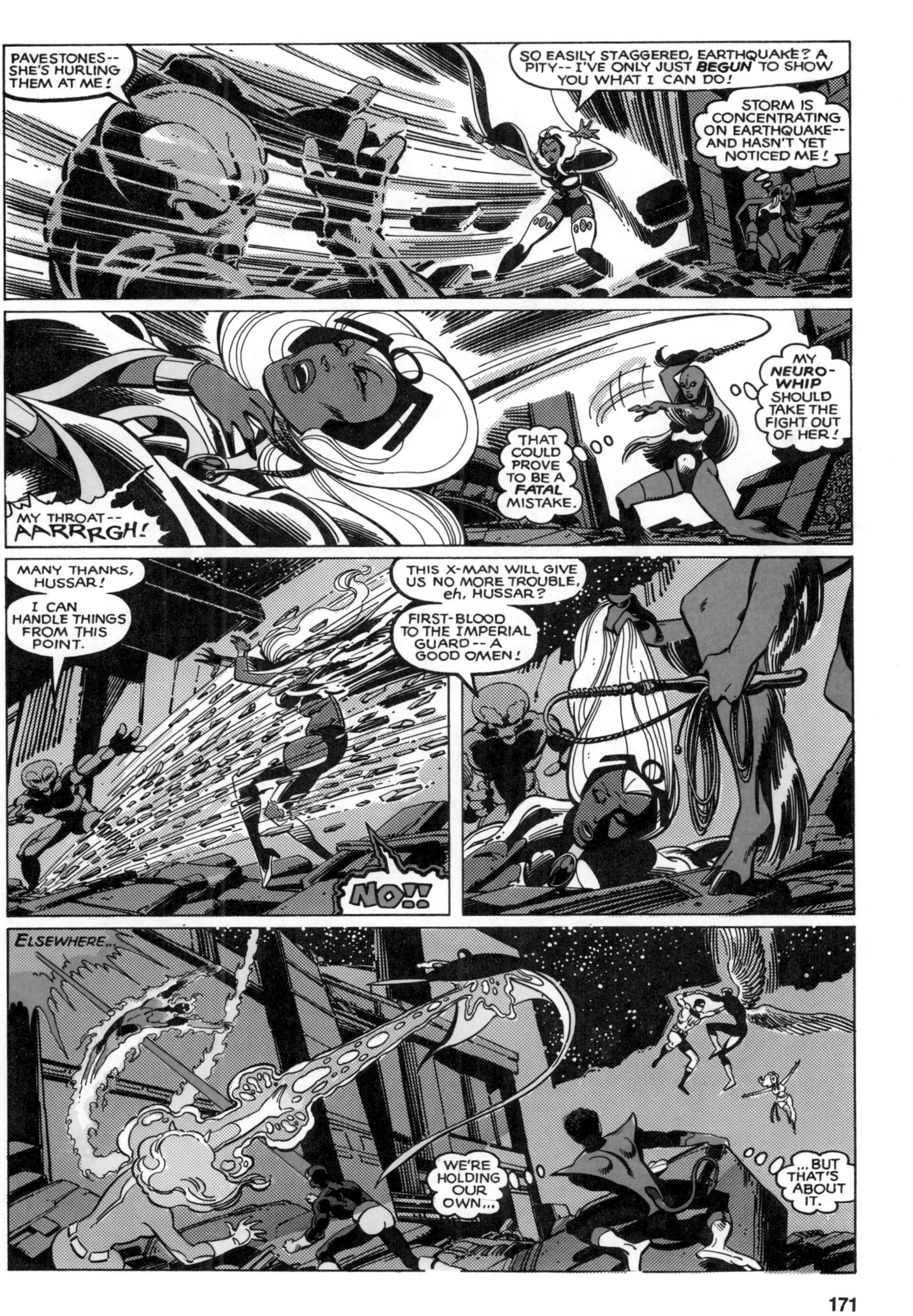
PAVESTONES-- SHE'S HURLING THEM AT ME!
SO EASILY STAGGERED, EARTHQUAKE? A PITY-- I'VE ONLY JUST BEGUN TO SHOW YOU WHAT I CAN DO!
STORM IS CONCENTRATING ON EARTHQUAKE-- AND HASN'T YET NOTICED ME!
MY NEURO-WHIP SHOULD TAKE THE FIGHT OUT OF HER!
THAT COULD PROVE TO BE A FATAL MISTAKE.
MY THROAT-- AARRRGH!
MANY THANKS, HUSSAR!
I CAN HANDLE THINGS FROM THIS POINT.
NO!!
THIS X-MAN WILL GIVE US NO MORE TROUBLE, eh, HUSSAR?
FIRST-BLOOD TO THE IMPERIAL GUARD-- A GOOD OMEN!
ELSEWHERE...
WE'RE HOLDING OUR OWN...
...BUT THAT'S ABOUT IT.

OUR POWERS AND TACTICAL SKILLS ARE PRETTY EVENLY MATCHED-- EXCEPT THAT *ALL* OF OUR FOES CAN FLY.

CYCLOPS AND JEAN CAN STRIKE AT LONG-RANGE, AND ANGEL CAN FIGHT THEM IN THEIR ELEMENT.

BUT I'M JUST A GLORIFIED *ACROBAT*. ALL THE MANEUVERS I'VE LEARNED TO COUNTER AN AIRBORNE ATTACK, WERE WORKED OUT WITH *STORM*. ANGEL DOESN'T KNOW THEM, AND THERE'S NO TIME TO TEACH-- *WHAT?!*

ANGEL! *LOOK OUT!* ORACLE'S MOVING IN BEHIND YOU!

M-MY MIND-- EVERY...THING... SUDDENLY GONE ...*BLOOEY!*

TOO LATE, NIGHTCRAWLER! I'VE *STUNNED* HIM!

AND WHILE THIS ANGEL-BEING IS HELPLESS...

...*SMASHER* WILL FINISH HIM OFF...

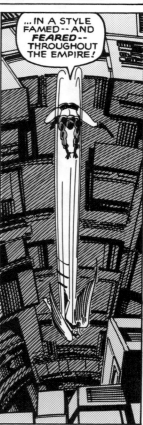

...IN A STYLE FAMED-- AND *FEARED*-- THROUGHOUT THE EMPIRE!

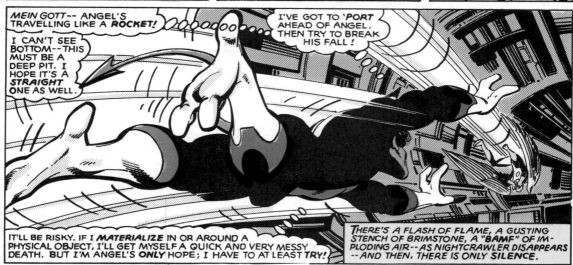

MEIN GOTT-- ANGEL'S TRAVELLING LIKE A *ROCKET!*

I CAN'T SEE BOTTOM--THIS MUST BE A DEEP PIT. I HOPE IT'S A *STRAIGHT* ONE AS WELL.

I'VE GOT TO 'PORT AHEAD OF ANGEL, THEN TRY TO BREAK HIS FALL!

IT'LL BE RISKY. IF I *MATERIALIZE* IN OR AROUND A PHYSICAL OBJECT, I'LL GET MYSELF A QUICK AND VERY MESSY DEATH. BUT I'M ANGEL'S *ONLY* HOPE; I HAVE TO AT LEAST *TRY!*

THERE'S A FLASH OF FLAME, A GUSTING STENCH OF BRIMSTONE, A "BAMF" OF IM-PLODING AIR-- AS NIGHTCRAWLER DISAPPEARS -- AND THEN, THERE IS ONLY SILENCE.

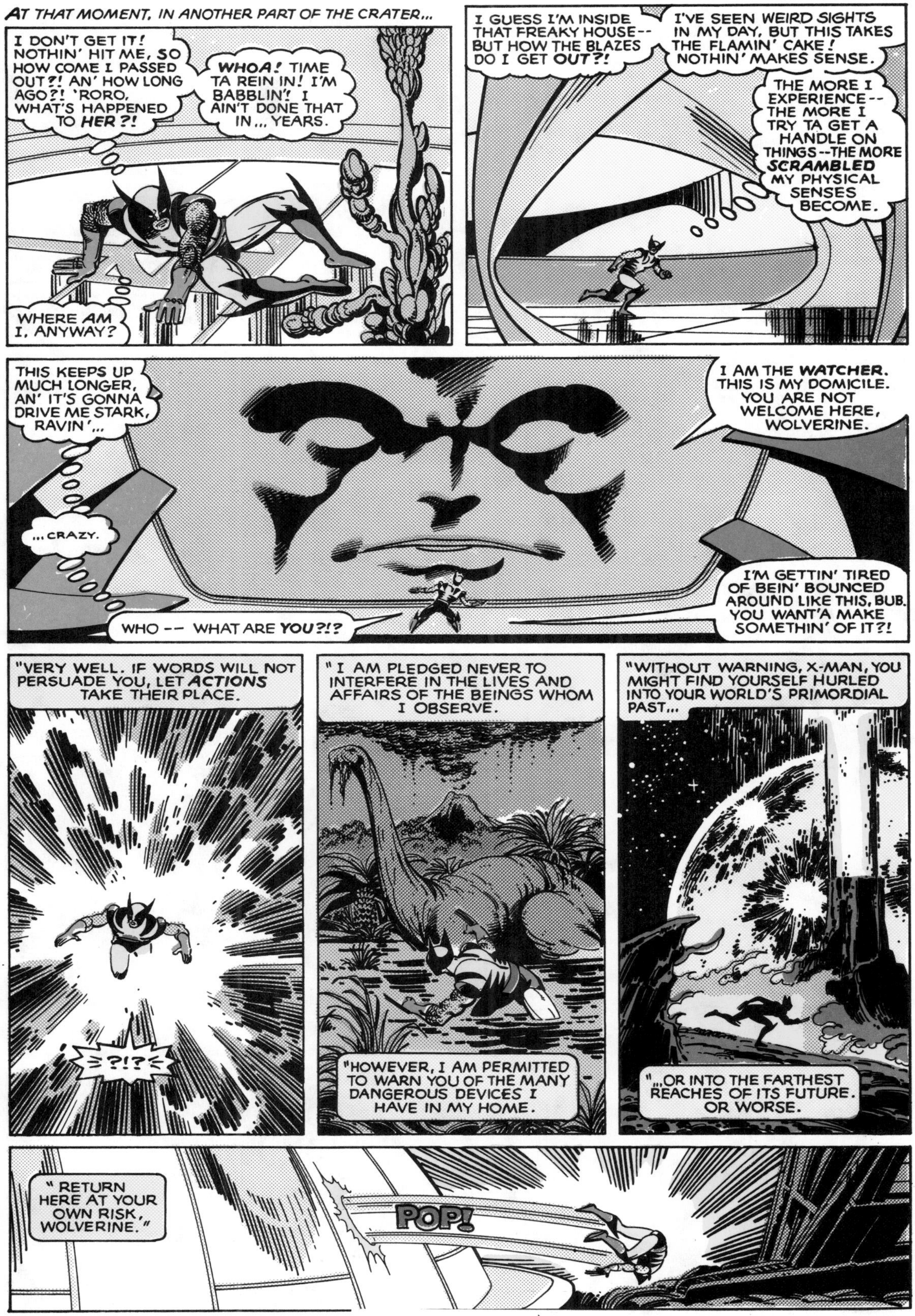
AT THAT MOMENT, IN ANOTHER PART OF THE CRATER...
I DON'T GET IT! NOTHIN' HIT ME, SO HOW COME I PASSED OUT?! AN' HOW LONG AGO?! 'RORO, WHAT'S HAPPENED TO HER?!
WHOA! TIME TA REIN IN! I'M BABBLIN'! I AIN'T DONE THAT IN... YEARS.
WHERE AM I, ANYWAY?
I GUESS I'M INSIDE THAT FREAKY HOUSE-- BUT HOW THE BLAZES DO I GET OUT?!
I'VE SEEN WEIRD SIGHTS IN MY DAY, BUT THIS TAKES THE FLAMIN' CAKE! NOTHIN' MAKES SENSE.
THE MORE I EXPERIENCE-- THE MORE I TRY TA GET A HANDLE ON THINGS--THE MORE SCRAMBLED MY PHYSICAL SENSES BECOME.
THIS KEEPS UP MUCH LONGER, AN' IT'S GONNA DRIVE ME STARK, RAVIN'...
...CRAZY.
WHO -- WHAT ARE YOU?!?
I AM THE WATCHER. THIS IS MY DOMICILE. YOU ARE NOT WELCOME HERE, WOLVERINE.
I'M GETTIN' TIRED OF BEIN' BOUNCED AROUND LIKE THIS, BUB. YOU WANT'A MAKE SOMETHIN' OF IT?!
"VERY WELL. IF WORDS WILL NOT PERSUADE YOU, LET ACTIONS TAKE THEIR PLACE.
?!?
"I AM PLEDGED NEVER TO INTERFERE IN THE LIVES AND AFFAIRS OF THE BEINGS WHOM I OBSERVE.
"HOWEVER, I AM PERMITTED TO WARN YOU OF THE MANY DANGEROUS DEVICES I HAVE IN MY HOME.
"WITHOUT WARNING, X-MAN, YOU MIGHT FIND YOURSELF HURLED INTO YOUR WORLD'S PRIMORDIAL PAST...
"...OR INTO THE FARTHEST REACHES OF ITS FUTURE. OR WORSE.
"RETURN HERE AT YOUR OWN RISK, WOLVERINE."
POP!

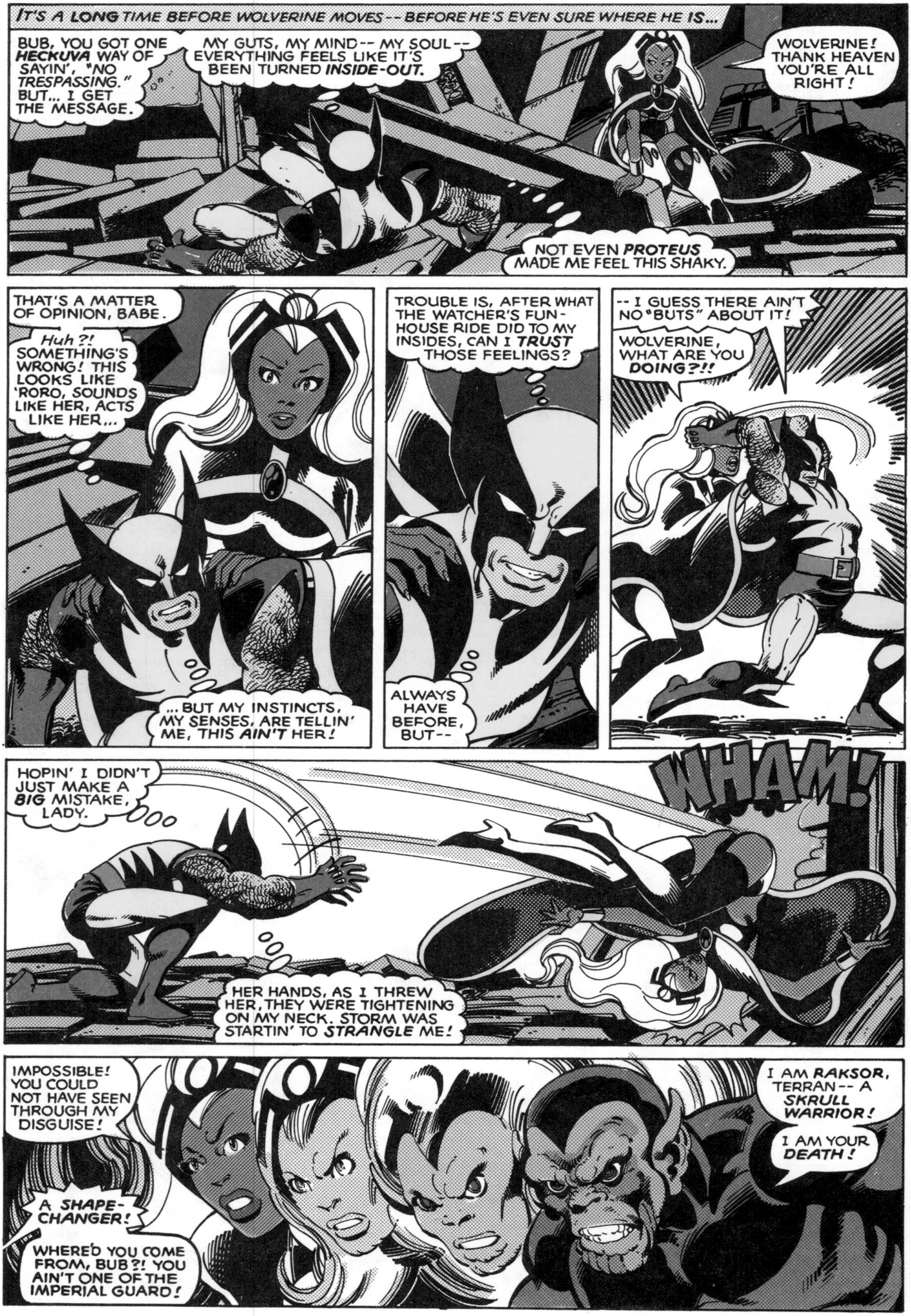

IT'S A LONG TIME BEFORE WOLVERINE MOVES -- BEFORE HE'S EVEN SURE WHERE HE IS...
BUB, YOU GOT ONE HECKUVA WAY OF SAYIN', "NO TRESPASSING." BUT... I GET THE MESSAGE.
MY GUTS, MY MIND-- MY SOUL-- EVERYTHING FEELS LIKE IT'S BEEN TURNED INSIDE-OUT.
WOLVERINE! THANK HEAVEN YOU'RE ALL RIGHT!
NOT EVEN PROTEUS MADE ME FEEL THIS SHAKY.
THAT'S A MATTER OF OPINION, BABE.
Huh?! SOMETHING'S WRONG! THIS LOOKS LIKE 'RORO, SOUNDS LIKE HER, ACTS LIKE HER...
...BUT MY INSTINCTS, MY SENSES, ARE TELLIN' ME, THIS AIN'T HER!
TROUBLE IS, AFTER WHAT THE WATCHER'S FUN-HOUSE RIDE DID TO MY INSIDES, CAN I TRUST THOSE FEELINGS?
ALWAYS HAVE BEFORE, BUT--
-- I GUESS THERE AIN'T NO "BUTS" ABOUT IT!
WOLVERINE, WHAT ARE YOU DOING?!!
WHAM!
HOPIN' I DIDN'T JUST MAKE A BIG MISTAKE, LADY.
HER HANDS, AS I THREW HER, THEY WERE TIGHTENING ON MY NECK. STORM WAS STARTIN' TO STRANGLE ME!
IMPOSSIBLE! YOU COULD NOT HAVE SEEN THROUGH MY DISGUISE!
A SHAPE-CHANGER!
WHERE'D YOU COME FROM, BUB?! YOU AIN'T ONE OF THE IMPERIAL GUARD!
I AM RAKSOR, TERRAN-- A SKRULL WARRIOR!
I AM YOUR DEATH!

WANNA *BET?!*

ZAP!

JUST BECAUSE MY *SKRULL* ALLY IS TOO *TERRIFIED* TO DEFEND HIMSELF, X-MAN, DOES NOT MEAN THAT HE IS COMPLETELY *HELPLESS.*

AT LEAST, NOT SO LONG AS HE HAS A *KREE WARRIOR* TO PROTECT HIM.

BE THANKFUL I DID NOT LEAVE YOU TO YOUR FATE, *SKRULL.* WE WERE MEANT TO BE *OBSERVERS* HERE, NOT COMBATANTS.

YOU!

YOU SAVED ME, KREE-- *YOU?!!*

THAT INSULT, I WILL NOT *ENDURE!*

HALA--!

MEANWHILE... I DON'T BELIEVE IT. I'VE *LOST* ANGEL!

HE SHOULD HAVE DROPPED RIGHT INTO MY ARMS, YET, DURING THE SPLIT-SECOND IT TOOK ME TO TELEPORT, HE *DISAPPEARED!*

I'VE BEEN SEARCHING FOR HIM, BUT THESE CATACOMBS HAVE MORE TWISTS AND TURNS THAN ARCADE'S *MURDERWORLD.*

AND NOW I HAVE THE UNCOMFORTABLE FEELING THAT *I'M* LOST.

Hmmm -- IT SEEMS I'M NOT ALONE DOWN HERE. THIS *FRAÜLEIN* IS ONE OF THE IMPERIAL GUARD. I BELIEVE SHE'S CALLED *MANTA.* AND I'LL LAY ANY ODDS THAT *THEY* ARE BEHIND ANGEL'S VANISHING ACT.

175

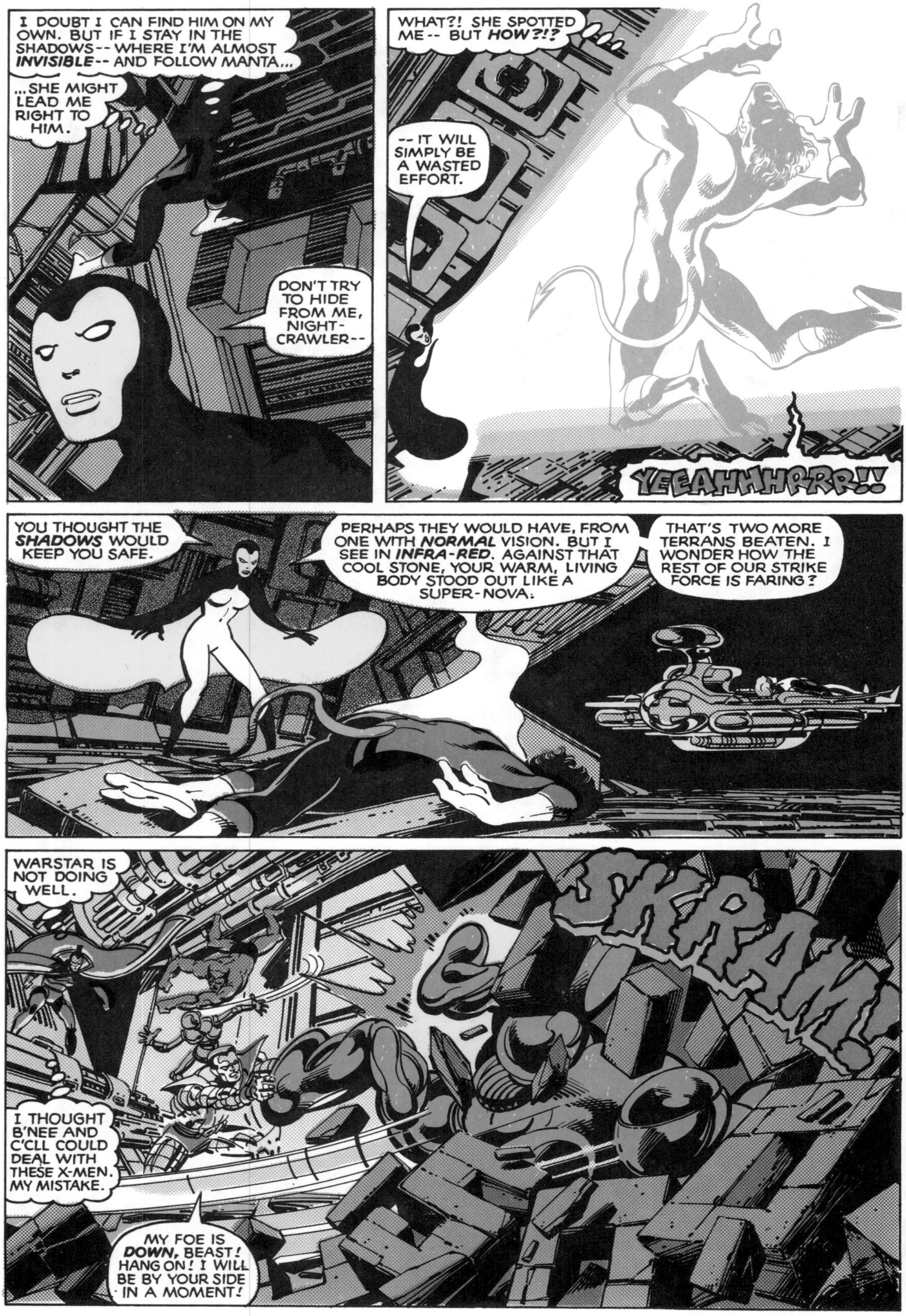
I DOUBT I CAN FIND HIM ON MY OWN. BUT IF I STAY IN THE SHADOWS-- WHERE I'M ALMOST INVISIBLE-- AND FOLLOW MANTA...
...SHE MIGHT LEAD ME RIGHT TO HIM.
DON'T TRY TO HIDE FROM ME, NIGHT-CRAWLER--
WHAT?! SHE SPOTTED ME-- BUT HOW?!?
-- IT WILL SIMPLY BE A WASTED EFFORT.
YEEAHHHRRR!!
YOU THOUGHT THE SHADOWS WOULD KEEP YOU SAFE.
PERHAPS THEY WOULD HAVE, FROM ONE WITH NORMAL VISION. BUT I SEE IN INFRA-RED. AGAINST THAT COOL STONE, YOUR WARM, LIVING BODY STOOD OUT LIKE A SUPER-NOVA.
THAT'S TWO MORE TERRANS BEATEN. I WONDER HOW THE REST OF OUR STRIKE FORCE IS FARING?
WARSTAR IS NOT DOING WELL.
SKRAM!
I THOUGHT B'NEE AND C'LL COULD DEAL WITH THESE X-MEN. MY MISTAKE.
MY FOE IS DOWN, BEAST! HANG ON! I WILL BE BY YOUR SIDE IN A MOMENT!

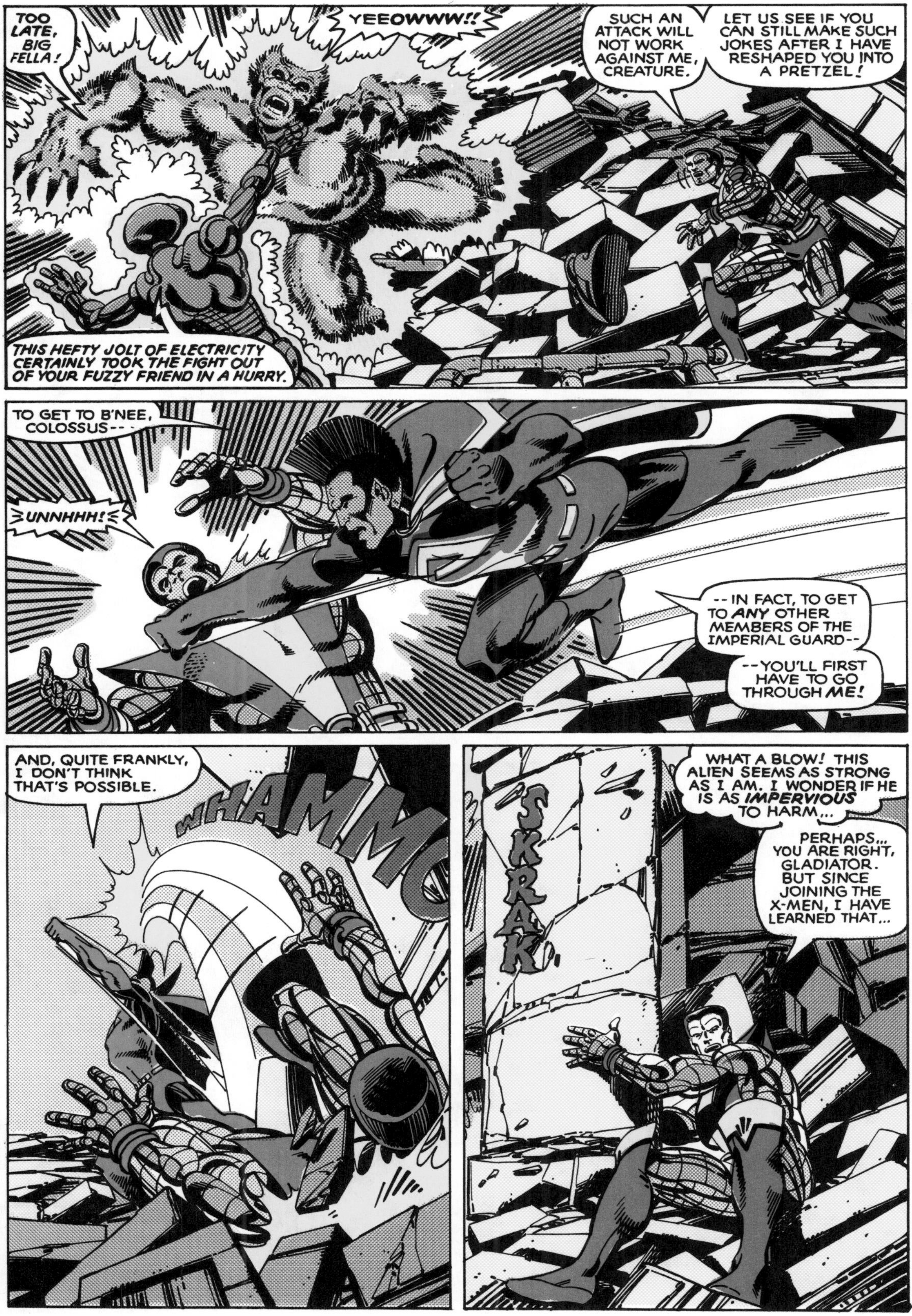
TOO LATE, BIG FELLA!
YEEOWWW!!
SUCH AN ATTACK WILL NOT WORK AGAINST ME, CREATURE.
LET US SEE IF YOU CAN STILL MAKE SUCH JOKES AFTER I HAVE RESHAPED YOU INTO A PRETZEL!
THIS HEFTY JOLT OF ELECTRICITY CERTAINLY TOOK THE FIGHT OUT OF YOUR FUZZY FRIEND IN A HURRY.
TO GET TO B'NEE, COLOSSUS--
UNNHHH!
--IN FACT, TO GET TO ANY OTHER MEMBERS OF THE IMPERIAL GUARD--
--YOU'LL FIRST HAVE TO GO THROUGH ME!
AND, QUITE FRANKLY, I DON'T THINK THAT'S POSSIBLE.
WHAMMO
WHAT A BLOW! THIS ALIEN SEEMS AS STRONG AS I AM. I WONDER IF HE IS AS IMPERVIOUS TO HARM...
SKRAK
PERHAPS... YOU ARE RIGHT, GLADIATOR. BUT SINCE JOINING THE X-MEN, I HAVE LEARNED THAT...

...ANYTHING IS POSSIBLE!

SO LONG AS WE STAND, WE FIGHT! AND SO LONG AS WE FIGHT-- NO MATTER WHAT THE ODDS--

--WE WILL PREVAIL!

THEY STAND TOE-TO-TOE, NEITHER OF THEM YIELDING AN INCH AS THEY TRADE PUNCH AFTER PUNCH OF AWESOME POWER.

THEIR FIGHT IS BRUTAL-- A CLASH OF MODERN TITANS.

TWO MEN OF STEEL -- ONE AN IRRESISTABLE FORCE, THE OTHER AN IMMOVABLE OBJECT-- BATTLING WITHOUT LETUP, GIVING EVERYTHING THEY HAVE.

IN THE END, THOUGH, IT IS NOT THEY WHO DECIDE THE ISSUE.

RATHER, IT IS THE ANCIENT, FRAGILE STRUCTURES AROUND THEM.

AT FIRST, THE OUT-COME IS IN DOUBT, AS SHOCKWAVES FROM THE SKYSCRAPER'S COLLAPSE THUNDER ACROSS THE GREAT CRATER, TO BE FOLLOWED MINUTES LATER BY AN UNNATURAL *SILENCE.*

THEN, AMID THE MOUNTAINS OF RUBBLE, A BOULDER MOVES...

...AND SLOWLY, PAINFULLY, RELENTLESSLY...

...THE *VICTOR* EMERGES.

AND, ON LILANDRA'S FLAGSHIP...

NO!

NO. NO. NO. NO. NO.

Oh, MY X-MEN-- I THOUGHT... I FELT... THAT YOU HAD A CHANCE. I NEVER DREAMED THINGS WOULD END LIKE THIS. FORGIVE ME, MY CHILDREN.

I KNOW I WILL NEVER FORGIVE MYSELF.

I WARNED YOU, CHARLES.

AS EACH X-MAN FALLS, ANOTHER PIECE IS CUT FROM YOUR HEART, AS ONE IS CUT FROM MINE.

I WANT TO COMFORT YOU, *BE* WITH YOU IN YOUR HOUR OF NEED...

...BUT I CANNOT. I AM EMPRESS. I MUST DO MY DUTY.

NO MATTER WHAT IT COSTS.

179

SCOTT, I'VE LOST TELEPATHIC CONTACT WITH ALL THE OTHER X-MEN! I THINK WE'RE THE ONLY ONES LEFT!

SO MUCH FOR MY BRILLIANT STRATEGY.

MY OPTIC BLASTS ARE MAKING THESE IMPERIALS KEEP THEIR DISTANCE. THEY'RE NOT REALLY ATTACKING US ANYMORE, JUST MARKING OUR POSITION UNTIL REENFORCEMENTS ARRIVE. THEN, WE'LL SEE FIREWORKS.

JEAN, WE HAVE TO LOSE THEM!

IN HERE!

THIS ALCOVE SHOULD HIDE US!

HOW?!

IT'S TOO SHALLOW TO DO US ANY GOOD. WE'LL BE SPOTTED IN AN INSTANT.

NOT AFTER I'VE USED MY TELEKINETIC TALENT TO COVER THE ENTRANCE WITH A WALL OF LUNAR DUST-- VOILÀ!

THERE THEY GO, NONE THE WISER.

WE'VE GOT BREATHING SPACE, SCOTT-- BUT, SOONER OR LATER, WE'LL HAVE TO COME OUT.

I KNOW.

THERE'S SO MUCH I WANT TO SAY TO YOU-- SO MUCH THAT I FEEL. I... DON'T HAVE THE WORDS.

WHERE I'M CONCERNED, IT'S THE THOUGHT THAT COUNTS. AND YOURS-- LIKE YOU--

--ARE BEAUTIFUL.

YOU'RE A SPECIAL MAN, SCOTT SUMMERS.

NO MORE SPECIAL THAN THE WOMAN I LOVE.

READY?

READY.

THEN... LET'S GO!

AS THEY MAKE THEIR LAST STAND, THEY FIND THEMSELVES REMEMBERING THE DAY THEY FIRST MET-- SO LONG AGO, SO FAR AWAY.

BDOW!

ZARK!

THEY REMEMBER ALL THAT'S HAPPENED SINCE-- GOOD TIMES AND BAD--

--AND DREAM OF WHAT MIGHT HAVE BEEN.

ONCE UPON A TIME, THERE WAS A WOMAN NAMED *JEAN GREY*, A MAN NAMED *SCOTT SUMMERS*.

THEY WERE YOUNG. THEY WERE IN LOVE.

THEY WERE HEROES.

TODAY, THEY WILL PROVE IT-- BEYOND ALL SHADOW OF A DOUBT.

MAJESTRIX-- SOMETHING IS HAPPENING! OUR INSTRUMENTS ARE REGISTERING OFF THEIR SCALES!

NO! SHARRA AND K'YTHRI--*NO!!*

THE ENERGY FLARE LIGHTS UP HALF A LUNAR HEMISPHERE, A PLASMA BOLT OF MONSTROUS PROPORTIONS, PUNCHING THROUGH THE STARSHIP'S DEFENSIVE FORCE FIELDS LIKE THEY DON'T EXIST...

... ANNOUNCING TO ALL THE UNIVERSE THAT--

--PHOENIX IS REBORN!

AND, ABOARD THE GREAT DREADNOUGHT -- INSTANT, TOTAL CHAOS!

GRAB HANDHOLDS, EVERYONE! THE ARTIFICIAL GRAVITY'S GONE!

DAMAGE CONTROL-- REPORT! HOW BADLY ARE WE HIT?!

CAPTAIN-- ALERT THE GRAND FLEET! PLAN OMEGA!

IF WE FAIL IN OUR MISSION...

--TO ENSURE THAT PHOENIX IS DESTROYED!

...BURN THIS WORLD, THIS SYSTEM, THIS ENTIRE STELLAR CLUSTER! DO WHATEVER IS NECESSARY--

LILANDRA... IS RIGHT. THINGS HAVE GONE TOO FAR. I HAVE DONE ALL I COULD -- TOO LITTLE, FAR TOO LATE -- FOR JEAN.

NOW, I MUST ACT TO SAVE THE HUMAN RACE!

HEAR ME, MY X-MEN! HEAR ME!

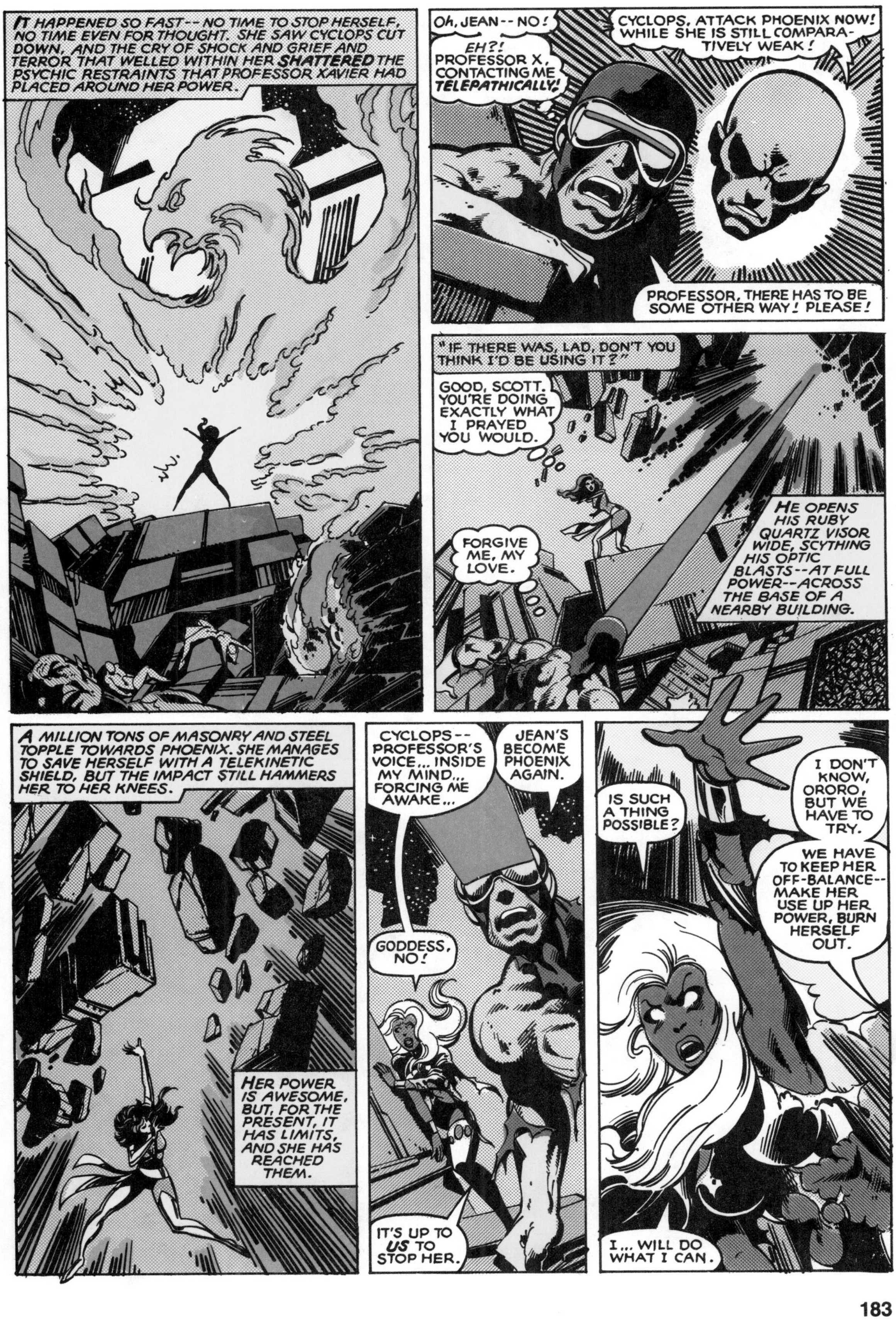
IT HAPPENED SO FAST-- NO TIME TO STOP HERSELF, NO TIME EVEN FOR THOUGHT. SHE SAW CYCLOPS CUT DOWN, AND THE CRY OF SHOCK AND GRIEF AND TERROR THAT WELLED WITHIN HER SHATTERED THE PSYCHIC RESTRAINTS THAT PROFESSOR XAVIER HAD PLACED AROUND HER POWER.
Oh, JEAN-- NO!
EH?! PROFESSOR X, CONTACTING ME TELEPATHICALLY!
CYCLOPS, ATTACK PHOENIX NOW! WHILE SHE IS STILL COMPARATIVELY WEAK!
PROFESSOR, THERE HAS TO BE SOME OTHER WAY! PLEASE!
"IF THERE WAS, LAD, DON'T YOU THINK I'D BE USING IT?"
GOOD, SCOTT. YOU'RE DOING EXACTLY WHAT I PRAYED YOU WOULD.
FORGIVE ME, MY LOVE.
HE OPENS HIS RUBY QUARTZ VISOR WIDE, SCYTHING HIS OPTIC BLASTS--AT FULL POWER--ACROSS THE BASE OF A NEARBY BUILDING.
A MILLION TONS OF MASONRY AND STEEL TOPPLE TOWARDS PHOENIX. SHE MANAGES TO SAVE HERSELF WITH A TELEKINETIC SHIELD, BUT THE IMPACT STILL HAMMERS HER TO HER KNEES.
HER POWER IS AWESOME, BUT, FOR THE PRESENT, IT HAS LIMITS, AND SHE HAS REACHED THEM.
CYCLOPS-- PROFESSOR'S VOICE... INSIDE MY MIND... FORCING ME AWAKE...
JEAN'S BECOME PHOENIX AGAIN.
GODDESS, NO!
IT'S UP TO US TO STOP HER.
IS SUCH A THING POSSIBLE?
I DON'T KNOW, ORORO, BUT WE HAVE TO TRY.
WE HAVE TO KEEP HER OFF-BALANCE-- MAKE HER USE UP HER POWER, BURN HERSELF OUT.
I... WILL DO WHAT I CAN.

STORM CONCENTRATES, AND THE AIR *STIRS* WITHIN THE HUGE CRATER, SWIRLING FASTER AND FASTER UNTIL -- LITERALLY IN THE BLINK OF AN EYE -- A *TORNADO* APPEARS AROUND PHOENIX, BATTERING HER MERCILESSLY.

NICE MOVE, 'RORO. BUT EVEN FROM HERE, I CAN SEE HOW BADLY YOU'RE HURT. YOU CAN'T KEEP UP THIS KIND OF PRESSURE FOR LONG.

I... "HEARD" PROFESSOR XAVIER,... YELLING IN MY HEAD... WAKING ME UP,... TELLING ME TO JOIN YOU...TO FIGHT...

I KNOW, MISFIT. HE PULLED THAT STUNT WITH ALL OF US.

DON'T YOU GUYS SEE?! WE'RE NOT FACIN' JEANNIE ANYMORE, BUT PHOENIX! LIKE IT OR NOT, IT'S US-- AN' MAYBE ALL HUMANITY-- OR HER!

WOLVERINE, WHAT ARE YOU DOING?!

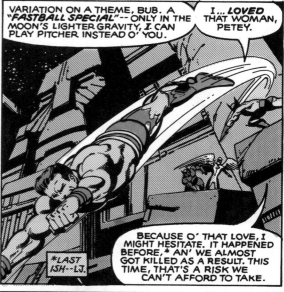

VARIATION ON A THEME, BUB. A *"FASTBALL SPECIAL"*-- ONLY IN THE MOON'S LIGHTER GRAVITY, *I* CAN PLAY PITCHER INSTEAD O' YOU.

I... *LOVED* THAT WOMAN, PETEY.

BECAUSE O' THAT LOVE, I MIGHT HESITATE. IT HAPPENED BEFORE,* AN' WE ALMOST GOT KILLED AS A RESULT. THIS TIME, THAT'S A RISK WE CAN'T AFFORD TO TAKE.

*LAST ISH--L.J.

YOU ASK ME TO *KILL,* WOLVERINE--SOMETHING I HAVE *NEVER* DONE.

WORSE, YOU ASK ME TO KILL A *FRIEND.*

IT'S UP TO *YOU,* COLOSSUS. YOU'LL PROBABLY ONLY HAVE ONE SHOT. MAKE SURE THAT WHEN PHOENIX GOES DOWN, SHE *WON'T* BE GETTIN' UP!

≥UNNNGNH!≤

I...

...I... CANNOT DO IT.

WOW. YOU... *PULLED* YOUR PUNCH, PETER. AND EVEN SO... I'M SURPRISED MY HEAD'S STILL ATTACHED TO MY BODY. THANKS, THOUGH, FOR KNOCKING SOME "SENSE" BACK INTO ME.

NOW, FINALLY, I TRULY UNDERSTAND WHAT I AM, AND WHAT HAS TO BE DONE...

TWO BEINGS -- JEAN GREY AND PHOENIX... SEPARATE... UNIQUE... BOUND TOGETHER. A *SYMBIOTE*, PETER; NEITHER CAN EXIST WITHOUT THE OTHER.

PHOENIX PROVIDES MY LIFE-FORCE, WHILE I PROVIDE A LIVING FOCUS FOR ITS INFINITE POWER.

SO LONG AS I LIVE, THE PHOENIX WILL MANIFEST ITSELF THROUGH ME. AND SO LONG AS THAT HAPPENS, I'LL EVENTUALLY, INEVITABLY, BECOME *DARK PHOENIX*.

THE PHOENIX IS A COSMIC POWER. IT CAN NEITHER BE CONTAINED NOR CONTROLLED -- ESPECIALLY BY A HUMAN VESSEL. RETURN IT TO THE COSMOS WHICH IS ITS HOME.

KILL ME!

NO!

IT DOESN'T HAVE TO BE LIKE THIS!

YOU HAVE AN INTELLECT, JEAN, A WILL, A SOUL -- *USE THEM!* FIGHT THIS DARK SIDE OF YOUR-SELF! WE'LL HELP YOU!

THE POWER...

...CHANGING ME -- IT'S TOO SOON!

JEAN -- *WAIT!!* YOU'RE NOT GIVING US ANY CHOICE!

THE CHOICE WAS NEVER *YOURS* TO BEGIN WITH.

TELEKINETIC FORCE BOLT--! I CAN'T MOVE!

YOU SEE, SCOTT? I TOLD YOU.

JEAN TO PHOENIX TO DARK PHOENIX -- A PROGRESSION AS INEVITABLE AS *DEATH*.

YOU OF ALL PEOPLE SHOULD KNOW HOW I FEEL, THROUGH THE PSIONIC RAPPORT WE SHARE.

I'M *SCARED*, SCOTT. I'M HANGING ON BY MY FINGERNAILS. I CAN FEEL THE PHOENIX WITHIN ME, TAKING OVER PART OF ME... *WELCOMES* IT.

185

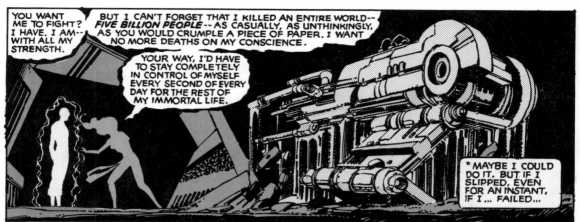

YOU WANT ME TO FIGHT? I HAVE. I AM-- WITH ALL MY STRENGTH.

BUT I CAN'T FORGET THAT I KILLED AN ENTIRE WORLD-- *FIVE BILLION PEOPLE* -- AS CASUALLY, AS UNTHINKINGLY, AS YOU WOULD CRUMPLE A PIECE OF PAPER. I WANT NO MORE DEATHS ON MY CONSCIENCE.

YOUR WAY, I'D HAVE TO STAY COMPLETELY IN CONTROL OF MYSELF EVERY SECOND OF EVERY DAY FOR THE REST OF MY IMMORTAL LIFE.

"MAYBE I COULD DO IT. BUT IF I SLIPPED, EVEN FOR AN INSTANT, IF I ... FAILED...

... IF EVEN *ONE* MORE PERSON DIED AT MY HANDS...

IT'S BETTER THIS WAY. QUICK. CLEAN. FINAL.

I LOVE YOU, SCOTT.

A PART OF ME WILL ALWAYS BE WITH YOU.

JEAN, NO. DON'T!

NO!

SCOTT!

JEAN!

YOU... *PLANNED* THIS, DIDN'T YOU?! FROM THE MOMENT WE LANDED ON THE MOON. YOU SHIELDED YOUR INTENTIONS FROM OUR RAPPORT, BUT JUST THE SAME I SHOULD HAVE GUESSED, I SHOULD HAVE REALIZED...

... THAT YOU COULD NOT BECOME DARK PHOENIX AND REMAIN TRUE TO YOUR *SELF*, THE JEAN GREY I KNEW, AND FELL IN LOVE WITH. SO, YOU TOOK STEPS TO ENSURE THAT, IF LILANDRA COULDN'T STOP YOU, YOU'D DO THE JOB YOURSELF.

YOU MUST HAVE PICKED THE MINDS OF THE KREE AND *SKRULL* OBSERVERS, LEARNED WHAT ANCIENT WEAPONS WERE HIDDEN HERE. THEN, YOU USED YOUR FIGHT WITH THE X-MEN TO DRAIN YOU OF ENOUGH ENERGY TO MAKE YOU VULNERABLE. AND, FINALLY, WHEN YOU WERE READY, YOU... YOU...

OH, JEAN...

JEAN...

STATEMENT: I AM THE *RECORDER*, A NON-CELLULAR HUMANOID, CREATED BY THE COLONIZERS OF RIGEL TO THINK AND TO RECORD. I HAVE OBSERVED ALL THAT HAS TRANSPIRED HERE, YET I DO NOT COMPREHEND THE MEANING OF THESE EVENTS.

MY HISTORICAL CIRCUITS INFORM ME THAT JEAN GREY WAS COUNTED A FORCE FOR *GOOD* ON EARTH. AS PHOENIX, HER POWER SAVED THE ENTIRE UNIVERSE FROM EXTINCTION. YET SHE WAS HOUNDED UNTO DEATH.

INTERROGATIVE: WHY?

BECAUSE SHE WAS HUMAN.

INSUFFICIENT ANSWER, WATCHER. PLEASE ELUCIDATE FURTHER.

ALL BEINGS CARRY WITHIN THEM A CAPACITY FOR GOOD AND EVIL. ALL OUR ACTIONS RESULT FROM THE INTERACTION OF THESE TWO FUNDAMENTAL FORCES.

THIS CHILD ACHIEVED A LEVEL OF POWER THAT PLACED HER AS FAR ABOVE HUMANITY -- ON THE EVOLUTIONARY SCALE -- AS THEY ARE ABOVE THE AMOEBA. SHE HAD ONLY TO *THINK*, AND THAT THOUGHT WOULD BECOME INSTANT REALITY

BUT THE PHOENIX IS ALSO A FORCE OF *PRIMAL PASSION*, AND *HOMO SAPIENS* IS STILL AS MUCH A CREATURE OF PASSION AS OF INTELLECT. SUCH PASSION IS BY ITS VERY NATURE SEDUCTIVE AND VIOLENT. JEAN COULD NOT HELP BUT RESPOND TO IT, BE CHANGED BY IT, AND IN TIME, *OVERWHELMED.*

OUR *REASON* MAKES US AWARE OF THESE FORCES AND LIKEWISE GIVES US THE RESPONSIBILITY OF CHOOSING BETWEEN THEM. REGRETTABLY, NOT ALL CHOICES ARE CLEAR-CUT, NOR ALL CONFLICTS OBVIOUS.

SO, SHE BRIEFLY BECAME THE *DARK SIDE* OF PHOENIX: THE BLACK ANGEL, CHAOS-BRINGER. YET, WHEN FACED WITH A CHOICE BETWEEN KEEPING HER GOD-LIKE POWER -- KNOWING SHE WOULD THEN WREAK DEATH AND DESTRUCTION ACROSS THE STARS -- AND DYING HERSELF, SHE CHOSE THE *LATTER.*

THAT IS WHAT MAKES HUMANITY VIRTUALLY *UNIQUE* IN THE COSMOS, MY FRIEND -- THIS EXTRA-ORDINARY CAPACITY FOR *SELF-SACRIFICE...*

...THIS ABILITY TO TRIUMPH OVER SEEMINGLY INSURMOUNTABLE OBSTACLES IF THE CAUSE BE JUST, KNOWING ALL THE WHILE THAT TO DO SO MEANS CERTAIN DEATH.

THE X-MEN DO NOT REALIZE IT -- THEY MAY *NEVER* REALIZE, OR ACCEPT IT -- BUT THIS DAY THEY HAVE WON PERHAPS THE GREATEST VICTORY OF THEIR YOUNG LIVES.

JEAN GREY COULD HAVE LIVED TO BECOME A GOD. BUT IT WAS MORE IMPORTANT TO HER THAT SHE DIE... A *HUMAN.*

187

Also by Stan Lee

Origins of Marvel Comics

Son of Origins

Bring On the Bad Guys

The Superhero Women

How to Draw Comics the Marvel Way

The Incredible Hulk

The Silver Surfer

The Mighty World of Marvel Pin-Up Book (with John Buscema)

Marvel's Greatest Superhero Battles

The Amazing Spider-Man

The Mighty Marvel Jumbo Fun Book (with Owen McCarron)

Dr. Strange

The Fantastic Four

Captain America, Sentinel of Liberty

Mighty Marvel Team-Up Thrillers